SCHOOL DEVELOPMENT SERIES
General Editors: David Reynolds and David Hopkins

THE EFFECTIVE CLASSROOM

OTHER TITLES IN THE SCHOOL DEVELOPMENT SERIES

R. Bollington, D. Hopkins and M. West:
An Introduction to Teacher Appraisal

D. Aspin and J. Chapman with V. Wilkinson:
Quality Schooling

P. Dalin:
Changing the School Culture

P. Dalin:
How Schools Improve

M. Fullan:
The New Meaning of Educational Change

D. Hargreaves and D. Hopkins:
The Empowered School

D. Hopkins, M. Ainscow and M. West:
School Improvement in an Era of Change

D. Hopkins and D. Hargreaves:
Development Planning for School Improvement

K. S. Louis and M. B. Miles:
Improving the Urban High School

J. Murphy:
Restructuring Schools

D. Reynolds and P. Cuttance:
School Effectiveness

P. Ribbins and E. Burridge:
Improving Education

J. Scheerens:
Effective Schooling

H. Silver:
Good Schools, Effective Schools

M. Wallace and A. McMahon:
Planning for Change in Turbulent Times

THE EFFECTIVE CLASSROOM

Bert P. M. Creemers

CASSELL

Cassell
Villiers House   387 Park Avenue South
41/47 Strand   New York
London WC2N 5JE   NY 10016–8810

First published 1994. Parts of this book have previously appeared in Dutch (see Acknowledgements).

British Library Cataloguing-in-Publication Data
A catalogue record for this book is available from the British Library.

ISBN 0–304–32707–7 (hardback)
    0–304–32709–3 (paperback)

Typeset by Fakenham Photosetting Ltd, Fakenham, Norfolk
Printed and bound in Great Britain by Redwood Books, Trowbridge, Wiltshire

Contents

Series Editors' Foreword   vii

Acknowledgements   viii

1   Can Education in the Classroom Be Improved?   1

2   Effective Instruction: Theoretical Framework   9

3   Traditions in Research on Instruction   36

4   The Effectiveness of Curricula   47

5   The Effectiveness of Grouping within Classrooms   57

6   The Effectiveness of Teacher Behaviour   73

7   The Effective Classroom   90

8   Effective Instruction in Effective Schools   100

9   Towards a Theory of Educational Effectiveness   109

References   126

Index   148

Series Editors' Foreword

We are pleased once again to be able to bring to the attention of researchers and practitioners work from a leading international expert in the field of school effectiveness. This book is based upon an original version published in Dutch and represents a unique summary of the published literature on classroom and teacher factors that influence children's achievements at school, together with an original and innovative theoretical analysis that links together the classroom level with the other educational levels that affect learning.

Creemers' position is that we have a known-to-be-valid knowledge base concerning the factors that make for 'effective instruction', and he proceeds interestingly through areas such as grouping practices, curriculum factors, teacher behaviours, the availability of learning time and the opportunity given students to learn as factors that can affect achievement levels. This literature comes from societies as diverse as the United States, Australia, the Netherlands, Belgium and Israel, as well as from the United Kingdom, and Creemers makes a powerful case for the importance of the classroom level – indeed, the variance in achievement explained at classroom level is considerably larger than that explained by the school level. Rather than being an important influence in its own right, Creemers argues for the school to be seen as important in terms of its facilitation of the classroom level to potentiate learning. Indeed, Creemers outlines a sophisticated and highly creative thesis which links together the macro, meso, school and classroom educational levels under the conceptual notions of the importance of consistency, constancy, cohesion and ultimately control.

The book opens up a fascinating literature on the classroom or 'instructional' level, a literature that is particularly important in a British context where *school* effectiveness is better appreciated than the *teacher* effectiveness literature. It is an accessible, creative and well argued presentation which we are sure will have a considerable input upon thinking in many countries.

David Hopkins
David Reynolds

July 1994

Acknowledgements

This book is in part a re-edited and updated version of my earlier Dutch book, *Effectieve instructie: een empirische bijdrage aan de verbetering van het onderwijs in de klas* (Effective instruction: An empirical contribution to improvement of education in the classroom). The Hague: SVO, 1991. Its publication was made possible by a grant from the Institute for Educational Research (SVO) and this institute funded the translation of the part of this book that originally appeared in Dutch.

I owe a great debt of gratitude to: Gerry Reezigt for the translation of the parts of the Dutch book included in this publication and her comments on the original version, which contributed greatly to the improvement of the manuscript; David Reynolds for linguistic editing and his critical support for the book.

Table 2.1 is reprinted from J. Scheerens, *Effective Schooling: Research, Theory and Practice*, Table 6.1, Copyright © 1992, with the kind permission of Cassell.

Table 3.1 is reprinted from G. D. Borich, *Effective Teaching Methods*, 2nd edn, Table 1.1, Copyright © 1992, with the kind permission of Macmillan Publishing Company.

Table 4.1 is reprinted from J. J. H. van den Akker, *Ontwerp en Implementatie van Natuuronderwijs*, Table 8–5, Copyright © 1988, with the kind permission of Swets Publishing Service.

Tables 6.1 and 6.2 are partly reprinted from B. J. Fraser *et al.*, 'Synthesis of educational productivity research', *International Journal of Educational Research*, vol. 11, no. 2, Tables 4.3 and 4.1, Copyright © 1987, with the kind permission of Pergamon Press Ltd.

Table 6.3 is reprinted from B. Rosenshine and R. Stevens, 'Teaching functions', in M. C. Wittrock (ed.), *Handbook of Research on Teaching*, 3rd edn, Table 13.1, Copyright © 1986 American Educational Research Association. Used by kind permission of Macmillan Publishing Company.

Tables 9.1 and 9.2 are reprinted from M. P. C. van der Werf and M. G. Weide, 'Effectief onderwijs voor allochtone leerlingen', *Tijdschrift voor Onderwijsresearch*, vol. 16, no. 4, Tables 3 and 4, Copyright © 1991, with the kind permission of Swets Publishing Service.

Figure 2.1 is reprinted from H. J. Walberg, 'Improving the productivity of America's schools', *Educational Leadership*, vol. 41, no. 8, Figure 1, Copyright © 1984 The Association for Supervision and Curriculum Development. Used by kind permission of the author and ASCD, all rights reserved.

Figure 2.2 is reprinted from E. De Corte *et al.*, *Beknopte Didaxologie*, p. 21, Copyright © 1974, with the kind permission of Wolters-Noordhoff bv.

Figure 2.4 is reprinted from M. J. Dunkin and B. J. Biddle, *The Study of Teaching*, Figure 3.1, Copyright © 1974, with the kind permission of Holt, Rinehart and Winston Inc.

Figure 2.5 is reprinted from J. Scheerens and B. P. M. Creemers, 'Conceptualizing school effectiveness', *International Journal of Educational Research*, vol. 13, no. 7, Figure 1.2, Copyright © 1989, with the kind permission of Pergamon Press Ltd.

Chapter 1

Can Education in the Classroom Be Improved?

COMPLAINTS ABOUT EDUCATION

Whenever I remember my childhood in the early 1950s, I see the classroom where I sat. It was in a school in a small rural area in the southern part of the Netherlands. The mixed-age class contained almost fifty children, all silently bent over their work. The windows were so high that through them you could see only the blue of the sky. That is what we did for most of the time, waiting for the ring of the bell that meant freedom for the rest of the day. In front of that class, the teacher (a female teacher in only the first class – in all the other classes in this boys' school the teachers were male) was always right. Even when teachers punished you unfairly, there was no discussion about their behaviour, their decisions and their teaching. On the contrary, when you as a child dared to make comments, you were punished even by your own parents, because the teacher and the school were always right, not only within the walls of the school but also in the village. As a high-ranking person placed immediately behind the mayor and the doctor, the teacher was important in our community: he was chairman or treasurer of several committees and a leading director of the chorus or the brass band. There was no discussion about education, or about the people who were responsible for it.

In all the countries of the world that picture was more or less the same, but times have changed. Nowadays education is under pressure and is criticized in a number of countries. Quite a lot of the criticism is directed to the outcomes of education. The complaint is that the outcomes are not as good as they should be, and that they are worse than in the past. Education is said to favour high-ability and high socioeconomic status (SES) students and to be unfair to low-ability, low-SES children. On the one hand, it is argued that children learn things in schools that they do not need for their further education or for their future lives, and on the other hand it is said that they do not learn things that are useful in further education or in their professional careers. In this respect, the criticisms and the complaints come from different directions. Some complaints concern the fact that children do not learn basic skills, cannot read or are illiterate, or cannot carry out basic mathematical operations. On the other hand, education is criticized for the fact that it is directed *towards* these kinds of basic skills: it is said that children cannot use a pocket calculator and other technical devices. Education is directed too much towards vocational education, or not enough, and so on.

Except for the outcomes, the aims and the objectives of education, most of the criticism is directed at the processes of education within schools and within classrooms. Teachers are sometimes said to be underskilled and underexperienced. Schools and classrooms are said to be not as well equipped as they should be. There is too much freedom in schools, teachers do not know how to teach and do not even

1

know the subject areas they are teaching in. Most of the time the arguments for these kinds of complaints are based on the results of education: on too many referrals to special education and on difficulties in the transition between different types of schools. In summary, from an untouchable place, the school became an institution under heavy pressure and very severely criticized.

EMPIRICAL EVIDENCE AND COMPLAINTS

Quite a lot of the criticism has nothing to do with the actual schools where education takes place, but is merely a signal of the interest of society in educational affairs. From an important but not very interesting part of life, education turned into an important issue that deserved a public debate. This can be illustrated by the introduction by Graubard, the editor of *Daedalus*, the journal of the American Academy of Arts and Sciences, to a special issue entitled 'America's Childhood'. Commenting on the report of the National Commission on Children, he states: 'I seriously wonder whether anything can be done to resolve concrete social problems until we deal honestly with real institutional issues – inadequate schools . . .' (Graubard, 1993, p. x).

The background to such statements about schools can be found in opinions about the place of education in a society. The society expects that schools, or education in general, can more or less compensate for initial differences between the students. The results of research have shown that differences between student outcomes depend heavily on ability, family background and other factors outside the school. As we will see in the next chapter, the contribution of education, schools and classes is relatively small. Although these variables are alterable, even in an optimal condition schools and classes have a minor influence and cannot compensate substantially for the initial differences between students. Apart from the question of whether this compensation is too difficult a demand for schools, one cannot expect that school can really contribute to the reduction of educational inequality in countries like the United States, where the availability of financial resources and therefore the quality of education depend on the 'wealth' of the neighbourhood in which the school is situated. Except for special programmes, for example for the disadvantaged, schools are mainly financed by a property tax which is based on the value of the real estate in a certain area.

In an opinion poll in the Netherlands, it turned out that education ranked second in an ordering of important social issues, with the health service in first place (Creemers *et al.*, 1993). It also turned out that, generally speaking, people with a higher level of education or people in the professions, like teachers, are more critical of education and schools than are others. Perhaps that is an indication that criticism of education comes specifically from more highly educated people and professionals, although these groups also blame parents and students for not participating enough in education. In particular, employers complain about the level of competence of their employees.

It is not easy to reject the complaints about education. In general, however, the world's population is more educated than in the past: more people are educated, but there are increased demands for people with higher levels of knowledge and skills. Especially when we take into account the time devoted to education and learning, together with the attendance of students in schools, the results of education and of schools are reasonable. Of course, almost every parent and teacher complains about the competence level of students in specific areas, but they should take into account the fact that schools now have more objectives and more topics to cover than in the past. For example, in primary education in the Netherlands we now have almost twice as many school subjects as in 1950. At the same time, school hours have been reduced by at least 20 to 30 per cent, and in some countries by even more. For example, in the Netherlands between 1950 and 1993 the time spent by primary students in school was reduced from 1300 to 1040 hours per year. There are differences between countries, as the studies of the International Association for the Evaluation of Educational Achievement (IEA) have shown. In these research studies, countries in the Pacific show better results compared with some countries in the Western world, but there are also great differences between Western countries, which proves that education can be improved within countries with comparable contexts, or at least that students can achieve better. But even in countries with quite reasonable results in these international comparative studies, general complaints about the results of education still exist or are made about something specific. As an example, in the Netherlands, which has quite good results in mathematics education, a point of criticism is the existence of a differentiated secondary school system, and linked with that is a large variation in the results of students.

It is also important to note that countries with high results in one area do not show those kind of results in another area. Dutch students, for example, achieve quite well in mathematics (Robitaille and Garden, 1989), but their results in language are far behind those in other countries, even towards the bottom end of the continuum. Other countries in Western Europe, such as Finland, achieve very well in this area (Elley, 1992; Postlethwaite and Ross, 1992). The same holds for science. In the second IEA study of science, the results of Hungarian students were the highest, even better than those of Japan (Postlethwaite and Wiley, 1992). These results can be interpreted as empirical evidence for the statement that the results of education can be improved by education itself, because we cannot expect that students in different countries have different abilities in specific areas (in general). It also points at the fact that we should investigate the contextual differences between countries.

From the results of educational research, we know that quite a high proportion of variance is explained by external variables, such as the ability of students and their socioeconomic backgrounds. In fact, schools and education in schools do not contribute that much to the explanation of variance in educational results. So, on the one hand, we need education to achieve results, because most of the students do not learn very much outside schools and do not master the objectives, but on the other hand mastering the objectives depends quite a lot on other sources of variance. Education in schools is unable to compensate for initial capacities of students. So, even when the complaints about education and educational results are valid, we have to take into account that most of the results are explained not by the schools, but by other sources of variance, and that schools cannot reduce the importance of these sources.

The differences between countries with respect to their results in different school subjects can be interpreted as an indication that school education can contribute to outcomes and that the contextual differences between countries can cause a higher level of education in general. Schools are burdened with all kinds of

3

tasks – more school subjects, achieving compensation for initial differences – and also have to face an increasing variation between students, for example with respect to their cultural background. In this respect, it is perhaps even encouraging that, contrary to some opinions within society, educational research cannot prove that educational results have worsened substantially. It is quite impossible to make comparisons every year for all students. However, indications in studies that, for example, the relative results of ethnic minorities are improving (slowly) and that participation in higher levels of education of specific groups (for example, low and middle SES students, and girls) is increasing, can be interpreted as counter-evidence for the supposed low quality of school education, although the critics will argue that these results could also be achieved by lowering the standards of examinations and tests.

In summary, we can conclude that complaints about the quality of education, with respect to the results of students, do not have a very firm basis, in general.

IMPORTANCE OF CLASSROOM EDUCATION

Complaints address schools or education in general. In fact, the discussion about education is very diffuse. Society expects learning results from education as an institution, and from the school as an organization, but in fact the results of education are achieved in a specific place within schools. Education is provided in the classroom. Once situated, it is understandable why we talk about 'education' and not about classrooms, because we expect that conditions can be arranged at the institutional level or at the school level, and that the effects of these can spread out through the whole system, the school(s) and classes. In this way it is expected, for example at the policy level, that results in education can be achieved by large numbers of students, independently from teachers, classrooms and classroom environments. However, for learning, the classroom is the nucleus where other influences on the learning of students and their educational results are found, like classmates, peer groups in general and also teachers and textbooks. In fact, all the factors or variables that contribute to educational outcomes exist in one way or another in the classroom.

What we have to do to make intellectual progress is to look at the different components, especially at components connected with education as a system, which can contribute to learning outcomes and to learning processes. We have to take into account the ability of students and their social background, because these influence results, but the central focus of this study is on the teaching–learning process at classroom level. We can look at other components and other levels in education, like the school, and at education as a system as conditions for what happens at classroom level. Issues and variables at state level and at school level, such as a national curriculum, educational policy-making, school working plans, school activity plans, school development plans, school teams, management and the principal as an educational leader, all influence what happens at classroom level, but we should not overestimate these influences. For example, teacher behaviour is partly determined by the school working plan, but what the teacher does is far more determined by what the individual teacher makes out of this plan. We would also expect that at classroom level teacher behaviour is determined more by the textbooks teachers are using than by the school working plan, which is especially influential at the higher school level, for example, by providing a common base for the teachers in choosing textbooks. That means that the school level and even the institutional level can create conditions and influence the educational outcomes by influencing factors and elements at classroom level, such as teacher behaviour, availability of textbooks and grouping procedures. Multilevel research in school effectiveness provides empirical evidence for this position. Factors at school level explain variance in educational outcomes, but this variance is reduced when factors at classroom level are introduced to the analyses. By the introduction of factors at classroom level, some of the variance can be explained at that level and the amount of total variance that is to be explained is reduced, so for the school level less variance is left over to be explained.

Although this study is primarily concerned with student outcomes, which are attained at classroom level, the class(room) is also important for the affective functioning of students. It is the place that students see as their 'home' at school, as studies on the well-being of students show (Stoel, 1980). Students' well-being depends on their class, their classmates, the teacher(s), activities both within the class and outside the classroom with their classmates, and less on school characteristics like size and organizational factors.

From a theoretical and empirical point of view, the classroom is the predominant place in the school where learning and teaching take place, and in this way the classroom level is more important for learning and outcomes than other levels in education.

IMPROVEMENT OF CLASSROOM LEARNING

When we accept that classroom learning is the main determinant of educational outcomes, we can expect that the considerable differences between classes within and between countries (as the IEA studies show) can be reduced, and education in classrooms in general can be improved, by taking advantage of experiences in other countries and knowledge that can be provided by educational research. For that reason, we have to know what actually happens at classroom level and what the important components are that constitute and contribute to educational outcomes at classroom level. We especially need evidence about the characteristics of these components that contribute to the effectiveness of classroom learning. For example, we might expect that an important element or component in education at classroom level is the teacher, and especially teacher behaviour. But then we also need knowledge about what the characteristics of the effective behaviour of teachers are or what the characteristics of effective teachers are, what kinds of behaviour they show and what the characteristics of that behaviour are. The same holds for other components at classroom level. For the improvement of classroom instruction, it is also important to know which these key characteristics are. Some of them, like teacher experience, cannot be influenced at all but others, especially with respect to textbooks, grouping procedures and the organization of the classroom, can be changed more easily.

Educational research already has quite a long history in many different countries. There are in fact many different traditions. For example, the American tradition in educational research was strongly quantitative. In the past, the research tradition in continental Europe, especially in Germany but also in the Netherlands, was more qualitative, with an emphasis on a hermeneutic and phenomenological approach. The British tradition in educational research is famous for in-depth socio-logical analysis of the participation of different social classes in education and all the problems connected with the position of school education in the society (see, for instance, Pollard, 1985, 1990; Woods and Pollard, 1988). In the United States, contin-ental Europe and the United Kingdom, research in classrooms was carried out from an educational–psychological point of view, which contributes to our body of know-ledge about instructional processes.

This study depends heavily on all these kinds of studies, although perhaps less on the sociological tradition, the importance of which I take for granted, as is clear from the previous section. At this time, different research traditions are converging. I would like to consider the results of British, European and American research in this area. As said before, there are different components in classroom education. The most important component is the teacher; the others are textbooks and group-ing procedures, including the organization of the classroom. There are interrelation-ships between the three components, including with respect to their effective characteristics. In that respect, it is quite strange that empirical research is restric-ted to one of these components most of the time. There is a vast amount of literature about teachers and teacher behaviour. The same holds for research on the cur-riculum, and for textbook-based research and research on different kinds of organ-ization of classrooms, especially with respect to the possibilities of adapting instruction to differences between students. It is striking that the results of studies in these areas are hardly ever interrelated. An explanation may be that research can make progress based on splitting of the complexity of education into smaller parts that are easily accessible for research. However, we can expect that the improve-ment of education cannot be achieved by changing one component in the instruc-tional process, or even, on a smaller scale, just one or two effective characteristics of such a component. Educational improvement is not that easy.

PROCEDURE

In addition to studies about the problematic situation of education in schools and classrooms, like *A Nation at Risk* (National Commission for Excellence in Edu-cation, 1983) and *A Place Called School* (Goodlad, 1984), quite a lot of studies have been published about the improvement of education. Some of these studies take a very broad scope, for example the *Handbook of Educational Ideas and Practices* (Entwistle, 1990). Almost half of this handbook describes ideas on the context of the school, before it deals with the school and the educational process itself. Other publications take a narrower scope and advocate a single solution for educational problems, like the organization and management of the school, or even the adoption of a specific teaching behaviour, such as a specific grouping procedure or higher-order questioning.

This study stems from a background of school effectiveness and instructional effectiveness studies. That means that it takes the outcomes of learning as the point of departure, and that we are looking for elements and characteristics which can contribute to effectiveness in this respect. As we will see in the forthcoming chapters, quite a lot of research is carried out in the field of effectiveness, as, for example, shown by the review by Levine and Lezotte (1990). They have found hundreds of correlates for effectiveness, based on their review of separate individual studies. My study differs in two respects from these kinds of studies. First, I intend to develop a theoretical framework that allows the studies to be given an appropriate classification. Although it is apparent from these studies that many factors may contribute a small amount to educational outcomes, we are looking for as few factors as possible, which can explain as much as possible, and which can be interpreted on the basis of a theory about education. Second, when possible I will make use of reviews of studies. Primarily I am interested in empirical research on classroom instruction; if possible, quantitative studies are used, but more qualitative case studies are also included, because they can expand our knowledge about the topic under consideration.

Some of the studies are reviews of research carried out in the past and sometimes we can make use of a meta-analysis. In a meta-analysis, studies are put together, which means that larger numbers of teachers and students are available for the analysis. Meta-analysis is the statistical analysis of large accumulations of results from separate unique studies; it aims at integrating conclusions from these studies, in order to reach conclusions about effect sizes. According to Glass (1976), meta-analysis should meet the following criteria:

1 Studies that are included in the analysis should be selected by means of an objective method.
2 Important features of these studies are described quantitatively or quasi-quantitatively.
3 Effects of all studies are described using one similar scale of effect sizes.
4 Statistical techniques are used to relate study features to study results (Glass, 1976, p. 3).

Kulik and Kulik (1989, pp. 228–9) emphasize the point that meta-analysis is about reviewing results; in this process, statistical data like mean scores and standard deviations, not raw scores, are the objects of analysis. Moreover, effect sizes are the issue, not mere levels of statistical significance. Finally, not only effect sizes are important, but also the influence of study features on the effect sizes.

Slavin (1987a) states that this kind of meta-analysis unfortunately takes into account studies that are not carried out properly. He developed another procedure: the best-evidence approach. This means that, for the selection of studies, strict criteria should be formulated. In most of the meta-analyses carried out by Slavin and his colleagues, fewer studies have been included than in other meta-analyses.

In summary, I will first develop a theoretical framework. I will make use of the following studies: meta-analyses and best-evidence studies, literature reviews and research reports. Finally, I will develop a contribution to an empirically validated body of knowledge about education.

CONTENTS OF THIS STUDY

The main goal of this study is to look for characteristics of effective education at classroom level. For that reason I will develop a conceptual framework for education at classroom level in the first part of this study (Chapters 2 and 3). In that framework, I also have to take account, as mentioned before, of the other factors that influence educational results and that explain more variance than education factors in schools and classrooms can ever do. In this first part of the study, I will also deal with the question of what is meant by educational effectiveness, especially what we mean by instruction and effectiveness. Effectiveness is closely related to the outcomes of education that are determined by the learning processes of students, so we have to look for components and characteristics of components in the classroom situation that can be related to these learning processes. Effectiveness in itself is also a problematic term and needs some definition and elaboration, especially because it has been closely related to academic outcomes and even to 'basics' in education in the past. I will argue that educational outcomes can be defined in quite a broad way, but also that education and schools should as a basic minimum contribute to academic outcomes, i.e. the cognitive behaviour of students.

In the second part of this study (Chapters 4, 5 and 6), I will look in more detail at the different components at classroom level and look for the effective characteristics of these components, based upon empirical research. When possible, I will make use of reviews of research and meta-analyses that allow us to look at many empirical studies at the same time and that enable us to have a more condensed view of the characteristics, but I will also look at some illustrative studies in the different areas.

In the third part of this study (Chapter 7), I will look at the possibilities of developing educational arrangements, taking into account the effective characteristics of the different components in the instructional process. It is expected that these arrangements will provide a greater chance for the development of educational effectiveness than just effective characteristics from isolated components like teacher behaviour or the use of textbooks in the instructional process. I expect that an integration of the effective characteristics of these components has more effect than the separated components and characteristics.

Finally (Chapters 8 and 9), I will look at the possibility that other levels, such as the school level, the institutional level and the context of classroom education, can provide conditions for effective classroom instruction. We can find, especially in this area, much empirical evidence in the school effectiveness and the school improvement literature, and that leads to the question of how this research base can facilitate improvement of education.

The study intends to review and summarize the empirical research on effective instruction. Although it depends heavily on empirical studies, it tries to be more than a simple review by also developing a theory about effective classroom instruction in relation to the other levels in education from the very first until the final chapter. This theory is supported by empirical arguments as much as possible, but it also provides, it is hoped, some ideas for further research and for further theorizing, and may be directly helpful in the improvement of educational practice.

Chapter 2

Effective Instruction: Theoretical Framework

INTRODUCTION

In everyday language, different terms are used to refer to the output of education; for example, the effectiveness of education, the effects of education, instructional effectiveness, teacher effectiveness and educational effectiveness. The same term is used for different notions: educational effectiveness is sometimes meant to describe the output of the total educational system, as well as the effects of education within a specific classroom. The same holds for the term 'instruction', which is sometimes used in a very specific way related to educational technology, as, for example, in the case of programmed instruction. In other cases, the same term is used for all the arrangements with respect to education; for example, instructional environments. Then the term covers everything related to the micro-level and meso-level (like school organization and innovation) of education (Walberg, 1979). Sometimes different terms are used to describe the same thing: educational effectiveness, instructional effectiveness and teacher effectiveness are used interchangeably when the effectiveness of education is described.

The term 'effectiveness' can also lead to confusion. It is used simultaneously to refer to effects and efficiency. Moreover, the criterion for effectiveness in education can cause a dispute. This means that not only instruction, but effectiveness as well, should be more clearly defined, because widely divergent effects (very general effects as well as concisely delineated student outcomes) are meant.

This study concerns the effectiveness of education at the classroom level, described by the term effective instruction. The terms 'effectiveness' and 'instruction' are discussed in the following sections. It is made clear that 'instruction' is used in a broader sense than simply teaching and teacher behaviour. 'Effectiveness' will be used in relation to the objectives of education, and covers the multiple outcomes of education.

In the past, teacher behaviour was frequently studied, sometimes from the (inaccurate) perspective that teachers and the way they behave were the sole determinants of the effectiveness of education at classroom level. Even though teachers play a central part, it is clear that other factors influence learning processes and student achievement as well, directly or indirectly (mediated by teachers). In the second part of this chapter, this point of view is developed into a theoretical framework for this study. First, we will look at factors at classroom level, then at factors at other levels, because the classroom is embedded in a wider educational context.

This analysis provides the elements of the basic theoretical framework. Because the theoretical framework is intended to explain the differences between students in learning outcomes, two variables are of the utmost importance: time and opportunity to learn, which will be discussed in the final sections of this chapter.

INSTRUCTION

As yet, the term 'effective instruction' is not widely accepted. 'Effectiveness of teaching' and 'educational effectiveness' are more commonly used phrases. However, educational effectiveness does not specify which element of education is meant: education at the school level, educational policy, the educational system or education at the classroom level. All these different aspects of education, separately and in combination, are indicated. The term 'effectiveness of teaching' was introduced to emphasize education at classroom level, which is determined by teacher behaviour to a large extent. Teaching was meant to include notions such as preparation of lessons, actual teacher behaviour and the evaluation of teacher behaviour. This meaning of teaching implies certain problems: effectiveness of teaching is narrowly related to teacher behaviour and does not adequately refer to other components of education at classroom level, such as curricula and grouping. Although curricula and grouping are influenced to some extent by the way teachers behave and make use of them, they should be distinguished as separate components of education at the classroom level.

An advantage of the term 'effective instruction' is that it indicates teacher-initiated activities, as well as the other components of education at classroom level aimed at eliciting and consolidating student learning, more strongly than terms such as educational effectiveness or the effectiveness of teaching. An objection to the term 'instruction' could be that it is used in a narrower sense. Instruction then refers to a stepwise and controlled change of student behaviour by means of learning, as the derived terms 'instructor' and 'programmed instruction' show. In that case, 'teaching' is used to indicate all teacher activities (such as the grouping of students, the use of media, instructing and practising) aimed at eliciting and consolidating student learning activities. Instruction is supposed to be just one aspect of teaching.

Several authors in the Anglo-American literature make a distinction between teaching and instruction. Teaching is a general, commonly used pedagogical term, not apt for scientific purposes because it is not clearly defined. Instruction is meant to indicate the transfer of knowledge (Smith, 1987). However, the distinction between teaching and instruction is not generally accepted. This shows, for instance, in the third edition of the *Handbook of Research on Teaching* (Wittrock, 1986), where 'teaching' is described in great detail in the index, but 'instruction' is described only by reference to teaching. This leaves the impression that the two terms are interchangeable. In addition, other generally accepted terms, such as 'instructional leadership' (the education-related tasks of school principals), underline the impression that the distinction between teaching and instruction should not be so strict.

In the following chapters, the term 'instruction' is meant to describe education at classroom level in a broad sense. Teacher behaviour is most important in this respect, but there are other components at classroom level contributing to education and its effectiveness as well.

Teaching is an issue of passionate debate, more or less independent of empirical arguments, but related to ideas about 'art', 'craft' or 'professionalism'. Opinions differ on the possibility of making statements on teacher behaviour that have a general validity, based on empirical research. Eisner (1979) emphasizes the pedagogical attitude of teachers, and the transfer of values concerning both cognitive and creative skills. He also focuses on 'artistic' aspects of teaching, like creativity and intuition, and pays less attention to technical aspects, although he considers these aspects important as well. Gage (1966) emphasizes cognitive goals, skills and instrumental training, and focuses on generalizing statements on teacher activities leading to these educational goals, rules, formulas and algorithms (series of instructions that have to be carried out in a specific order). However, he acknowledges that teaching also concerns intuition, creativity and expressiveness. Anyone who puts the artistic aspect, intuition and creativity of teaching in the forefront will look for other methods and techniques for education. Eisner and Vallance (1974) make a plea for 'educational connoisseurship' and 'criticism', in order to study what they see as the essential aspects, the value aspects of teaching. In their opinion, this is a desirable addition to empirical studies on education. Flinders (1987) tried to make the art of teaching concrete at the instructional level. In his view the art of teaching contains the art of communication, the art of perception, the art of cooperation and the art of appreciation.

The importance of these approaches for the development of transferable knowledge can be questioned, especially when the disappointing results of research traditions aimed at the discovery and description of these aspects and their relation with students' learning processes are taken into account. Another argument that speaks against an over-concern with the aesthetic aspects of teaching is their uniqueness and their strong relationship to the personality of the teacher. The aesthetic aspects of teaching are more related to the personality characteristics of the teacher, such as 'humour, creativity and sensibility', than they are to the attributes that can be acquired in a learning process. In contrast to those who acknowledge the aesthetic aspects of teaching, those who think teaching is a skill that can be learned will emphasize the necessity to look for rules and algorithms and the importance of testing these in empirical research.

Teachers' teaching certainly has more, and other, aspects than those already discovered by empirical research. However, this study aims to look for rules that can enhance successful instruction; including not only teachers' teaching behaviour, but their curricula and policy on grouping as well. Instruction is the sum of the intended processes, including all components going on at classroom level, that have the intention of starting or maintaining the learning processes of students.

EFFECTS AND EFFECTIVENESS OF INSTRUCTION

Everything happening in a classroom has some effects: curricula, grouping and teacher behaviour all lead to effects on students. Dealing with the effectiveness of instruction means relating curricula, grouping, teacher behaviour and educational goals. These goals concern student knowledge and skills in certain domains.

Effective instruction results in the reaching of educational goals, primarily student academic achievement goals. Achievement can be operationalized in several ways. Effective schools research especially concerns mathematics, reading and national language, although initially a lot of attention was directed to school careers, examination success rates, grade retention, school dropout and referral to special education. The effectiveness of classroom instruction is also fairly often measured by rather crude indicators, such as grade retention and referral to special education. When school effectiveness is being looked at, these measures may be acceptable.

When the effectiveness of instruction is being determined, measures directly related to educational practice in specific grades or in specific classrooms should be used.

With regard to student achievement, it is clear that not only the mean scores of classes should be studied. The specific extent to which low-achieving students actually achieve educational goals should especially be taken into account, given the assumption that education is able to and should compensate for the unfavourable starting positions of some students. This can be done by checking the variance in student achievement, especially by looking at the extent to which the size of variance is reduced during education (although this may not happen often).

Effectiveness is related to preset goals or objectives, preferably measured by achievement tests. Educational goals are not limited to mathematics and language achievement, but can also encompass other school subjects and the basic and higher cognitive skills. Apart from these outcomes, education yields other outcomes: social cognition, interest in school subjects and students' sense of well-being. Effective schools research is now paying more attention to non-academic goals. However, there is no consensus in education about the extent to which non-cognitive goals should be pursued. In fact, statements of educational goals seldom refer to affective elements; student well-being and other affective outcomes are seen as not necessarily intended. It is pleasant when students like their schools and show some interest, because this can enhance their motivation and (indirectly) their achievement, but affective outcomes are rarely explicitly stated, although research in the field of educational psychology shows that motivation and self-regulation can have substantial positive effects on student achievement, especially in secondary education (see, for example, Weinert, 1990).

Nowadays, multiple criteria are used to determine the effectiveness of instruction and of schools: basic skills, higher cognitive outcomes, outcomes in different subject areas, social and affective outcomes, and finally the extent to which instruction and schools contribute to equity in education. Some of them are explicitly well defined in advance but, especially in the case of social and affective outcomes, the objectives of education are often implicit. However, it is difficult to relate goals and means in the case of these non-intended educational outcomes, more difficult than in the case of the preset goals aimed at by teacher behaviour, curricula and grouping.

The following chapters focus on effective instruction from the perspective of preset goals and outcomes that can be measured by achievement tests. In this study, 'effectiveness' is related to these well-defined educational outcomes, and consequently effective instruction addresses the factors and variables in instruction that contribute to these educational outcomes. Rephrased in empirical terms, effective instruction is directed to 'find' the factors and variables in the instructional process, which can explain the differences in the intended outcomes of comparable groups of students.

A problem in effective schools research concerns the size and stability of effects (Mandeville, 1988; Bosker and Scheerens, 1989; Bosker, 1991; Blok, 1992; Blok and Hoeksma, 1993). Stability varies rather strongly with grades: schools can be effective in grade two but this does not imply automatically that they are effective in grade three. Furthermore, schools that are effective in one year are not automatically effective in another year, and schools are not automatically effective for all subjects taught. Research on effectiveness at classroom level shows here it is also not necessarily stable: teachers and curricula that are effective in one year are not necessarily effective in subsequent years. Studying the effectiveness of education means searching for materials, procedures and teacher behaviours that are stable over time; that is, for teacher behaviour that is regularly shown by teachers and is related to educational outcomes in repeated measurements of that relationship.

The size of school effects should be seen in relation to the variance in student achievement that education can account for. Variables like ability and socioeconomic status (SES), which can hardly be manipulated, account for a major proportion of variance. The same holds for prior achievement, because this factor reflects the influence of background variables and the results of school learning. Educational factors can explain an average of 20 per cent of the total variance, although there are variations in this estimate that can be attributed to measurement models. Based on multilevel analysis, it is possible to estimate the proportion of variance that can be explained by the different levels adequately. Stringfield and Teddlie (1989), for example, report that in their study 75 per cent of the variance could be attributed to students, 12 per cent to teachers and 13 per cent to schools. In a Dutch dataset, Bosker found for mathematics that 75 per cent of the variance could be attributed to student variables, 11 per cent to teachers and 15 per cent to schools. For language, the results were slightly different: 83 per cent could be explained by the student level, 6 per cent by the teacher level and 13 per cent by the school level (Bosker, 1992).

The studies mentioned above dealt with the percentage of variance that could be attributed to the different levels in an empty model. Far more important is the percentage of variance that can be explained by factors and variables at the different levels. In the context of this study, it is an important notion that factors at the classroom level account for a larger proportion of variance than do factors at the school level. Proportions of variance explained are generally small (see, for example, Hoeben, 1989; Scheerens *et al.*, 1989), but even minor proportions of variance explained are important, in the light of the total proportion of variance educational factors can account for. They are important not only from a scientific point of view, but also because minor proportions can exert a large influence in educational practice; for example, in relation to student achievement and the effects of decisions based on student achievement (grade retention, referral to special education, advice for secondary education, for example). Walberg (1984) developed a model for educational productivity, based on meta-analyses of a number of empirical studies. Figure 2.1 shows his model, which is a graphical representation of the statements previously made.

The variables in Walberg's model relating to student aptitude and environment explain more variance than those relating to instruction, and the relationship between these variables and educational outcomes is supported constantly in empirical research. The strong relations with learning, however, are caused by variables that can hardly be manipulated. Relations with learning at school level and class level are not so strong. In addition, there are many variables, each contributing only a little to the relation between the more global variables in the model and student achievement.

Goals of education are, in the end, legitimized by society. Instruction can be

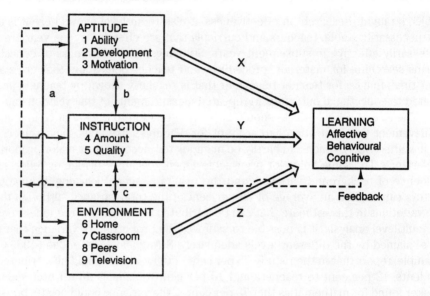

Aptitude, instruction, and the psychological environment are major direct causes of learning (shown as double arrows X, Y and Z). They also influence one another (shown as arrows a, b and c), and are in turn influenced by feedback on the amount of learning that takes place (shown as broken arrows).

Figure 2.1 *Causal influences on student learning (Walberg, 1984).*

considered effective when students succeed in reaching the general goals of education and the more specific goals of lessons derived from them. Criteria can be set, such as the (absolute) criterion that 80 per cent of materials taught should be mastered by all or most of the students. In order to compare effectiveness between schools and classes, corrections and controls are made for background variables (prior achievement, ability, socioeconomic status and gender). Another (relative) criterion is comparing student achievement between classes or schools. Sometimes effective instruction is expected to enhance equity, i.e. enlarge educational opportunities for students of low SES versus high SES. The effective schools movement originally started explicitly with equity as a major educational goal. The first research studies started in this context, and concluded that some schools offered black students more opportunities and achieved better results than did others. Research in later years showed the compensatory power of effective schools to be not so large (Brandsma and Knuver, 1989a). Effective schools seem to benefit all their students. The same can be expected of effective instruction.

Evaluation of the Educational Priority Programme in the Netherlands generally confirms this idea. The programme is especially directed to improving educational opportunities for minority groups. Actually, the other students benefit at least as much from any effective instruction in this programme (Weide, 1993). However, there is also research evidence for the statement that some factors in schools and classrooms benefit specific groups more than others do (Nuttall *et al.*, 1989). The same evaluation study in the Netherlands revealed some schools that did better in specific areas, such as language education.

WHICH FACTORS INFLUENCE THE EFFECTIVENESS OF INSTRUCTION?

When factors at the classroom level influencing student achievement are concerned, the teacher and the curricula used in education are often mentioned. Correlational studies show that there are many other variables in the learning environment that are related to student achievement one way or another. Many factors (from the temperature in the classroom to teacher activities) might influence student achievement or might explain variations in student achievement.

However, since the studies of Coleman *et al.* (1966) and Jencks *et al.* (1972), it has become clear that a major part of variance in student achievement is accounted for by initial differences in ability, SES, ethnicity and gender. Most of these variables can hardly be influenced, in any case not at short notice. This led to a certain scepticism in educational sciences and educational research, and to resignation in schools: it was thought that education hardly matters, and looking for factors that might explain variance in student achievement and that could be of interest for educational practice seemed like looking for a needle in a haystack.

It is a fact that ability and SES, two interrelated factors, account for a major part of the variance in student achievement and explain most of the later variations in student achievement. Education will have to accept that the influence of ability and SES cannot be set aside. However, there are research studies showing that schools can vary in their student achievement, controlling for ability and SES. This proves that schools and teachers do matter.

The key concept in education, in educational research and, in this case, in education at classroom level is whether there are factors that can be manipulated; in other words, that they can be changed by educational interventions in order to raise educational quality and output. Apart from ability and SES, there are other variables that may explain variations in students' achievement but that can hardly be changed (for example, the place where students live). But there are also variables that can be changed, and there are factors that can be influenced. Teaching paradigms try to put these variables and factors in a framework.

Especially important in education are the so-called prescriptive models, which do not describe educational practice by explaining how teaching takes place but prescribe how teaching should take place. Most of these models, on which the training of teachers is based, depart from educational goals and try to analyse, based on the 'intake' characteristics of students, how teaching should proceed. Especially in the 1970s and 1980s, the influence of the notion of educational objectives prescribing how teaching should be done was quite strong. Bloom (1963), for example, advocated educational objectives and relatively specific statements about what should be achieved by education as a useful tool that gives direction to the teaching–learning process. It is striking that after a lot of emphasis on educational objectives, the third edition of the *Handbook of Research on Teaching* (Wittrock, 1986) shows only one reference to educational objectives and goals. Perhaps this is the other end of the continuum.

One of the most well-known prescriptive paradigms is the model of didactical analysis (De Corte *et al.*, 1974), which has several American predecessors (Figure 2.2). Such models are heavily criticized (see, for example, Creemers *et al.*, 1981; Westerhof, 1989) because of their prescriptive nature. They do not reflect actual educational practice, but they depict what educational practice should look like. This is most clearly shown by the position of goals and teacher activities in these models. Goals are the guiding principles for teacher activities and the selection of curricular materials and contents; subsequently, effects are examined by means of evaluation.

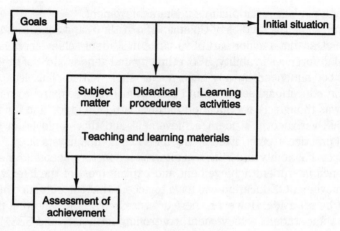

Figure 2.2 *Didactical analysis (De Corte* et al., *1974).*

In daily educational practice, goals do not play such an important part. As research in teacher cognition has shown, teachers are more occupied with curricular contents, techniques, materials and strategies. Goals are implicitly present in the subject matter: students should learn the contents that are taught to them. The explicit attention that was given some years ago to the formulation and establishment of goals for education at classroom level by teachers is not supported by their daily educational practice. Goals are present as general guidelines, but they are no longer as important as they were in the formulation of goals for education at classroom level. Goals are now more implicitly present, derived from curricular contents and textbooks.

Yet goals for lessons are important for the effectiveness and improvement of education at classroom level, as will be shown later in this book. Major parts of teacher behaviour and the way teachers use curricula are, or should be, related to their goals for their lessons. Guarding these goals for lessons proved to be an important method for achieving or raising the effectiveness of education. Goals for lessons are not an isolated component in the teaching–learning process, however. On the contrary, they are a part of it, a way to achieve educational goals that are further away, the final goals of education. Goals for lessons have become ways to realize goals that are more long term, and they form a basis for teaching and for teacher activities.

In addition to goals for lessons, goals for units of curricular contents can be distinguished; by this, I mean goals for integrated units that can include several lessons. Those lessons together form a unity, related to goals as well as to curricular contents. Even though the goals of lessons are not always visible in education at classroom level, they are implicitly present and constitute an essential component in teacher behaviour, in curricula and in textbooks.

The effectiveness of teaching especially concerns curricula, textbooks and other resources such as computers and audio-visual media. Textbooks, along with materials such as student workbooks, influence what goes on in teaching and learning at classroom level. The influence of planning documents, such as the curriculum, the school working plan or other activity plans, is much smaller (van der Werf, 1988). For a long time, it was thought necessary and possible to structure education at classroom level completely by means of textbooks. Teachers were to use textbooks according to guidelines that were as strict as possible, in order to achieve the goals set by textbooks and curricula. A lot of attention was paid to the so-called implementation of textbooks and curricula. In this vision, effective education would be achieved by the designing of curricula of a higher quality, which teachers would have to use according to the intentions of the curriculum designers.

In the following chapters, the ways in which effective instruction can be achieved by means of textbooks will be discussed. The ways in which teachers use curricular materials will be investigated as well. With regard to classroom organization, the same kind of question will be asked, namely which ways of organizing are more or less effective in relation to certain criteria. Examples of different ways of organizing are whole-class instruction, or forming homogeneous or heterogeneous groups based on student characteristics such as interest or ability. Criteria mostly refer to the achievement of educational goals, as will be clear by now. However, in the case of grouping and curricula, financial aspects (for example, the cost of curricular materials) as well as time aspects (preparation and implementation by teachers) can come into consideration.

Finally, and most characteristically of education at classroom level, the following chapters will discuss teacher behaviour. Teacher behaviour points towards various aspects. One aspect is goals that are not immediately visible in classrooms, but implicitly present in the educational activities of teachers. Literature on teaching, especially handbooks used in the initial training of teachers, often draws a distinction between preparation, the actual teacher activities and the evaluation. This distinction has more of a prescriptive than an empirical nature. It remains to be seen (see, for example, Clark and Yinger, 1977) whether teachers actually behave like this. Research shows that teaching is not such a straightforward process. Not everything that is planned is carried out, and not everything that is done is planned. Evaluation seems to be a neglected activity. Planning, actual behaviour and evaluation are strongly interrelated in teaching activities.

In the context of educational activities at classroom level, teacher activities can be divided into management and instructional behaviour. Management refers to everything teachers do to organize their classroom in order to make teaching possible. In addition to management, and often related to it, teachers show instructional behaviour: general teacher activities, didactic approaches that characterize teaching (for instance, 'discovery learning') and several other strategies or techniques, such as asking questions and providing corrective feedback. These techniques are often incorporated in general didactic approaches, which consist of a conglomerate of more or less effective strategies or techniques, or techniques fit for a certain

17

context. There is a great diversity in strategies and techniques, and educational philosophies and ideas about education promote new strategies time and time again.

A clear relation exists between ideas about education and educational strategies and approaches. When, for example, certain affective goals are thought to be very important, teacher enthusiasm, creativity and affective behaviour will be more strongly emphasized than when goals reflect cognitive and instrumental domains. This is yet another indication of the strong relationship between educational goals, the goals for lessons and the means that are used to achieve those goals (grouping and curricula), and teacher activities. In the achievement of effective instruction, different components at classroom level seem to be interrelated: the curriculum, grouping procedures and especially teacher behaviour. It is essential for effective instruction to detect the characteristics of these components that make them effective, and to find out in which ways they are related to each other.

EDUCATION AT CLASSROOM LEVEL AS A PART OF A LARGER COMPLEX

Education at the classroom level is essential for student achievement. The learning processes of students take place in classrooms, students are confronted with subject matter in classrooms and students are instructed in classrooms. However, education at the classroom level is not an island, without any connection with other parts of the school. Education at the classroom level is embedded in schools. In schools, education is prepared and organized by teams of teachers, under the direction of headteachers. In schools, policies for teacher behaviour in classrooms are developed, creating frameworks for teacher behaviour, even though teachers remain responsible for their own classrooms. The school level itself is embedded in a context. This context is conditional for ongoing processes at the school level and eventually at the classroom level.

Creemers (1985) adapted a model developed by Lundgren (1979) and revised by Hoeben (1985). This relatively simple model indicates the most important components of the teaching–learning process (Figure 2.3). The frame system provides a structure for the teaching–learning process. It encompasses conditions for the teaching–learning process, such as the physical environment, the organizational characteristics and the available time for education. The goal system encompasses specific plans, laid down in a specific curriculum, and guides teacher and student behaviour in the teaching–learning process. The actual teaching–learning process is created under the influence of the restrictions and guiding influences of the frame system and the goal system, and is an adaptation of the goal system in most cases. The output of the teaching–learning process, student learning, is important in this model. A distinction can be made between short-term content-specific realization of goals and long-term general societal effects of instruction.

Although the model specifies the relationship between educational outputs at classroom level and the external environment, in general it is not specific enough about the nature of the relations between different levels in the educational system, especially their relations with classroom learning. Dunkin and Biddle (1974) present a model for 'classroom teaching', based on the model of Mitzel (1960); their model is exhaustive because it includes different global groups of variables and numerous variables within these groups (Figure 2.4).

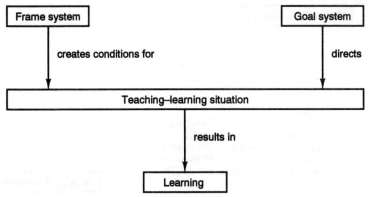

Figure 2.3 *Categories of variables in the evaluation of education (Creemers, 1985).*

Dunkin and Biddle mention four groups of variables:

1 Presage variables, such as teacher characteristics (experience, training) and other properties influencing teacher behaviour.
2 Context variables, such as characteristics of students, schools, communities and classrooms (class size, textbooks, presence of educational television).
3 Process variables, observable activities of teachers and students in classrooms.
4 Product variables, immediate and long-term effects of student learning, such as students' intellectual, social and emotional development.

The completeness of this model is a drawback, because it is not clear whether these variables are empirically important and, if so, to what extent. Another drawback of this model is the minimal amount of attention paid to the different levels within education, and the model's exclusive concentration upon education at the classroom level. School and community variables, and even classroom variables, are treated as contextual variables instead of as process variables, which are the variables that can influence the process and in that respect are part of, or contribute to, the throughput.

Some elements, such as classroom composition and its effects on school policy, are located at the school level and are conceptually at a distance from the actual classroom situation. At the school level, these elements can clearly influence educational practices in classrooms within schools. There are components even further away from the classroom level that are still important for the effectiveness of instruction: the educational policies of governing boards at district level and at national level (for example, their teacher employment policies, the availability of curricular materials, their guidelines for timetables and the national educational guidelines).

Kyriacou (1985) developed a framework of three complementary levels of analysis to 'unpack' effective teaching. At the surface level, the maximization of learning time and the quality of instruction are the key factors of teaching that 'explain' students' outcomes. At the psychological level, factors connected with

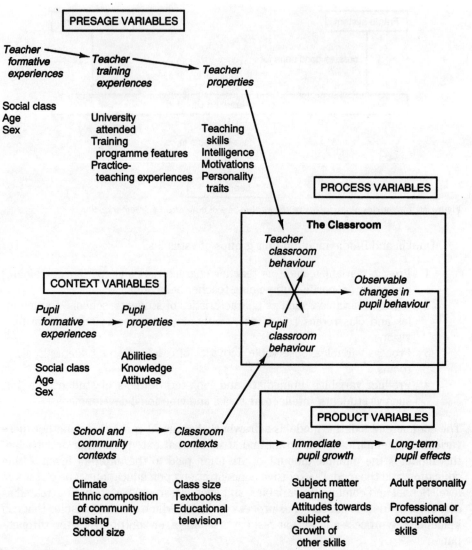

Figure 2.4 *A model for the study of classroom teaching (Dunkin and Biddle, 1974).*

learning are important. At the pedagogical level are teacher perceptions and strategies, pupil perceptions and strategies, and the characteristics of the learning experience itself. It is unclear, though, how the levels are interrelated.

Scheerens and Creemers (1989) have presented a model that tries to connect several levels of the educational system, with respect to the possible contributions of the levels to effectiveness of education (Figure 2.5). As yet, the model is formally not very well elaborated. The various levels need more specification, especially concerning the way elements of one level may be conditional for elements of other levels. Probably there are more relations to specify than has been done as yet, such as between background characteristics and the school level (Brandsma, 1993).

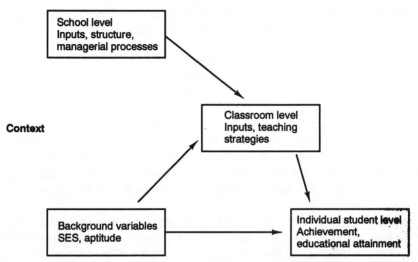

Figure 2.5 *A contextual multilevel model of school effectiveness (Scheerens and Creemers, 1989).*

However, the model makes it possible to relate divergent theoretical insights and theories on education (educational policy, educational management, school organization, instruction) and integrate them into a 'total' scheme. The model shows that, ultimately, student learning and learning outcomes are what education is all about. It also shows that factors at the classroom level and the school level, as well as at other levels, embedded in a specific educational context, influence student learning and learning outcomes in addition to background factors. These factors should be related to each other. For example, educational policies aimed at achieving national goals and evaluating these goals systematically might lead to the development and implementation of an evaluation policy at the school level, which might eventually lead to regular control of achievement in classrooms and to the use of corrective, remedial materials.

CONDITIONS FOR AND ELEMENTS OF EFFECTIVE INSTRUCTION

The model presented in Figure 2.3 showed the important role of the frame system and the goal system, and therefore the context of educational policy, in the organization of education. This certainly applies to the Netherlands. Education is decentralized, yet the organization of education is strongly influenced by national policy. The national government has to guard the quality of education and fulfils this task in many ways, for example by assigning financial means, by taking care of examination regulations and by maintaining the Educational Inspectorate. National policy contributes indirectly to education as well, by financing centres for the development of curricula and tests, and the huge network of advisory centres for primary and secondary education. Starting and promoting debates on educational topics (for example, on educational goals) can also be considered as a new policy instrument, used to give guidance to the organization of education, yet without strictly dictating how schools should be organized.

Examination regulations are an important instrument for national governments.

This instrument will probably become even more powerful when national goals are established and examinations are adapted in line with these goals. Considering the disappointing results of recent large-scale educational innovations in primary education and especially in secondary comprehensive schools, it can be questioned whether the formulation of national goals will result in guidelines for educational organization in individual schools. Regulations can be too strict, and ultimately they can defeat their own aims when the professional skills of teachers are not adequately acknowledged. When teachers feel this way, they will not bother about national goals, unless they are forced to do so by continuous internal and external control. In addition to examination demands, national goals and exam regulations, national governments influence education by regulations for timetables and by financial mechanisms. In short, the organization of education is intensively guided by the national level.

In terms of educational effectiveness, regulations for examination demands the development of an evaluation system, and feedback concerning achievement of educational outcomes contribute to an increase in the effectiveness of education. When more knowledge about how to increase effectiveness is available, and when this knowledge influences the direction of educational policy, national governments can enhance the effectiveness of education more strongly, by rewarding effectiveness and by stimulating the development of effectiveness-increasing factors. This will certainly contribute to the development of a school-level policy to increase educational effectiveness.

Studies on effective schools and evaluations of school improvement projects, although the latter were not totally based on effective school variables, produced factors that could increase the effectiveness of education. Not all these factors turned out to be as important in the Dutch context as they were in the United States context. Probably this shows the existence of general cultural differences between the two countries, and, in particular, educational cultural differences between them. Some factors, such as high expectations, appear to be important in both countries. Parent involvement, especially support of educational activities, can also contribute to the effectiveness of education. Other factors, such as educational leadership and a strong evaluative capacity in schools, supported to some extent by American and British research, are not as important in Dutch studies, as Scheerens's (1992) summary shows (Table 2.1). It should be noted that some elements, such as structured teaching, effective learning time and opportunity to learn, are probably more apparent at the classroom than the school level. Moreover, a characteristic like effective learning time is not only a factor resulting in student achievement, but the result of other characteristics, like educational leadership, as well.

Apart from contextual and cultural differences, there are probably two more factors responsible for the smaller importance of some school-level factors in Dutch research, in comparison with American and British studies. First, research in the Netherlands started later and could make use of improvements in instruments for data collection and data analysis. A second, and probably more important, reason is a sharper distinction between characteristics at school level (or other levels) and at classroom level, partly because of multilevel analysis and the theoretical conceptualization involved. Explanations for school achievement have therefore shifted to the classroom. However, the classroom context is not a sufficient condition for success

Table 2.1. *The degree to which the most important school and instruction characteristics relevant to effectiveness have been confirmed by empirical research*

Characteristic	Multiple empirical research confirmation	A reasonable empirical basis	Doubtful empirical confirmation	Hypothetical
Structured teaching	x			
Effective learning time	x			
Opportunity to learn		x		
Pressure to achieve		x		
High expectations		x		
Pedagogic leadership			x	
Assessment ability			x	
School climate			x	
Recruiting staff				x
Organizational/structural preconditions			x	
Physical/material school characteristics		o		
Descriptive context characteristics			x	
External stimuli to make schools effective				x
Parental involvement		x		

x, a meaningful influence; o, a more marginal influence.
From Scheerens (1992).

in school careers. Arrangements between classes and arrangements at school level are necessary as well. For example, a school policy emphasizing academic orientation is necessary, accompanied by high expectations of student achievement that are in line with such a policy. At the school level, structured teaching, effective learning time and opportunity to learn have to be promoted. This can be accomplished by a further specification in schools of evaluation policies and the national goals of national governments, related to previously mentioned elements, such as structured teaching, the opportunity to learn and effective learning time.

STUDENT LEARNING

The elements described in the previous section all concern an increase of student knowledge and skills. Student background characteristics account for a major proportion of variance in student achievement. British (Mortimore *et al.*, 1988) and Dutch (Brandsma and Knuver, 1989b) studies show that factors at school level and classroom level can explain between 9 and 27 per cent of the total variance in attainment at a point in time and about 20 per cent for progress over time (Brandsma, 1993). Adequate use of factors and variables that start learning and keep it going is necessary to utilize this proportion of variance optimally. As Carroll (1963) stated, this requires that the organization of education should be based on a theory which can explain the school learning of students, and which is sufficiently empirically supported. In the previous section, education at the classroom level was viewed from the perspective of national regulations. To find out if teachers' activities are effective, it is necessary to view education at classroom level from the perspective of school learning.

Carroll developed a theory that takes student learning in classrooms and schools as a point of departure. Variables at classroom level were explicitly involved in this theory. Later, in the 1960s and 1970s, several other important models were introduced, such as those of Bruner (1966), Bloom (1976), Glaser (1976), Harnischfeger and Wiley (1976) and Bennett (1978). All these models acknowledge students' aptitude, background and motivation and, in addition, instructional factors at the school site as important constructs for (school) learning (Haertel *et al.*, 1983).

Some of these models of school learning were sufficiently supported empirically during the past decades. Therefore, they can be used as a point of departure for the evaluation of factors that contribute to learning. Furthermore, it is possible to extend these models of school learning to educational theories contributing to effective education, by adding elements at the classroom and school levels.

Despite all the variations in teacher behaviour, curricula and grouping procedures, in the end one goal is of central importance: student learning. When we speak about learning, we can make a distinction between learning as a process and the outcomes of learning. We need to know how learning takes place in order to design instruction in such a way that we can enhance student learning in order to achieve the objectives of education, which are multiple outcomes. In psychologically based research, especially, quite a lot of attention is given to theories about learning, but not to theories about teaching. Gage (1963), for example, refers in the first *Handbook of Research on Teaching* to the fact that at that time there were three times more studies on learning than on teaching, and that the relationship between learning theories and teaching theories was quite weak. Nowadays there are quite a lot of theories or theoretical models concerning the learning of students in schools, as well as attempts to connect learning theories and teaching theories in educational learning theories, but an instructional theory or theory about teaching is not well developed. The proponents of a specific learning theory draw conclusions about how teaching and instruction should proceed, but the relationship is mostly quite weak. Gagné (1977) provided a description of the learning process based on information processes and on theories of learning and memory, but these instructional events strongly depend on learning prerequisites and a hierarchy of learning. These learning events, such as drawing the attention of students to what happens in the instructional process and providing feedback about their performance, are quite general and have to be better specified by the designers of instructional processes. In more recent theories about learning, emphasis has been put on the specific elements of learning, including the influence of motivation on learning processes outlined by Keller (1983), Boekaerts (1988) and Boekaerts and Simons (1993).

Some of the theories, such as Ausubel's (1968) and Bruner's (1966), strongly influenced curriculum development in the United States, although they were rarely tried out in educational practice or empirically tested. Gagné (1977) concludes, probably correctly with respect to his own strongly formalized cognitive theory, that the influence of these theories upon educational practice and instruction is small. Perhaps the influence should be small, because the models and ideas do not offer many possibilities for direct application in educational practice. Walberg's (1986a) review of learning theories in education also points out that, although all theories yield some good ideas, theories were not sufficiently supported empirically, and research and practice did not have enough valid ideas to develop.

This applies to a lesser extent to Carroll's model. In developing his model, Carroll explicitly aimed at designing a learning theory that would be of use for educational practice. Because of the elaboration Bloom provided within a broadly instructional framework (although Carroll (1989) thinks this is a rather mechanical and technical elaboration of his original intentions), the influence of these learning theories on educational practice was substantial. The Carroll model states that the degree of student mastery is a function of the ratio of the amount of time students actually spend on learning tasks to the total amount of time they need. Time actually spent on learning is defined as equal to the smallest of three variables:

1   Opportunity (time allowed for learning).
2   Perseverance (the amount of time for which students are willing to engage actively in learning).
3   Aptitude (the amount of time needed to learn, under optimal instructional conditions).

This last time is possibly increased because of a poor quality of instruction and a lack of ability to understand less than optimal instruction (Carroll, 1963, p. 730).

The Carroll model can be criticized for being more an instructional than a learning model. In fact, it does not provide information about how learning itself takes place, only that learning takes time and that this depends on multilevel interrelated factors. On the other hand, the general framework provides possibilities for elaborating on the different components.

In recent years the idea of how to learn as an objective of education has been given more emphasis. In addition to knowledge and skills, students should acquire learning strategies. A strategy concerns the knowledge and skills necessary to proceed in a task and to acquire knowledge. Strategies are also called meta-cognitive skills. A meta-cognitive skill consists of activities such as orientation, planning, testing, evaluation and reflection. From a review by Wang et al. (1990), it can be concluded that meta-cognitive skills can predict learning outcomes. So far we expect that the same factors that are contained in Carroll's model contribute to the achievement of objectives in the area of learning strategies. Perhaps the quality of instruction differs between the different sets of objectives. Authors writing about meta-cognition state that the learning processes and other instructional strategies that are required for meta-cognition are different from those needed for the achievement of lower-level objectives, like skills and knowledge (Palincsar and Brown, 1989; Prawat, 1989). On the other hand, Prawat emphasizes the fact that 'ordinary' cognitive knowledge and skills are required for this more active learning directed at meta-cognitive knowledge and skills.

In educational psychology, there are many theories that are clearly subject-specific; for example, psychological theories concerning learning to read and learning mathematics. This book, focusing on the general characteristics of the design of learning environments and teaching–learning processes, is based upon general psychological principles. These principles were discussed above, in reference to Carroll and Bloom. Three principles are important. The first concerns the construction of learning: by acquiring simple skills, one can acquire more complex skills. This means that subject matter has to be ordered in such a way that subordinate skills are learned first, because mastery of subordinate skills is expected to enhance the learning of superordinate skills. A second principle of an educational psychological nature, important for effective teaching processes, is feedback. Learning processes will take place adequately when students are informed on the progress of their learning and when corrective procedures are provided. Students are not only told whether they performed learning tasks adequately, they are also informed on how the improvement of learning tasks can take place. A third general principle of the learning process is the principle of practice, and the principle of mastery learning based on this. Learning rates are individually determined and are, especially at the start of school education, related to intelligence. However, when basic skills are sufficiently practised, which may imply that slow learners clearly need much more time than faster learners, the time needed for acquiring new skills will decrease gradually because students learned to master the learning tasks conditional for learning new tasks at an earlier stage (see, for example, learning hierarchies: Starren *et al.*, 1988, pp. 20–7).

As was formulated in previous sections, when education predominantly aims at an increase of student knowledge and skills, the achievement of intellectual skills is important, but the development of learning itself, as specified in the Carroll model, is of a more fundamental importance. The Carroll model points at important student factors associated with success in learning, especially student capacities and perseverance, and educational factors such as quality of instruction, time spent on learning and opportunity to learn.

The next section will offer more information on this model. For the development of a model for effective education, effective schools and, in this study, effective instruction, it is important not only to take a top-down view (from educational policy via its influence on schools to the classroom contexts where learning takes place), but to start from a bottom-up viewpoint (from student learning to classroom contexts to the schools and to the educational policy) that influences classrooms. The way learning processes take place has to be taken into especial account. The Carroll model is chosen as a theoretical basis, because it explicitly takes instruction and teachers into account. Moreover, several elements of the model offer possibilities for improvement of learning conditions or conditions of the instructional processes.

A PRELIMINARY CONCEPTUAL MODEL

The elements discussed in the previous sections are reflected in Figure 2.6. This model will be elaborated in the following chapters, on the basis of the insights described so far. The model is a combination of various components that can contribute to achievement to a greater or lesser extent. It is essential that student achievement is influenced by effective learning time and the opportunity to learn, in addition to several student background factors. Education at the classroom level (in terms of curricula, grouping and teacher behaviour) is supposed to influence learning time and student achievement (directly or indirectly, via an extension of learning time). The following chapters will discuss which characteristics related to the quality of these components of education at classroom level can increase effectiveness.

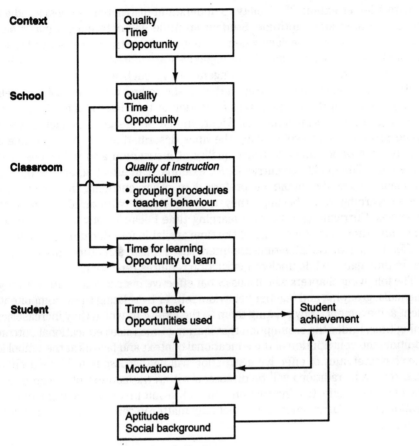

Figure 2.6 *The basic model of educational effectiveness.*

Factors at school level influence education at classroom level, in the same way that factors in the societal context of education influence the school level. I expect that components at the school level and at the contextual level influence the quality of instruction, the available time and the opportunity to learn. Besides these indirect effects of the context and the school level on educational processes at the classroom level and on effective learning time, there may be direct but weak influences as well. At the classroom level academic learning time and the opportunity to learn mediate the influence of all the other variables at school level, except the student variables. At the student level these two variables appear again, this time in the ways students make use of their time for learning (academic learning time) and their opportunities to learn (opportunities used). I shall elaborate these two constructs further in the next section.

The model emphasizes the influences of variables in the teaching and learning process at the classroom level that can be manipulated, such as curricula. It is clear, however, that other variables, also integrated in the model, influence student achievement directly and indirectly (such as student aptitude, social background and motivation), although these factors themselves are influenced by educational

27

factors to a lesser extent. The ability to understand instruction is considered a part of the factor of student aptitude. Student aptitude will determine a major part of student achievement, especially when there are no constraints set on ability levels or student pacing. When educational objectives are stated at a specific level, it is important to design educational arrangements in such a way that students are provided with enough time to work on their tasks, in line with their ability levels.

The essence of the model is that education at the classroom level, in terms of curricula, grouping and teacher behaviour, should be designed in such a way that learning processes can evolve along the lines described above. Next to time allocation and the opportunity to learn, quality of instruction also influences student achievement. The quality of curricula, for example, can affect actual learning time. High-quality curricula should be preferred to other curricula that may actually decrease learning time, because they are not clearly structured or show other deficiencies. Curricula can increase learning time because they are more efficient and because they make better use of the time available for education. Available time and effective use of available time are interrelated. Clear, structured instruction will result in time gains, while unclear instruction requires repetition.

The following chapters will discuss what effective instruction means with regard to curricula, grouping and teacher behaviour, either by relating these components to student achievement or by relating them to the extent to which they increase actual learning time, under the assumption that learning time raises educational outcomes. In addition, the contribution of the educational context and factors at the school level to the characteristics of effective instruction will be discussed. In the next chapter, several research traditions will be discussed within the context of a search for the characteristics of effective instruction. This will result in an overview of elements of education at the classroom level that actually matter in terms of affecting children's achievement.

ACADEMIC LEARNING TIME AND OPPORTUNITY TO LEARN

In Carroll's model the terms 'time' and 'opportunity' are both used; for Carroll, the opportunity to learn is the same as time allowed for learning. In the literature, time on task and the expansion of this concept, 'academic learning time', both refer to the 'time' dimension, but 'opportunity to learn' refers more to the content dimension. Together, these concepts stress the fact that time for learning is important and that possibilities for learning within that time framework should be offered. In this section I will discuss both concepts, because they are at the root of the basic model of educational effectiveness developed in this book.

Academic Learning Time

As a direct relationship between teacher activities and student achievement does not necessarily exist, researchers in the Beginning Teacher Evaluation Study (Berliner et al., 1978; Fisher et al., 1980) introduced the concept of academic learning time (ALT). This concept will be discussed first, because the ALT variable can be influenced by teachers in particular, and is related to student achievement as well.

From 1972 to 1978, the influence of teacher behaviour on student learning in schools was studied in detail in California. The Beginning Teacher Evaluation Study investigated (strangely unlinked with the issue suggested by the title of the study) the classroom characteristics and teaching activities of experienced teachers that positively influenced student achievement in primary schools. The study aimed to generate results that could be of use in the improvement of teacher training. Research on teacher behaviour is clearly problematic when achievement test scores are used to measure effectiveness, because the effects of learning in schools are partly determined by influences outside of schools, and because instructional activities that are hard to assess take place. Finally, test scores give information about the results of learning, but not about the process of learning itself. For these reasons, student learning is best placed between teacher instructional behaviour and the results of learning. Student learning is therefore best operationalized as the quantity of time spent on subject matter.

The attention given to academic learning time stems directly from the models discussed in this chapter. These models, for example Carroll's model of school learning and Bloom's more elaborated version, relate time spent on learning to achievement. Academic learning time (ALT) refers to four aspects: allocated time (learning time allocated to students by teachers), time on task (time students are really involved in learning tasks), student error rate (level of difficulty of tasks) and task relevance (relevance of the specific task to a certain part of the curriculum). Larger quantities of allocated time and time on task, a low student error rate and a high level of task relevance are expected to enhance achievement.

In a teaching strategy for effective reading instruction developed by Marzano *et al.* (1987), these four aspects were converted into teacher interventions. Several studies then related teacher actions to academic learning time. The study measured allocated time for a specific part of the curriculum (related to the achievement test), student learning time with respect to this part of the curriculum and student error rate. Task relevance was presupposed in the presentation of subject matter. Positive correlations appeared to exist between several aspects of ALT and achievement. The quantity of allocated time correlated positively with achievement for the specific tested part of the curriculum. The proportion of allocated time actually spent on learning (time on task) also correlated positively with achievement. Finally, for some students, the proportion of allocated time spent on tasks with a low error rate correlated positively with achievement. Allocated time, and especially the proportion of allocated time students spent on learning (time on task), seems to be essential in the relationship between ALT and achievement. This holds for the regular classroom situations of all students but especially for students at risk. This is underlined by recent research; for example, by Gettinger (1991) in an experiment with students with learning difficulties and Greenwood (1991) in a longitudinal study of low-SES students. At the school level, effectiveness can also be improved by a policy directed towards more academic learning time (Murphy, 1988, 1992; Levine and Ornstein, 1989).

Gage, among others, criticized the concept of effective learning time because of its psychologically empty and quantitative nature. According to Gage (1977, p. 75), it is necessary to investigate what kind of activities are offered during this academic learning time and which learning processes take place. Despite the fact that the ALT variables were partly based on criticisms of process–product research, Shulman

(1986) puts the Beginning Teacher Evaluation Study and the concept of ALT in the process–product tradition, and sets ALT as a merely intermediating variable between teaching processes and achievement. The ALT variables can be seen as a first step in the search for intermediary processes, such as the cognitive processes of students and mediating teacher activities. In our basic model, the ALT variables are put in such an intermediary position. Elements of education at classroom level, such as curricula and grouping procedures, can contribute to an increase in learning time when they are effective.

Opportunity to Learn

In order to achieve educational outcomes, students should at least have some opportunity to acquire knowledge, insights and skill. For curricula, this implies that the subjects students are supposed to learn have to be incorporated in curricular materials. For teachers, it implies that they should present these subjects. There must be some opportunity for students in classrooms to learn subjects.

In international research, the presentation of subjects in curricula and/or by teachers is called the 'opportunity to learn'. Research studies measure the opportunity to learn by checking whether subjects reflected in test items were presented in education. Large-scale studies often measure the opportunity to learn in a simple and therefore unreliable manner, for example by measuring years spent in education and by looking at the policies in the school curriculum on the topics to be covered in the attended grades. Another measurement technique is asking teachers whether they presented test items and how they taught the curriculum areas related to test items. Analysis of curricula is a more refined technique for measuring the opportunity to learn (Pelgrum, 1989a). Classroom observation is an even better technique, because teachers do not always stick to intended curricular contents; sometimes additional subjects are offered more or less extensively.

The opportunity to learn was included as a variable in several international comparative studies of the International Association for the Evaluation of Educational Achievement (IEA). The IEA aims at internationally comparative educational evaluation studies for several school subjects. Well-known evaluation studies were conducted for mathematics, science and the classroom environment (Pelgrum, 1989b). The opportunity to learn was defined in these studies in different ways. The first studies defined it as what teachers said they had presented to their students; more recent studies make use of curriculum analysis and classroom observation. In the preparatory notes for the Third International Mathematics and Science Study, the opportunity to learn is expanded to relate to the entire teaching process and includes characteristics of teaching quality, because it is expected that the opportunity to learn is promoted by the quality of teaching (Burnstein, 1993). Nevertheless, even when opportunity to learn is poorly operationalized, it turns out to be an important variable in explaining variations between schools and teachers. Husén (1967) concluded that the opportunity to learn was an important variable in an early IEA mathematics study. Teacher variables accounted for 5.4 per cent of the variance. However, when the opportunity to learn was excluded from the analyses, the proportion of variance explained fell to 0.2 per cent.

Variations between countries in the opportunity to learn are large. They are related to the age of selection and to the degree of tracking in the educational system. The opportunity to learn and student achievement are more closely related in countries with a tracked educational system, as Great Britain had in earlier years. A weaker relationship was found in Sweden, where tracking is absent in the educational system and therefore the variance in the opportunity to learn is reduced. This variance is one of the reasons why, among others, Oakes and Lipton (1990) criticize tracking in American education, where depending on their class levels, students will get different opportunities to learn. The lower-ability classes in the American educational system do not get homework assignments and their learning tasks involve lower-order activities only, like memorizing and repeating answers instead of critical thinking and problem solving, and a great deal of what is important is omitted from their curricula and their textbooks. This leads to an unequal situation in which pupils who need learning opportunities the most get the least (Oakes and Lipton, 1990).

Scheerens *et al.* (1989) concluded that variations between schools are smaller in countries with comprehensive systems, where tracking is absent. Variations between classrooms still remain, however, and this finding again supports the view that the effectiveness of education is determined by effective instruction. The importance of the opportunity to learn in international comparative studies is shown by other IEA studies as well, for example by the science study of Walker (1976) and by the Second Mathematics and Science Project (Pelgrum, 1989a). IEA researchers developed over a period of time techniques for estimating the opportunity to learn in relation to the evaluation of educational achievement (Pelgrum, 1989a; de Haan, 1992), and rather simple techniques that are available now can be used. At the end of a particular term or year, teachers can be asked to examine each item included in a measure of student learning, and respond to a series of questions (Did you teach it? If not, why not? If yes, with how much emphasis? Anderson, 1991).

Lugthart *et al.* (1989) present an overview of studies on the relation between the opportunity to learn and student achievement (Table 2.2). These studies show the importance of the variable 'opportunity to learn' in accounting for variations between schools and teachers. Relationships can vary from country to country, as the results make clear, and this is probably caused by the degree of individualization in school systems and in schools, resulting in the take-up of different subjects for different groups of students. When the same subjects are offered to the total student population, variance in the dependent variable 'quantity of subjects' no longer exists, and the variable 'opportunity to learn' loses its explanatory power (see, for example, the cases of Sweden and Finland in the Husén study of 1967). Outcomes are more dependent on other variables at the classroom level and/or at the student level. This is probably the cause of the smaller explanatory power of the opportunity to learn when variance at the classroom level is concerned, by comparison with explained variance at school level.

Students in the same classroom are mostly offered roughly the same opportunity to learn, because they are all instructed in school subjects for an equal number of hours and because they all use the same curriculum, although an exception should be made in this respect when within-class grouping procedures imply variations in curricular contents. The quantity of subjects presented by teachers and lessons will not vary substantially when classes are compared within schools of different categories.

Table 2.2. *Opportunity to learn*

Researcher(s)	Sample size/population	Research methods	Level of analysis	Operationalization of the independent variable	Dependent variable	Results
Husén (1967)	Average of 144 schools (3000 students) in 10 countries (age 13), IEA	Multiple regression for each age group and each country	Student	Mean score of all test items of opportunity to learn, varying from none to all of the students (scored by teacher)	Mathematics achievement	$r = 0.55$ $\beta = 0.33$ (UK) $r = 0.04$ $\beta = -0.05$ (Fin) $r = 0.26$ $\beta = 0.06$ (Fran) $r = 0.09$ $\beta = 0.04$ (Japa) $r = 0.56$ $\beta = 0.40$ (Scot) $r = -0.03$ $\beta = 0.00$ (Swed) $r = 0.19$ $\beta = 0.11$ (USA) $r = 0.29$ $\beta = 0.18$ (all)
	Average of 50 schools in 12 countries (800 students); exam grade secondary education, IEA					$r = 0.40$ $\beta = 0.16$ (Aust) $r = 0.13$ $\beta = 0.13$ (UK) $r = -0.09$ $\beta = -0.02$ (Fin) $r = 0.44$ $\beta = 0.30$ (Japa) $r = 0.18$ $\beta = 0.08$ (Scot) $r = 0.29$ $\beta = 0.12$ (USA) $r = 0.30$ $\beta = 0.14$ (all)
Fend (1984)	144 classes (9th grade) 67 traditional schools 44 *Gesamtschule* (2 levels) 44 *Gesamtschule* (3 levels)	Regression, all classes, each school type	Class	Content of test taught/practised, proportion of total contents of lessons	English language achievement (sum of scores IEA test and test EET 9)	$\beta = 0.079$, $R = 1.5$ ($P < 0.05$), all school types $\beta = 0.039$, $R = 0.5$ (n.s.) (traditional systems) $\beta = 0.049$, $R = 8.0$ ($P < 0.05$) (*Gesamtsch.* 2 levels) $\beta = -0.082$, $R = 0.82$ (n.s.) (*Gesamtsch.* 3 levels)

Table 2.2. *(cont.)*

Researcher(s)	Sample size/population	Research methods	Level of analysis	Operationalization of the independent variable	Dependent variable	Results
Horn and Walberg (1984)	1480 students (age 17) NAEP dataset (National Assessment of Educational Progress)	Correlations and multiple regression	Student	Number of maths courses, Highest level of maths course	Mathematics achievement	$r = 0.62$ $\beta = 0.94$ $r = 0.63$ $\beta = 2.05$
Pelgrum *et al.* (1983)	5350 students (237 teachers), 239 schools, sec. education, 2nd grade, IEA	Correlations	Class	% items taught (scored by teacher)	% items correct per class, maths test	$r = 0.22$ (sign.)
Bruggencate *et al.* (1986)	5165 students, 224 schools, sec. education, 3rd grade, IEA	Correlations	Class	% items taught (scored by teacher)	Mean score per class	$r = 0.14$ (biology) $r = 0.40$ (science) $r = 0.69$ (chemistry) $r = 0.31$ (geography)

From Lugthart *et al.* (1989).

Variation increases when students are the unit of analysis, but student characteristics still account for relatively higher proportions of variance than the factors 'duration of education' or 'number of subjects presented'. Differences in curricula can be expressed in the hours of instruction they require, which is an indication of the quantity of subjects in a curriculum and the opportunity to learn offered to students. Goodlad (1984) reports an enormous range in the time spent on instruction in elementary schools and in the allocation of teachers to subjects in secondary schools. In elementary schools there is a difference of between 19 and 27 hours of overall instruction per week. Within the hours spent on instruction overall in the different schools, language and mathematics receive the most attention, with about 54 per cent of all the instructional time. In other curriculum areas there is an enormous amount of variance, from paying virtually no attention to subjects such as physical education and the arts, to giving the latter more time than science and social studies (Goodlad, 1984).

Analyses of Dutch curricula show distinct differences in the hours of instruction and in the quantity of subjects for instruction. For example, the total number of lessons in the English language curriculum in primary education varies from 39.6 to 71.1 (with an average of 50.8). Differences in the mean percentage time for those subjects actually presented (in relation to the total number of activities for grammar, reading, speech etc.) are even more evident: percentages vary from 22 to 60 (with an average of 43; Edelenbos, 1990).

It seems justified to conclude that the opportunity to learn is an important variable in relation to student achievement, especially when variations in the quantity of subjects presented to students occur. Variations can occur between school types, within classes (as a result of grouping procedures) and between different curricula and textbooks (with regard to the amount of learning time they require and to the presentation of subjects).

The relationship between the presentation of subjects and the level of aspiration of curricula on the one hand and the tests measuring effectiveness of education on the other hand deserves further attention. When two different operationalizations of educational goals, operationalization in tests for the evaluation of education and didactic operationalization in curricula, are accepted (de Groot, 1961), no correspondence between the two is necessary. However, this may result in discrepancies between actual instruction and student achievement as measured by tests. Sometimes students will achieve more goals (mediated by curricula) than measured by their tests, or, which happens more often, they will achieve fewer goals. The results of the Dutch Education and Social Environment Project (OSM; Slavenburg et al., 1989) give a striking example. In the evaluation of the curricula developed in the project, it appeared that students did meet the criteria for the curriculum to be deemed successful (in most cases, 80 per cent of the students scored an 80 per cent correct response rate), but the same students did not achieve as well on national tests. A low level of transfer of knowledge to the national tests may partly explain these results, although a low level of aspiration within the project curricula, lower than necessary for average achievement on national tests, is a more likely explanation. This finding implies a discrepancy between didactic and evaluational operationalizations of goals and objectives, which may lead to the claim that tests should reflect educational contents and goals. Another implication of the study concerns curriculum designers: in developing curricula, they should strive for the achievement of national goals.

A striking argument can be found in the results of an evaluation of Dutch textbooks with respect to the national objectives. It turned out that for an extremely important subject in primary education, language, only for the component 'spelling' was enough relevant material offered to students; for the other components, such as reading, speaking, listening and writing, this was not so. For mathematics, the provision of adequate material was sufficient and in accordance with the national objectives in this area. The outcomes of education, measured by a national test given at the end of the eighth grade (i.e. to 12-year-olds), were in line with this analysis of the learning material. Except for mathematics, physical education and the expressive arts (like drawing), all the other teaching and learning materials provided in textbooks were more or less insufficient and it is doubtful whether the Dutch national objectives can be achieved by the learning experiences offered by the textbooks (Harskamp and Suhre, 1993; Commissie Evaluatie Basisonderwijs, 1994).

SUMMARY

Following a discussion of two basic concepts, instruction and effectiveness, this chapter presented a basic model of educational effectiveness. This model provides a framework for the coming chapters, which deal with the components of effective instruction in more detail, and which outline the contribution of the levels above the classroom level, which will be discussed in the final chapters.

In this chapter I dealt especially with two fundamental components of the model at classroom and student level. Essential at both levels are the time and the opportunities allowed and offered to students and the use students make of that time, which induces their learning outcomes. In this way, time and opportunity mediate the other variables.

Chapter 3

Traditions in Research on Instruction

INTRODUCTION

Research on instruction deals with aspects of education at the classroom level mentioned in Chapter 2: curricula, teacher behaviour and classroom organization. In research on instruction, several traditions can be distinguished. These traditions concern not only the way research is done (process or product), but also the dominant issues within teaching. In one period, for instance, research concentrated on curricula and textbooks, in another period on teacher behaviour, and in yet another period on the implementation of curricula. Often a new research tradition arises as a reaction to disappointing results, generated by a previous period and another research issue. The constant changing of research issues is an illustration of the not so stable character of a science. De Groot (1976) illustrated the short history of educational research by comparing it with the characteristics of 'weak young' sciences, such as underdeveloped disciplinary organizations and a proliferation of theories.

In educational research, a constant changing of interest and the development of new theories can be seen, with little emphasis on convergence or stability in research traditions. This study makes an effort to gather findings from several research traditions, which may lead to a somewhat flattering picture of developments in the history of educational research. However, several traditions in educational research are converging at this moment, and the interest in effective schools, effective instruction and most of all the further development of theory in this tradition all reflect the movement towards convergence. Stability, for one thing, has increased, influenced by Gage's (1963) process–product paradigm, especially in the narrower field of research on teacher behaviour. This stability has also promoted progress in research.

The following sections offer a short historical overview of the rise of three research traditions and the different approaches of these traditions: curriculum research, research on grouping and research on teacher behaviour. It will be shown that these three subjects have become more and more interrelated in the history of research. Curricula cannot be studied independently of the way teachers use them; teacher activities are, to a certain extent, prescribed and structured by curricula and textbooks. The same holds for grouping procedures in education. Grouping in itself is not content-related, but implications for grouping are often integrated in curricula, which point out how subjects should be taught. Moreover, effects of grouping are dependent on the way teachers implement grouping.

A major part of the research presented in this chapter and the next chapters is from the United States, because the majority of relevant studies took place in that country. European empirical research is mostly of a more recent date and also shows specific traditions. In Germany, the influence of the hermeneutic approach and phenomenology is still important. Dutch educational science, although dominated by the empirical approach, is influenced by this German tradition and, in the field of teaching and learning theory, by the Russian constructivist approach. In the United Kingdom a strong qualitative sociological tradition in education can be found in addition to educational psychology. This has led to special attention being given to societal influences on schools and to the differential effects of school education on students of different backgrounds. These traditions still give a specific colour to the educational research going on in the different countries, although, as in educational effectiveness, the programme of research is also determined internationally.

It is very important, though, that research does take place in different national contexts. In the development of the integrated model for educational effectiveness in the previous chapter, I pointed at the importance of the school context. This certainly applies to the review of results of research on teaching, since there are (cultural) variations between, for example, education in the United States and education in European countries. These variations apply to areas such as the autonomy of teachers, the decentralization of educational policy, the influence of local educational boards, the influence of individual schools, the influence of curricular materials on educational practice and state-determined obligations to use materials. Such variations have to be taken into account when results of research on the effectiveness of teaching are interpreted in a specific national context.

THE CURRICULUM

Over the years, the term 'curriculum' has been used to indicate quite different documents, especially in the European tradition. Originally a curriculum was a document at school level, containing information about the time schedule, aims, objectives and methods. Later, the term was also used for textbooks. Nowadays, other terms are introduced to distinguish documents at the different school levels. The school working plan contains the information originally in the curriculum at school level (aims and goals, overview of methods). The school activity plan provides information about the way the school will achieve its purposes. At classroom level, terms such as textbooks, methods, student workbooks and teaching–learning material are used. In this study, I will use the terms 'curriculum', 'curricular materials' and 'textbooks' interchangeably to refer to the documented material at classroom level used by teachers and students in the instructional process.

In education, several related approaches to the learning of skills or the transfer of knowledge exist. Traditionally, different approaches were adhered to. For instance, in the field of beginning reading instruction, a debate took place on the merits of global versus analytic–synthetic approaches. Nowadays, debates like these are still continuing in the area of foreign-language instruction (communicative versus grammatical approaches) and mathematics instruction (realistic, such as mathematics in daily life, versus traditional, the so-called mechanistic approach). Such debates are often based on ideological principles and conducted with great vigour, but they can only be settled with the help of empirical data. This is one of the reasons for comparative research on curricula, for example on the curricula for beginning reading instruction, that started at a fairly early stage. For a review of research in the past see, for example, Chall (1967) and for European research see Müller (1964).

Comparative research on curricula soon showed the existence of large variations in results within one and the same curriculum. Sometimes curricula that clearly exhibited shortcomings or errors resulted in good achievement despite these, while curricula that looked sound resulted in relatively lower achievement. This indicates that teachers and classrooms differ strongly from each other, even when the same curriculum is used. Some of the variation between classrooms could be attributed to differences in student characteristics such as ability, socioeconomic status and gender. But even classrooms that were relatively comparable with regard to these characteristics showed achievement differences. This situation raised the question of whether teachers, rather than the curricula, produced these differences.

In addition, research on teacher behaviour and research on the differences between teachers using the same curriculum was initiated, as well as the development of so-called 'teacherproof' material, especially after Coleman *et al.* (1966) and Jencks *et al.* (1972) concluded that teachers and schools hardly mattered. Porter and Brophy (1988) explained the development of 'teacherproof' curricula as a result of the low expectations held of schools and teachers.

Another explanation is the involvement of specialists, such as reading and mathematics specialists, in the school improvement projects launched by President Johnson's Great Society Program, while specialists in the field of research on teaching were not involved. Subject specialists wanted to codify subject-specific knowledge in curricula and textbooks. The development of curricular materials was also enhanced by the supposition of deficiencies in American education, which arose from the setback for the United States in comparison with the Soviet Union in the development of space programmes (the so-called Sputnik effect). Curricula that teachers should follow obediently were developed, in order to achieve better results. The ideas of teachers were considered disturbing to the effects the curriculum aimed at, and were to be eliminated as much as possible. The development of 'teacherproof' curricula generated research on the way teachers applied curricula, the way curricula should be implemented and the importance of factors that generate precise following of directions in curricula and textbooks.

The studies of the Rand Corporation (Berman and McLaughlin, 1977; Hall and Loucks, 1977) and most of all the analyses of Fullan and Pomfret (1977) on these implementation studies became widely known. These studies focus on factors that can promote or hinder the implementation of educational innovations (federal policy programmes, curricula or textbooks). As well as non-use or mechanical use (routine following of guidelines), several stages of use are distinguished: leading from the first orientation via degrees of implementation to the integration of educational innovations in teacher behaviour, in such a way that adaptations of innovative materials (curricula, textbooks) can take place.

Fullan and Pomfret mention a number of factors, on the basis of the research literature, that decide whether an innovation will be implemented or not. The extent to which the changes in schools and classes are in line with the aims of the designers of the innovation was not taken into consideration. The factors concern the efforts necessary for implementation (explicitness, complexity, strategy, resource support) and the context of innovations (for example, innovation experience, the role of the principal, relations between team members).

These factors contribute to the implementation of the innovation, but it will be clear that the correspondence of implementation with the aims of curriculum designers is even more important. That is why projects like the Education and Social Environment Project (OSM) in Rotterdam attach great value to the implementation of innovations as they were meant to be implemented. Curricula developed in the project were important means to achieve the project goals: improvement of the outcomes of disadvantaged students. OSM used school support services to make teachers implement curricular materials in the way they were intended. Implementation of a programme was thought sufficient when 70 per cent or more of the programme activities were implemented. The way actual implementation took place was not of fundamental importance, the implementation itself of elements of the programme was regarded as the key. A study by Slavenburg (1986) shows that three out of seven programmes on which data were collected were implemented sufficiently. The provision of strictly structured programmes, and school support services aiming to ensure that guidelines are followed by teachers and students, seem to contribute to fidelity in the use of a programme, defined as the implementation of programme activities. On the other hand, the results of the study make clear that more effective strategies than guidance provided by the school support service are needed.

Another way to stimulate implementation is the training of teachers. A study by Stokking *et al.* (1987) shows disappointing implementation results in Dutch education, when the criterion is implementing the essential aspects of the innovation at hand (in this study, it is dealing with individual educational needs). The authors conclude that training did not meet the preferences of teachers well enough. A study by Snippe (1991) shows that training sessions together with classroom consultation resulted in a higher quantity of time spent on lessons and subject presentation. In comparison with effects on teachers who visited training sessions but did not receive classroom consultation, consultation in itself did not have an effect on teacher behaviour. Well-defined interventions seem to be capable of influencing implementation positively.

Recent studies on variations between curricula for school subjects point to the need to pay more attention to the way teachers use curricula. Van Batenburg (1988), in a study on the use of language curricula, concludes that curriculum designers provide few imperative directions for educational practice. Directions within the units of curricula as well as the overall curricula are often given in an eclectic manner. Variations in curricula do not necessarily lead to variations in instructional behaviour, and ultimately student achievement is not affected either (after control for initial student differences). Harskamp (1988) studied variations in mathematics curricula. Differences in use were found; however, teachers using traditional curricula individualized instruction to a higher degree but showed little variation in the presentation of subject matter, while teachers using more realistic or culturally relevant curricula emphasizing mathematical reasoning in real-life assignments varied subject matter more but individualized instruction less. These differences in use were dependent on content-related variations between traditional and more realistic curricula. However, differences in curricula did not result in achievement differences.

Edelenbos (1990) studied English-language curricula within Dutch primary education. Views on the way English language should be taught in primary education differ explicitly in the Netherlands. One approach emphasizes the teaching of grammar, while the other puts communication between students at the centre of attention. In this study, teachers again turn out to follow curricula more or less strictly, and they often stick to their personal opinions on the way English should be taught. But the actual achievement variations between curricula are minimal: students taught by means of grammar-oriented curricula show more knowledge of grammar, but they also show adequate achievement in communicative skills.

The data described in this section do not permit the conclusion that school curricula are of no importance in determining students' cognitive gains. The importance of curricula for the design of education is beyond discussion. However, variations between curricula do not result in significant achievement differences. Teacher behaviour, the intensity of use of the curriculum and all the other things teachers do may be more important than the curriculum itself, and even more important than the implementation of the curriculum. Sound guidelines for implementation are often lacking. On the other hand, one can question whether, when they are provided, they are perhaps too restrictive in the views of the teachers, so that in any case they would not follow them.

Curricula do differ, but differences in what is actually consumed by students often disappear in spite of the emphasis on implementation: significant achievement differences that can be attributed to curricula or textbooks are not found. Comparative international research on curricula, intermittently showing up in educational research, establishes the importance of curricula, since the curriculum offers the (possible) objectives and content for education at the classroom level. However, the way teachers use curricula is important. The fidelity perspective on the implementation of curricula is probably an illusion that does not do justice to the professional skills of teachers. Teachers do not merely implement curricula: they also have to make independent decisions based on their classroom contexts, the children in their classrooms and their own professional views.

The disappointing results on the development and implementation of 'teacher-proof' materials have led, according to Porter and Brophy (1988), to renewed attention being given to teachers and to professional teacher training (see, for example, the Carnegie Forum on Education and the Economy, 1986). This is one of the reasons why directions, as they are provided by textbooks, are not studied as frequently as before. Attention has shifted to the principles of teaching that can improve education, increase effectiveness and reconcile complex and sometimes conflicting teacher tasks, such as the pursuit of higher achievement and the realization of more equity within and by education at the same time.

Goals like these can be achieved by developing textbooks and curricula, namely by explicitly incorporating rules and directions, and by taking teachers' knowledge and experience seriously in this process. However, many approaches and implementation strategies start from the opposite point of view. For example, some people consider teachers as adult learners with a lack of self-confidence. Therefore, it is believed they will suffer from fear of failure when learning new procedures, and they will quickly reject information that cannot be integrated in their existing frame of reference (Creemers et al., 1981). This view implies that new curricula should be more or less similar to the old ones.

Analyses of new textbooks often point to the monotony of materials and the lack of clear relations of the material with any principles concerning learning and effective teaching. The reason for this is, according to Muther (1987), that in every grade teachers want to teach, or have everything available to teach. Because of this, publishers include almost anything in every book (Muther, 1987).

GROUPING IN CLASSROOMS

Grouping of students, in order to meet differences in abilities, knowledge and skills, is frequently practised. A major part of the Dutch educational system, especially secondary education, is based on student differences. This results in a differentiated system for secondary education, with separate tracks for vocational and general education, both on three levels: lower, intermediate and higher. In primary education various within-class grouping procedures can be found in addition to whole-class instruction. Between-class grouping is not very common, but is increasing in primary education, with the renewed emphasis on students' needs. Within-class grouping procedures concern group-based mastery learning, ability grouping and individualized instruction. Individually based forms of mastery learning and self-paced instruction do not occur, at least not in Dutch primary education.

Between-class ability grouping, also known as streaming or tracking, was very common in primary and secondary education in the United Kingdom for a long time (Barker Lunn, 1970). In the years after 1970, this situation changed when comprehensive schools were set up. During that time, most forms of between-class ability grouping were considered 'sacrilegious' (Gregory, 1984, p. 209). The current situation in the United Kingdom concerning between-class and within-class grouping procedures is not very well documented and there may be differences in the grouping procedures used in the various parts of the United Kingdom (Kerckhoff, 1986).

In the United States, tracking is still 'nearly universal' in secondary education and fairly common in primary schools (Slavin, 1987b), although there is a growing movement towards de-streaming, especially in the middle grades (Slavin, 1991). Within-class ability grouping is commonly practised in primary education, particularly for reading instruction (Sørensen and Hallinan, 1986; Slavin, 1987b). Group-based mastery learning is practised in primary and secondary education to a lesser extent. Individualized forms of mastery learning are practised in post-secondary education in the United States (Slavin, 1987a). There is virtually no information available about the occurrence of relatively newer grouping practices, such as co-operative learning.

An extensive research literature on the effects of grouping is available, both internationally (see, for example, Block and Burns, 1976) and nationally in the Netherlands, for example (Wolbert et al., 1986; Reezigt, 1993). In addition to compilations of studies in reviews, meta-analytic studies offer larger research syntheses. Initially focusing on the question of 'does it work?', research on grouping now concentrates on the question of which components of grouping bring about effects, and in what way (Hymel, 1990). Just as comparative research on curricula showed, the implementation of grouping can take very different forms, concerning both school subjects and the way teachers apply grouping.

Concerning school subjects, Reezigt and Weide (1989) found large differences between language and mathematics. For example, 43 per cent of teachers use whole-class instruction for language and 13 per cent for mathematics; mastery learning is used by 19 per cent of teachers for language and by 31 per cent for mathematics. Both Reezigt *et al.* (1986) and Wolbert *et al.* (1986) conclude that grouping procedures are often dependent on the curricula teachers use, and the degree to which teachers can adapt instruction to individual needs in their classrooms depends on (among others) the following factors:

- the availability of instructional materials and possibilities for differentiation;
- the possibilities for grouping students within spatial constraints in a classroom;
- teachers' capacities to evaluate students (Janssens, 1986).

Teacher behaviour and teachers' capacities influence the effects that can be expected from grouping, as is shown by the occurrence of 'mixed' grouping procedures and the factors mentioned above influencing the implementation of grouping.

There is a political and quite emotional debate about grouping, especially about the disadvantages of a tracking system and ability grouping (Oakes and Lipton, 1990). The negative results at school level are quite obvious (Gamoran and Berends, 1987), but the grouping procedure at classroom level is more or less the consequence of the introduction of this grouping system at school level.

Research on grouping, just like research on curricula, shifted from effect studies connected with the sometimes emotional debate about the advantages and disadvantages of specific grouping procedures, to studies on the components of grouping that are related (in combination with other classroom variables) to the achievement of different groups of students.

RESEARCH ON TEACHER BEHAVIOUR

Research on teachers is traditionally an important issue in educational research. The person of the teacher has always attracted attention, whether the teacher was Socrates or Mr Chips. The picture arising from literature is that the personalities of teachers and their characters were very significant, not only during the time children spent at school, but lifelong. The literature on the personality characteristics of teachers is immense. In the first *Handbook of Research on Teaching*, Getzels and Jackson (1963) published a chapter on teachers' personality and characteristics, at a time when another approach to research on teacher behaviour came to the forefront, namely the process–product paradigm. Getzels and Jackson reviewed 800 studies, all published after 1950, on teacher domains such as attitudes, values, interests, needs, personality factors, the results of using projective techniques, cognitive skills etc. These studies yielded a wealth of data about teachers and their qualities, ranging from intelligence to heterosexual needs. Jackson and Guba (1957) concluded: 'The factor of low heterosexuality is considerably more pronounced in veteran teachers, as one might expect in view of the fact that experienced teachers are generally older and therefore subject to the usual sexual decline accompanying aging.'

Questions that should be asked with respect to the personalities and characteristics of teachers are: why should personalities and characteristics matter, what do they have to do with education? In the few studies in which relationships with student outcomes were postulated, the effects concerned estimations of effective-

Table 3.1. *Commonly studied teacher characteristics*

Personality	Attitude	Experience	Aptitude/achievement
Permissiveness	Motivation to teach	Years of teaching	National Teachers Exam
Dogmatism	Attitude towards children	experience	Graduate Record Exam
Authoritarianism	Attitude towards teaching	Experience in	Scholastic Aptitude Test
Achievement–	Attitude towards authority	subject taught	1 verbal
motivation	Vocational interest	Workshops attended	2 quantitative
Introversion–	Attitude towards self (self-	Graduate courses	Special ability tests,
extroversion	concept)	taken	(e.g. reasoning ability,
Abstractness–	Attitude towards subject	Degrees held	logical ability, verbal
concreteness	taught	Professional papers	fluency)
Directness–		written	Grade-point average
indirectness			1 overall
Locus of control			2 in major subject
Anxiety			Professional
1 general			recommendations
2 teaching			Students evaluations of
			teaching effectiveness
			Student teaching
			evaluations

From Borich (1988).

ness by principals and teachers about groups of teachers, divided into men versus women or young versus old. In addition, in the opinion of Getzels and Jackson research on the personalities and characteristics of teachers does not necessarily have to be connected with research on teacher effectiveness. This would put too much stress on the ambiguous concept of teacher effectiveness (Getzels and Jackson, 1963, p. 507). It seems that questions concerning the effectiveness of teacher behaviour were hardly raised in 1963, even though the word 'effectiveness' was used. A good teacher was someone living up to the ideal of a good citizen, parent or employee.

Research on personalities and psychological characteristics of teachers was an elaborated operationalization of this vision, although slowly characteristics more related to education were studied: directness, anxiety, motivation to teach, attitudes towards children and teaching, years of teaching experience, experience in the subjects taught, experience in specific grades and characteristics such as the level of training. Borich (1988) presents an overview of frequently studied teacher characteristics (Table 3.1).

Although some personality characteristics, such as emotional stability or the way teachers deal with problems, probably are important for effective teaching, the conclusion seems justified that there are no clear findings on which emotional or social characteristics, as measured by personality tests, are essential for effective teaching. With regard to attitudes, the fundamental problem is that teachers' attitudes do not give much information as to their actual classroom behaviours (Walberg, 1986b). It is more problematic to measure teacher attitudes in relation to effective teaching validly than it is directly to observe teacher behaviour that supposedly reflects attitudes. Teaching experience is also too global a characteristic to distinguish between effective teachers. Research shows that experience with specific curricula is of more importance than general teaching experience. Relationships between experience, achievement rates and the abilities of teachers on the one hand and effective teaching on the other hand are weak and not very meaningful with respect to actual classroom behaviour.

Even though research on teachers' personalities and characteristics was a step forward, compared with earlier definitions of 'good' teachers, this research turns out to be too far away from actual classroom events to be a good predictor of teachers' classroom behaviour. Therefore, research concentrated on the question of what an effective teacher might be in terms of growth in student knowledge and skills. This research tradition acknowledges the importance of teacher characteristics for teaching, but research during the past two decades no longer concentrated on these 'good qualities' of teachers. Actual teacher behaviour in classrooms was described and a search for the behaviour characteristics of effective teachers was started.

This research tradition admits that it is not possible to record all teacher behaviour, and that, in the end, it is not possible to create a purely scientific basis for teaching by extensively summing up factors, variables and the characteristics of effective teachers. However, scientific evidence can be collected to show which behaviours can be effective. Teachers themselves can make a choice from behaviours that have proven to be effective, depending on their classroom contexts.

The paradigm dominating research on teaching for several decades has been the process–product paradigm, also known as the 'criterion for effectiveness' paradigm (Gage, 1963). This approach looks for processes (teacher behaviour such as teaching styles, techniques or strategies) that predict or preferably cause products (educational results such as growth in student knowledge and skills). At first, most studies were of a descriptive nature. Later, many correlational studies were conducted, but experimental studies, which introduced certain behaviours and then checked whether these caused the expected effects on students, were also undertaken (Gage and Giaconia, 1983).

The process–product paradigm was the leading model for research on teaching for years, even though it was criticized from different angles. Because of the definitions of both process and product variables, the process–product paradigm preferred empirical research of a quantitative nature. Critical advocates of the qualitative approach stated that the quantitative approach did not do enough justice to the 'richness' of education at classroom level (Guba, 1978). Ethnographic, detailed descriptions of education processes at classroom level, with very little attention to the outputs of education, were presented as an alternative.

The process–product paradigm was also criticized by advocates of the empirical approach. For example, Doyle (1986) states that the paradigm is based on only two groups of variables: teacher variables (processes) on the one hand and output variables (products) on the other. No attention is paid to anything that might intervene between teacher behaviours and student achievement. Student behaviour in classroom and the means used in classrooms, like curricula, seem to be neglected.

Moreover, the process–product paradigm seems to assume causal links only from the teacher to the student, despite the fact that student behaviour also influences teacher behaviour in its turn. In addition to this, the paradigm seems to concentrate on the frequencies of teacher behaviour, which stems from a preference for the measurement of so-called 'low-inference' behaviour, which can be observed directly, without any interpretation by the observer. Doyle (1986) suggests that too little importance is attached to what behaviour means for the actors in education at classroom level. The process–product paradigm and the quantitative approach also prefer to deal with teacher behaviour that is consistent over time, while of course instability and inconsistency of behaviour are known to occur and can be of great influence on classroom procedures and student achievement. Results of research on teacher behaviour in the process–product paradigm might lead to overly directive recommendations for educational practice, the same kind of directions observed formerly with 'teacherproof' curricula. Alternative models or paradigms, trying to meet the restrictions of the process–product paradigm, emphasize the intermediary processes between teaching and learning (Doyle, 1986), the ecology of classrooms (which leads to descriptions of classroom contexts) and the necessity of finding out why students learn.

The process–product paradigm emphasizes the importance of directly observable teacher behaviour, although other variables in the general area of teacher variables, such as training and experience, were also considered important. Research on non-directly observable behaviour, related to the hidden factors of teacher thinking and judging, also took place, and research on a more cognitive approach to teaching, focusing on thinking, cognitive processes and decision-making, was promoted, based on studies by Clark and Yinger (1979), Shavelson (1983) and Shulman (1986). This approach concerns not only teachers but students as well, and shows some similarity to Doyle's (1986) mediating paradigm.

According to Winne (1987), the cognitive processes of teachers and students are a black box in process–product research. In the 'cognitive mediational methodology', it is not so much the process variables that are important (referring to anything happening in the teaching–learning process), but the cognitive processes of students. Because of the emphasis on these (unique) cognitive processes, Winne (1987) thinks it is possible to 'test' theories on the basis of the data from only one study. This is not possible in process–product studies, because only replications of research can constitute a preliminary affirmation of theories.

The fight between paradigms raged vehemently during the past few decades. Nevertheless, as a paper by Gage (1989) showed, paradigms are now growing closer again and are often considered complementary. The methodological controversies between quantitative and qualitative research, often related to preferences for overall scientific paradigms, are not as bitter as in recent years. This is shown, among other things, in models that integrate process–product studies and theories from a quantitative approach, together with models originally developed for other paradigms and other research traditions. Critics argue that models which integrate so much are not specific enough and are too complex. Furthermore, it is said that they do not fully take into account the results that a clash between conflicting opinions and ideas in this field, both in research and in theory development, might have (Creemers, 1983; Knoers, 1983; Veenman, 1987).

Shulman (1986) acknowledges that alternative approaches, often proclaimed with ardour and élan like the cognitive approach, did not result in the further development of theories as much as was suggested by their creators. This is a further argument against a too rapid integration of diverse theoretical insights and methodological approaches and paradigms, thereby eliminating contrasts. It may be more useful to let contrasts crystallize, and to check theoretical and methodological pretentions of ideas and insights. Traditions which are invalid may then fall into the background or even disappear, as happened to research on the personalities of teachers. In general, it is not detrimental to the development of sciences, and this also applies to research on teaching, when scientific insights and methodological traditions appear and disappear again after some time, sometimes leaving hardly any discernable traces.

CONCLUSIONS

With respect to the components of teachers and the curricula, the attention of researchers, theorists and educational practitioners has shifted from one component to the other. Curricula were expected to improve education, if only teachers would use materials as they were meant to be used. This approach aimed to find the most effective curricula. Even though it is possible to make empirically founded statements about curricula (Chapter 5), time and again research proves teachers not to be docile executors. They do not follow curricula, but use them in the way they want to in designing education at classroom level. Because of this, differences in teacher behaviours and student achievement are sometimes larger within curricula than between curricula.

A shift of the same kind took place in research on the effects of grouping in education, probably based on the conclusion that teachers do not always apply grouping as intended. More attention is paid now to the components in grouping procedures that contribute to effects, and to the other classroom factors that influence grouping.

Research on teaching developed from a period in which the personalities of teachers were the centre of interest, through research on the characteristics of good teachers, to process characteristics. Research on process characteristics focuses on the question of which teacher behaviour is effective; that is, results in the growth of student knowledge and skills. This effective teacher behaviour is related to the other components in education at classroom level: curricula and grouping.

The outcomes of various research traditions will probably have to be inter-related and integrated for the development of educational practice and educational theory, which can enhance the explanatory power of theory and improve educational practice. The professional responsibility and expertise of teachers and above all their actual teaching behaviours seem a good point to start, based upon the research studies of the past.

Chapter 4

The Effectiveness of Curricula

INTRODUCTION

Students are supposed to learn in classrooms. They learn different things, such as interacting with their classmates, or reacting to adults, such as their teachers; these are often the implicit outcomes of education. Explicit outcomes are acquiring knowledge and skills in various domains. Educational contents are chosen from an extensive domain. Educational contents in specific domains are laid down, more or less concretely, in school curriculum documents, which may include guidelines for the way contents should take shape at classroom level, but which mostly do not.

Subject matter in a specific field for a specific grade is recorded and codified in school curricula. Educational outcomes are highly dependent on the quantity of subjects and educational contents that are presented in lessons and grades. In addition to this, it is important whether subjects are presented in a way that makes it easier to acquire knowledge, insights and skills. Presentation of subjects can involve choices for specific ways of acquiring knowledge and skills: for example, the choice of an 'analytic–synthetic' or a 'whole-word' curriculum in early reading instruction, the choice of a 'grammatical' or a 'communicative' curriculum in foreign language instruction, and the choice of 'realistic' or 'traditional' mathematics instruction. Presentation of subjects also concerns the way goals are selected from educational domains and the way subjects are ordered. Variations in presentation are likely to lead to variations in student outcomes.

Research on school subjects such as language, reading and mathematics has yielded a massive quantity of data about the value and validity of the procedures for acquiring knowledge and skills. Long-term disputes on, for example, the appropriate curricula for early reading instruction were gradually settled. This study mainly focuses on more general insights into the way education at classroom level should take place, and therefore the way school subjects should be structured is not in the centre of attention. The same applies to studies on school subjects, which can be found in separate reviews and subject-specific publications.

The well-known American publication *What Works* (1986) gives a limited number of directions for policy on school subjects. This somewhat arbitrary list of suggestions does not provide a rationale on which education in a specific school subject can be built. The higher quality of the analytic–synthetic approach in comparison with the formerly popular whole-word method of teaching reading is mentioned. *What Works* stresses the necessity of using physical objects in order to teach abstract mathematical concepts in the lower grades. Biology and geography teachers should check for prior knowledge and experiences of students, it argues, but the document is rather short on subject-specific directions. Instead, it looks for general characteristics that may lead to directions for effective instruction in the field of curricula, grouping and teacher behaviour. Within each school subject, directions for teaching can be much more specific than these important yet rather general directions. However, general directions can be considered as higher-order directions, because they are valid for different subjects. Moreover, the effectiveness of subject-specific directions is dependent on the extent to which they reflect general directions.

The following sections offer information about the provision of educational contents in curriculum documents, especially what research has to say in this field. As mentioned before, this study is restricted to instructional processes and therefore primarily to the curriculum and textbooks at classroom level, since the influence of the normal or 'regular' school-level curriculum on what happens at classroom level is doubtful (van der Werf, 1988).

COMPARISON OF CURRICULA: CHARACTERISTICS OF EFFECTIVE CURRICULA

Curricula and textbooks vary in the quantity of subjects, which has consequences for the outcomes they achieve. Differences in the quantity of subjects, the opportunity to learn and the time necessary for learning will have consequences for achievement, even when national goals are pursued in school subjects. Curricula that maximize learning time within the boundaries of timetables, by utilizing learning time as efficiently as possible and by presenting as many subjects as possible, will probably result in higher achievement than other types of curricula.

In addition to, and related to, the opportunity to learn offered by curricula and textbooks, other aspects of curricula are important for achievement: these are curricular goals, and the translation of goals into subgoals and into goals for lessons. Both the level of aspirations of the curricula (see, for example, the experiences with the project curricula in the Education and Social Environment Project mentioned earlier) and the hierarchy of goals are concerned. Opinions differ as to the importance of starting teaching with an explicit formulation of goals. In this respect, a distinction must be drawn between curriculum development and the use of curricula. Since the work of Tyler (1949), to start with the formulation of goals and follow with the selection of subject matter relevant to these goals and the ordering of subjects is a widely accepted strategy in curriculum development. These basic principles are promoted in the development strategies of Taba (1962) and Wheeler (1967), as well as in the more recent strategies of Saylor and Alexander (1974) and Romiszowski (1984), and in the strategy for curriculum development in the education and Social Environment Project (Slavenburg *et al.*, 1989). However, research on the validity of these principles for curriculum development hardly took place. Experiences with an elaborated strategy for specific curriculum development in the Netherlands make it clear that following the principles of a strategy does not necessarily lead to intended outcomes of a 'better' curriculum (Hoeben, 1981). In educational practice, teachers appear not to follow such strategies (stating goals first, then selecting subject matter afterwards). Instead, they use curricula as a 'source' for subject selection; so, in order to be used by teachers, curricula do not need a very tight overall structure.

The meta-analysis by Kulik and Kulik (1989) shows the relative importance of behavioural goals for students, as suggested by Mager (1962). This meta-analysis is

Table 4.1. *Average use of time per lesson*

Lesson part	Condition	Mean minutes	%	SD	n	p
Starting phase	A	18.05	17.8	8.67	1.34	0.191
	B	15.10	12.6	4.67		
Task-oriented time	A	43.75	43.3	19.15	5.66	0.000
	B	71.00	59.0	9.85		
Evaluation discussions	A	18.40	18.2	8.64	−4.32	0.000
	B	32.25	26.9	11.58		
Non-academic activities	A	20.95	20.7	25.30	3.35	0.003
	B	1.85	1.5	2.86		
Total	A	101.15	100.0	15.87	−4.52	0.000
	B	120.30	100.0	10.33		

From van den Akker (1988).

based on two studies, one by Asencio (1984) and one by Klauer (1984), covering respectively 111 and 52 studies. In most studies small positive effects were found. The mean effect size found in Kulik and Kulik's meta-analysis is 0.30, a moderate effect size. This implies that the explicitness of goals can contribute to effectiveness, especially when goals are listed in a hierarchical way, as suggested within the objectives-based approach. However, behavioural goals are only one specific category of goals and, moreover, the effects of goals are analysed separately, not in combination with other components (such as curriculum structure, subject matter and evaluation; Kulik and Kulik, 1989, pp. 293–4).

The hierarchy of goals is reflected in the structure of a curriculum, starting with easy exercises and simple knowledge and building up to more complex exercises and knowledge structures. This structure of a curriculum is the second important aspect of curricula and textbooks. Research shows that clearly structured curricula are more effective than less clearly structured curricula. The clear structure is expressed in goals that should be achieved in succession: achieving the first goal is a condition for achieving later goals. The way subjects and activities *within* specific goals are structured is a further element of curriculum structure, as well as the sequence of subjects and activities meant to achieve specific goals.

The importance of structuring subjects is shown in a study on science curricula by van den Akker (1988). He compared two curricula, a curriculum developed by the Dutch National Institute for Curriculum Development (SLO) that was unstructured and a clearly structured curriculum developed by himself. Both curricula pursued the same goals. Table 4.1 presents outcomes of a comparison of mean time spent on activities in lessons in the SLO-curriculum (A) and in the structured curriculum (B).

Student learning activities take place during task-oriented time (when students are supposed to solve science problems) and during evaluative discussions of students and their teachers. Mean time spent on activities related to the achievement of goals is clearly higher in the structured curriculum. It is a pity that testing of student achievement did not take place in this study but, taking the relationship between time spent and student achievement into consideration, it could be assumed that achievement in the B type of curriculum would also be higher, especially because the proportion of activities that are not task-oriented (an indication of time not actively spent) is much higher in the less structured curriculum. Another advantage of structured curricula appeared in this study: that the time teachers spend on preparation of lessons decreases substantially. Moreover, of the total time, a higher proportion is spent on preparation for instruction than on the material or organizational conditions for lessons. For these reasons, the results of this study can be considered as an argument for structured curricula. In a study about innovatory practice in physics, biology and chemistry in secondary education, teachers preferred teaching and learning materials that provided all contents or even more contents than were necessary in a well-structured way (Kuiper, 1993).

The incorporation of tests in curricula and textbooks is an aspect of structuring that deserves special attention. Tests can be used to check whether students are achieving as they are expected to, with respect to the goals of the curricular units. The curricula of the Dutch Education and Social Environment Project offered possibilities for teachers to check student achievement from time to time. Tests were related to goals, which made it possible to find out every now and again if students achieved these goals. Regular evaluation of student achievement turned out to be an important condition for achieving curricular goals (Klaasman, 1989).

Evaluation of student achievement can take place at different stages of the learning process, for example after finishing a curricular unit. Including questions in texts is another option. Studies by Kulik and Kulik showed that testing can enhance learning, but testing in itself is not sufficient. Testing has to be integrated within the teaching–learning process, i.e. in curricula (Kulik and Kulik, 1986–7, 1987, 1989). Testing, if it is to be effective, should be not so much aimed at assessing students' achievement levels and knowledge, but at guiding and enhancing learning processes. Positive effects of this kind of testing were found in several studies (Hamaker, 1986), including that principle evaluation in curricular materials cannot be separated from the use of results in the instructional process by providing feedback and corrective instruction. In this way curricular materials can serve as real time savers for teachers (Eisner, 1987).

An important aspect of Ausubel's (1968) learning theory is the concept of 'advance organizers', which are indicators of concepts and of the way information is ordered. Advance organizers, which should relate what students already know and what they have to learn next, influence student achievement positively, in the short term as well as the long term. They act as structuring principles in subject presentation (for example, in curricula or presentations by teachers). They also act as structuring principles for the way students receive and process information. In a synthesis of research on educational productivity (Fraser et al., 1987), the use of advance organizers in curricula (in this case science curricula) appeared to have positive effects on student achievement.

The conclusion seems justified that curricula differ with respect to certain characteristics. The following characteristics of curricula, curricular materials and textbooks influence student achievement:

- explicitness and ordering of goals and content;
- structuring and clarity of content (in relation to goals);
- use of advance organizers;

- materials for evaluation of student outcomes, feedback and corrective instruction.

These characteristics are the features of the curriculum and textbooks that can influence learning opportunities. With respect to opportunity to learn, these characteristics determine how effective time is spent by students (as measured by learning outcomes), and also how effectively, in terms of learning outcomes, the opportunities are used.

THE PROBLEM OF IMPLEMENTATION

Some characteristics of curricula result in higher student achievement, as was argued in the previous sections. Some other characteristics of effective education might be incorporated in documents for the planning of education and teaching. When effective instruction is assumed to be achieved (exclusively or primarily) by effective curricula, the decision to employ financial and professional means in developing curricula is only justified if it can clearly be demonstrated that these curricula are subsequently used in education as they were intended to be used. Teachers should follow curricula closely and in fact their educational arrangements should be guided by their curricula. This belief led to the fidelity ideal for the implementation and use of curricula (see Chapter 3). Curriculum developers should clearly describe how teachers have to use curricula, and curricula should considerably structure the education at classroom level. Teachers should teach according to the curricular guidelines with regard to the subjects and the sequence of goals as well as the way subjects are presented.

Ideas about the fidelity ideal in the implementation of curricula were put under pressure by the studies of the Rand Corporation (Berman and McLaughlin, 1977, 1978) and Fullan and Pomfret's review (1977). Fidelity implementation turned out to be an unattainable ideal. However, results of these latter studies were based on curricula developed in the 1960s, a time of great innovation. These curricula fell short in two essential characteristics: the directions for teachers and the degree of structuring. In the implementation of these curricula, teachers were treated as 'mechanistic' users and not as responsible teachers to whom the ownership of the new curricula should be given. In the DESSI study (Dissemination Efforts Supporting School Improvement: Huberman and Crandall, 1982), more favourable conclusions, based on curricula developed after 1975, were reported on the fidelity of implementation. These curricula showed higher quality, were structured to a higher degree and were more adequately evaluated. Implementation was also accompanied by adequate support.

School support services have tried to accomplish the development of curricula that would accurately and clearly state how education should take place. These curricula were intended to provide teachers with explicit and clear directions. Support services tried to make teachers follow curricular directions as closely as possible. Even the fidelity perspective on implementation offered teachers some capability to make their own contributions and adapt curricula to their own classroom contexts and students, but strictly speaking this was not really necessary because curricula already incorporated ideas about student characteristics. Knowledge about the design of education and student learning was already codified in curricula and textbooks.

In the Netherlands, the Education and Social Environment Project is an example of the development strategies and implementation strategies mentioned above. School support services aimed to implement the project curricula as they were intended, without any teacher-determined change. Implementation was considered sufficient when 70 per cent of curriculum activities were performed. Sometimes this operationalization was extended by the addition of other criteria: for example, no more than 10 per cent of activities that are not mentioned in the curriculum are allowed. According to this criterion, the two most important curricula of language and mathematics were sufficiently implemented (Slavenburg, 1989, p. 98).

Apart from the question of whether 'sufficient implementation' might be better established empirically by relating the criterion to student achievement (van Tilborg, 1987), the criterion of only 70 per cent implementation of curricular activities can be questioned as a valid indicator of fidelity implementation. A maximum of 30 per cent of curricular activities may still not be implemented at all, and the way activities are performed is not measured by this criterion. This could be of considerable importance for fidelity implementation, and so for the achievement of educational effects as intended. A better criterion for implementation will probably have to be determined. Support services will also be necessary to increase fidelity implementation with respect to the characteristics mentioned.

It is questionable whether fidelity implementation can actually be realized in education. Freeman and Porter (1988) concluded that four teachers, engaged in their case study, used 58 per cent of curricular contents in their lessons, and had deliberately skipped 29 per cent of textbook contents at the end of the course. Within lessons, teachers used about one-third of the appropriate chapters in their textbooks, with a range from 13.2 to 60.5 per cent. Freeman and Porter conclude that curricula influence lessons most with respect to the selection of subjects and the order of subjects. The impact of curricula on decisions about time spent on subjects, the formulation of criteria for students to achieve and the adaptation of education for different groups of students is not very substantial.

The relationship between following and not following a curriculum and student achievement was studied in another publication, based on the same dataset (Freeman and Porter, 1989). Teachers who were following the curricula emphasized applications and comprehension more, while teachers deviating from the curricula put more emphasis on practising mathematics skills. This means that students are not necessarily better off with teachers deviating from the curricula. When the autonomy of teachers is acknowledged and they are not asked to follow curricula strictly, teachers should be involved in the process of determining standards for education (and teaching), and they should be supported in achieving those standards in their own professional activities, according to Porter (1989). These standards concern teacher skills, grouping procedures and (yet again) curricula.

Stodolsky (1989), in her study on maths and social science, draws similar conclusions. Although the six teachers involved in her study showed correspondence with respect to the subjects in curricula and the subjects presented in education at classroom level, similarities with respect to activities suggested in the curricula and the actual classroom activities were not very frequently found (Stodolsky, 1989, p. 175), especially in mathematics. In science instruction, not only did teachers differ in the presentation of subjects, but the presentation of subjects also differed from the presentation suggested in the textbooks.

These case studies do not show that teachers want to be guided by curricula and textbooks. Teachers act according to their own convictions and preferences, except for the selection of subjects and the sequencing of subjects. However, the case studies cited are field studies, which implies that teachers were not explicitly asked to implement curricula as intended. This applies for most of the studies of curricula and textbooks. Van Batenburg (1988), van den Berg (1987) and Edelenbos (1990) concluded, on the basis of studies of the use of language curricula, that curriculum developers do not prescribe very strictly how curricula should be used.

Teachers use curricula eclectically, thereby causing variations in use within the same curriculum area. Harskamp (1988) also reported variations in the use of curricula. In both studies (van Batenburg, 1988; Harskamp, 1988), variations in use did not lead to variations in student achievement. The study of Edelenbos (1990), concerning the effects of the implementation of English language curricula on teacher behaviour, also demonstrates that curricula are not fully implemented as intended. Teachers adhere to guidelines prescribed by curricula, but also take their own views on how language should best be taught into account (Edelenbos, 1988), which can partly be blamed on the frequent absence of explicit directions. However, as the use of curricula in the Dutch Education and Social Environment Project showed, even when explicit directions are available, fidelity implementation of curricula is not guaranteed. This can cause problems when teachers do not follow directions with respect to important aspects of education. Other Dutch studies on the planning and implementation of education by teachers (Ax, 1985) and Lager-weij's (1976) study on the way teachers use curriculum manuals support these findings. Teachers are willing to follow curricula, but this mostly means they are willing to follow the selection of subjects that should be presented, not the ordering or other directions.

In the United States, new and often exciting materials and media, including educational technology, are generally used within the traditional educational system (Cohen and Grant, 1992). This may be caused by the way the educational system is organized, and especially by the extent to which teachers are expected to use and follow centrally produced textbooks. In the old USSR teachers were required to do so. Curriculum leader John Lewis of the American Science Masters Association suggested, on the basis of his classroom visits, that even less expert teachers can give reasonably effective lessons if adequate textbooks and other materials guide them and carry some of the instructional burden (Walberg, 1991).

An alternative to the fidelity perspective on educational innovations in general and curricula in particular was the mutual adaptation perspective: the idea of the mutual adaption of curricular materials and users. The debate on fidelity versus mutual adaption looks like a pendulum: sometimes the first perspective stands out, sometimes the second, depending on the experiences of educational innovations. However, from the effective instruction viewpoint, the fidelity perspective is preferred, because in this perspective curricular characteristics that are important for effectiveness should be reflected in educational practice at classroom level. Fidelity implementation, in the sense of following curricula scrupulously and in all details, is not a realistic option, although only through it can the pure effects of curricula be estimated. Fidelity may be realized by the way curricula are designed and supported.

What we know so far is disappointing with respect to the influence textbooks and curricula can have on what happens in classrooms. Most of the curricula and textbooks do not offer suggestions on how to use the respective curriculum and the textbooks, so we cannot expect teachers to use the curriculum according to the intended goals. However, even when directions and guidelines are available, teachers do not follow them strictly. That is a pity, because, based on research, we can expect that curricula that show some of the specific characteristics mentioned in this chapter can contribute to effectiveness at the classroom level.

There are two possible solutions to this. Based on research on the implementation of curricula, we know that teachers use the curriculum for their selection and ordering of the subjects. In the development of curricula and textbooks, it is possible to include effective characteristics in the subjects, but even then it remains unclear whether or not teachers will make use of these directions. Perhaps the second solution should be preferred: the curricula and textbooks make clear what kinds of effective characteristics are included in the curriculum, and point out the advantage of using the curriculum in that way. The results of a science project (van den Akker, 1988) are an argument for this position, since the structuring of the material developed by van den Akker is a combination of the two solutions. One of the characteristics of effectiveness was included, and it was made clear to teachers why it was important. Teachers did follow the structure and the curriculum itself. However, another outcome of this project is a warning not to be too optimistic about the influence of a structured effective curriculum. In a follow-up questionnaire, almost half of the teachers who used the well-structured curriculum declared that they would prefer a less structured and more 'open' curriculum in the future. Later, this conclusion was confirmed by other research in this field (Gravemeijer et al., 1991; Kuiper, 1993).

Ultimately, these results lead to the conclusion that we need a combination of mutual adaptation, with an emphasis on the importance of the teacher's expertise, and fidelity, which stresses the knowledge base contained in curricula and textbooks. This means that the construction of effective curricula and textbooks in the way described above can go on (see, for example, Squire, 1988), but in the implementation phase it should be taken into account that, for fidelity, we need teachers who are effective, know how to teach and therefore know how to use the curricula and textbooks. In this way, mutual adaptation as an implementation strategy does not necessarily result in substantial deviations from the curriculum and textbooks, but can result in fidelity with respect to the basic goals and ideas of the curriculum and textbook. This can be achieved by the expert system in instructional consultation mentioned earlier. In their research, Fuchs et al. conclude that in this case teachers can adjust the curriculum material to their own instruction (Fuchs et al., 1991; Snippe, 1991).

CONCLUSIONS

Curricula are important instruments for the planning and implementation of education at classroom level and for the effectiveness of classroom instruction. What teachers will teach and what students will learn is laid down in curricula. Curricula create the opportunity to learn, and achievement is expected to be higher when curricula cover more subject matter. Research shows that the opportunity to learn is an important variable at school level, accounting for substantial variations in student achievement. As is apparent from Alexander's research, the substance of the curriculum needs more attention than do simple physical and organizational arrangements (Alexander, 1992, p. 57).

Comparative research on curricula and the elements of curricula has yielded characteristics that are important for the effectiveness of instruction. These characteristics concern not only the objectives curricula try to achieve, but also the structuring of objectives, in the hierarchy of learning objectives and in the ordering of subject matter as well. A related curricular characteristic is the degree of evaluative control of the achievement of the objectives of lesson units and the extent to which corrective procedures are offered to individual students or groups of students based on this evaluative control. These curricular characteristics enhance effective learning time and, by this, student achievement. Certain effective characteristics, such as evaluation and corrective procedures, also influence student motivation and by this, indirectly, effective learning time. However, the usefulness of effective curricular characteristics is related to the extent to which teachers actually make use of curricula and textbooks. When teachers are more or less free to act as they want to (because no support is offered to stimulate fidelity implementation of curricula, or because curricula do not incorporate guidelines for implementation), they think of curricula as a general source of ideas, especially concerning the subjects to be covered and the order of subjects, but in general they do not hold very strictly to the curricula when they are teaching. When curricula demand certain teacher activities, there are indications that teachers always want and need to have ample freedom to adapt education to their classrooms.

Therefore, capitalizing on the design of curricula through fidelity implementation does not seem to be a very successful approach to enhancing educational effectiveness. Nevertheless, a basis for effective instruction can be created by emphasizing educational elements that are inherent to curricula and are acknowledged by teachers as such in the design of curricula. These elements are the subjects to be taught in classroom instruction, the structuring and ordering of

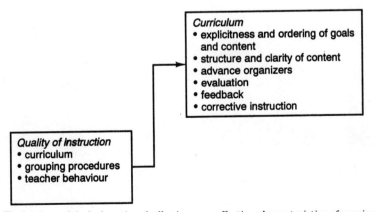

Figure 4.1 *The basic model of educational effectiveness: effective characteristics of curricula.*

educational objectives and subject matter, and, related to these, evaluation procedures. Support in the implementation of curricula should also focus on these elements. The further design of education should be regarded as the professional responsibility of teachers, which they should acquire in their pre-service training and later in-service education.

Summarizing, we can further elaborate the theoretical framework that we started to develop in Chapter 2 (see Figure 4.1).

Chapter 5

The Effectiveness of Grouping within Classrooms

INTRODUCTION

Students differ from each other with respect to characteristics that are relevant to and influence their learning, such as ability and socioeconomic status. At least 20 per cent of children have special needs and require special attention, although they can differ from each other in many other ways. They have in common that their learning progress or behaviour may be disturbing in the view of their teachers (Galloway and Edwards, 1991). In the Netherlands, about 4 per cent of children are referred to special education. Nowadays, as in many other countries, a policy has been started to retain most of these children within the regular school system, and to provide them with the instruction they need there. However, all the other students also deserve instruction that is appropriate to them, because they differ from each other too, perhaps not to such a degree that they disturb the teaching process, but enough to make it important to avoid inappropriate, 'general' instruction that is essentially the same for everybody.

Grouping of students is a way to deal with these differences between students. Grouping of students can take place between schools, within schools and within classes. In countries with a differentiated school system, like the Netherlands, grouping of students between schools takes place. For example, different types of schools are available in secondary education for lower, middle and higher forms of general and vocational education. Within schools, classes can be formed for students of a similar ability level or for students of mixed ability levels. Homogeneous ability grouping can be based on overall achievement, the so-called practice of streaming or tracking, or it can be based on subject-specific achievement, the so-called setting policy.

Within classrooms, the same can occur. Students can be grouped on the basis of achievement in homogeneous or heterogeneous groups within classes. A special form of heterogeneous grouping is cooperative learning, in which a special effect is expected from students working together in a heterogeneous group and taking responsibility for each other's learning. There is another way to deal with individual differences between students, especially differences in the time they need to master the objectives of education: students can be grouped on the basis of time differences within classrooms in several ways; for example, in heterogeneous groups, in a form of group-based mastery learning or in forms of more or less individualized mastery learning.

Within schools and within classrooms, grouping requires the organization of schools and classrooms, and this is where that comes into the area of effective education. Scheerens (1992) examined which organizational elements can raise educational effectiveness, especially at the school level. I will discuss this issue in

Chapter 8, when we look at the factors at levels above the classroom level that can provide conditions for effective instruction. At the classroom level, it is clear that the organization of the class and the management of the classroom by the teacher are important factors for the effectiveness of instruction. In the next chapter we will deal with classroom management as an element of teacher behaviour. In this chapter, we will look at the grouping of students within schools and classrooms relatively independently of teacher behaviour, with an emphasis on grouping within classrooms.

To start, we will pay some attention to the results of empirical studies on between-class grouping. Then we will turn to the effectiveness of within-class grouping. Mastery learning is not only a grouping procedure, but includes a specific organization of instruction as well. Therefore, we will discuss mastery learning in more detail, particularly looking at its recent forms, for example within the general area of educational technology.

BETWEEN-CLASS GROUPING

The wide variety of grouping procedures, and especially the occurrence of several grouping procedures within the same school (homogeneous grouping for some subjects, heterogeneous grouping for other subjects), have caused problems in research on grouping (van Laarhoven and de Vries, 1987; Slavin, 1987b).

In the United States in particular, grouping procedures have been studied very frequently and results have been summarized in reviews and meta-analysis (Table 5.1). Kulik and Kulik (1982, 1984a, b) published several meta-analyses on the effects of between-class ability grouping. They concluded that the mean effects of this type of grouping on achievement in primary and secondary education are so small that grouping cannot be considered very meaningful. However, their analyses showed a consistent positive effect of ability grouping on the achievement of the brightest students, enrolled in American honours programmes. In a separate meta-analysis of these kinds of programmes, summarized under the heading of acceleration, this positive effect became clearer. Especially when compared to students of the same age in regular classes, the accelerated students showed higher achievement. When they were compared to older students with the same ability level in non-accelerated classes, the effect size in primary education was much smaller, and in secondary education the effects disappeared totally. In a later meta-analysis, Kulik and Kulik (1987) did not find any differences in outcomes between the effects of setting for several subjects and setting for one subject.

According to Slavin (1987b), the results of the meta-analyses of Kulik and Kulik are difficult to interpret, because they do not make a distinction between different types of between-class ability grouping, and because they do not apply very strict methodological criteria for the selection of studies. He presents a research synthesis in order to reach conclusions as clearly as possible, the so-called 'best evidence synthesis' described in Chapter 1. He concludes that between-class ability grouping does not have any positive effects at all, either in primary or in secondary education. However, ability grouping for specific subjects (setting) has positive results for some subjects in primary education when students spend the major part of their day in a heterogeneous class.

In line with Dar (1981), van Laarhoven et al. (1986) concluded that clear effects of between-class grouping for the entire group of students are not found; however, it seems likely that differential effects do occur for groups of students. There are indications that heterogeneous grouping is beneficial to low-achieving students and harmful to high achievers; the opposite seems likely to apply to homogeneous ability grouping (Allan, 1991). In his research on ability grouping in British secondary schools, Kerckhoff (1986) found that students in high-ability groups gain more and students in low-ability groups gain less over a five-year period than would have been expected if they had not been separated into ability groups. In the United States, there exists a strong movement towards heterogeneity, because tracking is seen as damaging to almost all students (Oakes and Lipton, 1990, 1992; Slavin, 1991; Gamoran, 1992).

Another way of dealing with differences between children and responding to individual needs is the non-graded school, in which pupils are flexibly grouped according to performance level and proceed through the school at their own rate. In the Netherlands, the 'Jenaplan' school (based on the ideas of Petersen: see Boyd and Rawson, 1965), which integrates the setting for school subjects and grouping according to broad age categories for social and affective learning, is quite popular. A non-graded organization of the elementary school can have a positive impact on student achievement if cross-age grouping is used to allow teachers to provide more direct instruction to students (see Chapter 6). The positive effects of non-grading do not occur if cross-age grouping is used as a framework for individualized instruction (Gutiérrez and Slavin, 1992).

WITHIN-CLASS GROUPING

The grouping of students and the associated educational organization it generates will have to be realized at classroom level in order to result in effects on achievement. Whole-case instruction, teaching all students in a class in the same way, was often criticized in the past. Teachers were said to aim their activities at imaginary 'average' students or at a small group of students in their classes. They supposedly did not adapt instruction to individual students. Based on his research studies, Lundgren (1972) makes clear that instruction for so-called 'steering group' or 'middling' students is not adapted to their capacities either. In any case, whole-class instruction is not adapted to individual student's needs or learning problems.

Various forms of within-class grouping were developed over the years, as alternatives to whole-class instruction. De Koning (1973) mentions the following forms of grouping.

1   Grouping on the basis of ability: students are assigned to ability groups, which are as homogeneous as possible, on the basis of their ability levels.
2   Grouping on the basis of pacing: this kind of grouping is meant to do justice to students' different speed of learning. Teaching–learning situations are offered so that individual students or groups of students can work at their own pace on tasks or task systems.

In addition to these grouping procedures, aimed at individualization or homogenization of education, cooperative learning is a form of within-class grouping, specifically starting from the principle of heterogeneous groups. In cooperative learning, students cooperate in heterogeneous groups to achieve group objectives.

Table 5.1. *Between-class grouping*

Meta-analysis	Criteria for study inclusion	Grouping procedure	n of studies (achievement)	n primary	n secondary	n college	Time span covered
Kulik and Kulik (1982)	Control group (conventional) No methodological flaws	Between-class ability grouping	51	–	51	–	<1951–1980
Kulik and Kulik (1984a)	Experimental studies Relevance to topic	Between-class ability grouping	28	28	–	–	1928–1973
Kulik and Kulik (1984b)	Quantitative data Control group (not accelerated) Aptitude matching experimental–control	Acceleration	26	8	18	–	1932–1974
Kulik (1985)	Methodological adequacy Relevance to topic	Between-class ability grouping	85	40	45	–	No data reported
Slavin (1987b)	Comprehensive ability grouping Control group (heterogeneous) Standardized test data Initial comparability of samples Duration (1 semester) Minimum of 3 exp. and 3 control classes	Between-class ability grouping	12	12	–	–	1932–1972
		Ability grouping for subjects, within grades	5	5	–	–	1960–1969
		Ability grouping for subjects, across grades (Joplin Plan)	14	14	–	–	1946–1968
Slavin (1990a)	Comprehensive ability grouping Control group (heterogeneous) Standardized test data Initial comparability of samples Duration (1 semester) Minimum of 3 exp. and 3 control classes	Between-class ability grouping	29	–	29	–	1927–1978

Table 5.1. *(cont.)*

Meta-analysis	Achievement measure	Correction pre-test diff.	Mean effect size	Primary effect size	Secondary effect size	College effect size	Range effect sizes	Significant study features
Kulik and Kulik (1982)	Exam scores	No	0.10	–	0.10	–	–1.25 to 1.5	Type of programme (honours) Source of study
Kulik and Kulik (1984a)	Achievement test scores	No	0.19	0.19	–	–	–0.27 to 0.71	Type of programme (honours)
Kulik and Kulik (1984b)	Standardized tests	No	0.47 Control group same age: 0.88 older: 0.05	0.63 1.43 0.16	0.39 0.72 –0.01	– –	–0.37 to 2.68	Type of control group
Kulik (1985)	Achievement results	No	0.15	No data reported			0.05 to 0.33 (mean e.s. across types of studies)	Type of programme (honours) Source of study Year of study
Slavin (1987b)	Standardized achievement test scores	Yes	–0.03	–0.03	–	–	–0.34 to 0.21	–
	Standardized achievement test scores	Yes	0.18	0.18	–	–	–0.28 to 0.43	–
	Standardized achievement test scores	Yes	0.40	0.40	–	–	–0.02 to 0.89	–
Slavin (1990a)	Standardized achievement test scores	Yes	–0.02	–	–0.02	–	–0.48 to 28	Subject area

Although the distinction in grouping based on ability and the pacing of students can be found in educational practice in schools, classes and classrooms, it is a problematic one because there is a high correlation between ability and pacing. But whatever distinction is used, there is always a discrepancy between this formal distinction and what really happens in classrooms, which can be illustrated by the results of Dutch research on grouping in primary education.

In the Netherlands, the frequency of occurrence of grouping procedures was studied in a random sample of 220 primary schools (age groups 8–12, language and mathematics) (Reezigt and Weide, 1989). Grouping procedures used by 1034 teachers were defined by their answers to questions about components of the teaching–learning situation. Essential characteristics of specific grouping procedures (group-based mastery learning, within-class ability grouping and individualized instruction) were represented in pre-structured answers to these questions. The assignment of teachers to grouping procedures, based on their answers, was dependent on the strictness of criteria. When criteria for labelling answering patterns as grouping procedures were used strictly, only 20 per cent of the answering patterns could be classified as a grouping procedure. Therefore, some violations to the essential characteristics of each grouping procedure were permitted. This implied that teachers no longer had to show correct answers on all questions asked, i.e. show an answering pattern clearly representing one of the grouping procedures. They were allowed to show 'wrong' answers (answers that were meant to indicate characteristics of other grouping procedures). Their imperfect answering patterns were then considered as representing grouping procedures. When only those components that clearly discriminated between grouping procedures were taken into account, and when violations of two out of six components were permitted, 620 of the teachers could be classified for language and 575 of the teachers for mathematics. Even when violations were permitted, some teachers still could not be classified as using a specific grouping procedure. A substantial group of teachers showed answering patterns that indicated their use of elements of whole-class teaching as well as group-based mastery learning (273 teachers for language, 270 for mathematics). These teachers seemed to mix elements of both procedures constantly. Finally, a group of teachers could not be identified as using a specific grouping procedure at all, or even a mix of two procedures. These teachers (141 for language, 189 for mathematics) give the impression of randomly choosing elements of three or four grouping procedures at the same time, even though these elements are often not rationally linked and sometimes are even conflicting. Table 5.2 presents absolute frequencies and percentages for the different grouping procedures. Whole-class instruction is still very frequently practised in primary education in the Netherlands, especially for language instruction. Different grouping procedures are used in language instruction and in mathematics instruction.

In their study of the effects of grouping in Dutch primary education, Reezigt and Weide (1989) draw rather negative conclusions. The effects of mastery learning do not differ significantly from those of whole-class instruction. Within-class ability grouping and individualized instruction stand out in a negative way: students show lower language and mathematics achievement in comparison with students whose teachers apply whole-class instruction or mastery learning, even when achievement is corrected for student characteristics, such as social background and intelligence.

Table 5.2. *Frequencies and percentages of grouping procedures in language and mathematics instruction*

	Language		Mathematics	
	Freq.	%	Freq.	%
Whole-class instruction	382	42.8	110	13.0
Mastery learning	171	19.1	258	30.6
Ability grouping	22	2.5	91	10.8
Individualized instruction	45	5.0	116	13.7
Mixed procedures	273	30.6	270	31.9
Total	893	100	845	100

From Reezigt and Weide (1989).

None of the three grouping procedures in this study results in higher achievement than whole-class instruction.

Other studies examined grouping procedures in secondary education (Bonset, 1987; De Koning, 1987). The educational system of secondary education in the Netherlands is highly differentiated and consists of different types of schools (or sections within the same school) for vocational and general education at the lower, middle and higher levels. Some comprehensive school experiments in the 1970s and 1980s kept all students together and provided the same curricula, but this experiment ended, and in future all secondary schools will provide the same 'basic education' in the first two to four years of secondary education. Then, students continue in the traditional differentiated types.

Information is available about the tracking system in Dutch secondary education (for example, studies on the organization of the first grades by Vermeulen and de Koning, 1985). Less is known about within-class grouping, although a study by Bosker and de Vries shows that within-class grouping is practised more often in comprehensive schools, than in other differentiated secondary schools (the majority in that time) (Bosker and de Vries, 1982, 1984; de Vries, 1986).

With regard to grouping, Dutch education shows similarities with education in the United States. Within-class grouping is fairly often practised in primary education, especially in reading instruction and to a somewhat lesser extent in mathematics instruction. In secondary education, within-class grouping is hardly ever found (Barr and Dreeben, 1983; Hallinan and Sørensen, 1983). As far as grouping is practised in secondary education, between-class ability grouping is the predominant grouping procedure.

Several meta-analyses have been published on the effects of within-class grouping in education. These meta-analyses are summarized in Table 5.3. In this section and the next I will comment on the results.

The meta-analysis of Slavin (1987b) included only eight studies on within-class ability grouping in mathematics instruction. In them, ability grouping results in higher achievement than whole-class instruction, especially for low-achieving students and the effect size for lower achievers is somewhat higher (0.53) than for the total group of students. These results probably cannot be generalized to reading

Table 5.3. *Within-class grouping*

Meta-analysis	Criteria for study inclusion	Grouping procedure	n of studies (achievement)	n primary	n secondary	n college	Time span covered
Slavin (1987a)	Germaneness grouping / Control group (conventional teaching) / Equity experimental/control / Duration (4 weeks) / Objectives taught in experimental/control / Minimum of 2 exp. and 2 control classes	Mastery learning (within-class, group-based)	17	8	9	–	1970–1986
Guskey and Pigott (1988)	Grouping teacher-paced and group-based / Control group/time series design / No serious methodological flaws	Mastery learning (within-class, group-based)	43	11	21	11	1972–1985
Kulik et al. (1990)	Field evaluations / Control group (conventional teaching) / Mastery criterion 70% / No serious methodological flaws / Quantitative results	Mastery learning (within-class, group-based)	36	7	10	19	1970–1986
Slavin (1987b)	Comprehensive ability grouping / Control group (heterogeneous) / Standardized test data / Initial comparability of samples / Duration (1 semester)	Ability grouping (within-class)	8	8	–	–	1948–1985
Slavin (1990b)	Germaneness / Same materials in control groups / Initial equivalence experimental and control groups / Duration: 4 weeks / Standardized test or same objectives measured in experimental and control classes / Minimum of 3 experimental and 3 control classes	Cooperative learning	60	28	32	–	1972–1988
Kulik et al. (1979)	Equality experimental/control group / Fairness of comparison	Personalized System of Instruction (PSI)	61	–	–	61	no data reported
Bangert et al. (1983)	Individualized system in experimental class / Actual school classrooms grade 6–12 / Control group (conventional) / No crippling methodological flaws / Published after 1955	Individualized systems of instruction (IPI, PLAN, PSI)	49	3	46	–	1960–1978
Kulik et al. (1990)	Field evaluations / Control group (conventional) / Mastery criterion 70% / No serious methodological flaws / Quantitative results	Personalized System of Instruction (PSI)	67	–	–	67	1969–1985

Table 5.3. (cont.)

Meta-analysis	Achievement measure	Correction pre-test diff.	Mean effect size	Primary effect size	Secondary effect size	College effect size	Range effect sizes	Significant study features
Slavin (1987a)	Achievement test scores	Yes	0.26 Standardized: Experimenter made:	0.18 0.10 0.26	0.35 0.01 0.45	— — —	−0.11 to 0.90	Type of achievement test
Guskey and Pigott (1988)	Exam scores and grades Tests: crit./norm ref.	No	0.55	1.00	0.86	0.55	−0.77 to 2.27	Subject area Grade level
Kulik et al. (1990)	Exam performance	When possible	0.59 Standardized: Experimenter made:	0.40 0.17 0.68	0.55 0.02 0.61	0.68 — 0.68	−0.11 to 1.58	Mastery criterion Type of achievement test Subject area Amount of feedback in control group
Slavin (1987b)	Standardized achievement test scores	Yes	0.34	0.34	—	—	0.07 to 0.55	
Slavin (1990b)	Achievement test scores	No	0.38 Control group/ conventional: 0.52 Only standardized tests: 0.21 Conventional standardized: 0.20	0.15 0.20 0.20 0.19	0.56 0.88 0.25 0.21	— — —	−0.71 to 3.93	Type of cooperative learning Type of control group
Kulik et al. (1979)	Exam scores	No	0.49	—	—	0.49	−0.02 to 1.27	Subject area Accuracy of control Group teaching
Bangert et al. (1983)	Achievement scores	No	0.10	−0.24	0.12	—	−0.84 to 1.24	None
Kulik et al. (1990)	Exam performance	When possible	0.49 Standardized: 0.33 Experimenter made: 0.53	— — —	— — —	0.49 0.33 0.53	−0.22 to 1.19	Mastery criterion Type of achievement test Subject area Amount of feedback in control group

instruction, because students do not work as individually and independently as in mathematics instruction. In a meta-analysis of fifteen studies, Kulik and Kulik (1987) reported a very small positive effect of ability grouping.

Concerning grouping on the basis of pacing, there are clear indications that programmes, such as the Personalized System of Instruction (PSI) based on the strategy of Keller, yield positive results in post-secondary education (college level). Effects in primary and secondary education are much smaller and sometimes are even negative. However, strategies suggested by Bloom and Keller demand more than student grouping only (see, for example, Kulik and Kulik, 1986–7, 1987; Slavin, 1987a) since they are strategies for teaching and learning that include grouping, materials and teacher behaviour. For this reason, I will discuss these strategies separately in more detail in the next section.

The United States meta-analyses of group-based mastery learning present ambiguous conclusions. Slavin (1987b) argues that his best-evidence synthesis (in primary and secondary education) does not show significant effects on standardized tests; effects are found on tests constructed by the researchers. Guskey and Pigott (1988) and Kulik et al. (1990) report significant effects at all levels of education (primary, secondary and tertiary education), although differences based on the type of test used in experiments still remain.

On the basis of his research, Slavin, an advocate of cooperative learning, concludes that when cooperative learning is adequately implemented (the communal objective for all students cooperating in a group is a mastery of tasks or objectives by each participating student), it can achieve positive effects (Slavin, 1983, 1990b). The effects in secondary education are larger than in primary education. When effect sizes are computed for scores on standardized tests, the effects are much smaller, in primary as well as in secondary education. An experiment in Dutch education (Vedder, 1985) did not lend support to the positive conclusions of Slavin.

Other research on cooperative learning (Sharan, 1980; Johnson and Johnson, 1989) shows positive effects in the areas of academic achievement, and also in non-cognitive areas like self-esteem as a learner, cross-race friendship, social acceptance and social skill development, if social skills are taught and practised. Davidson and Wilson O'Leary (1990) plead for a combination of cooperative learning as a grouping procedure and direct instruction as a teaching strategy to increase effectiveness (Chapter 6).

The results on the effects of grouping on student achievement, although especially designed to handle differences between students, are somewhat disappointing. Generally the effects of within-class grouping are more favourable than the effects of between-class grouping. The results of mastery learning and within-class ability grouping on tests constructed by researchers are reasonable, and at college level (the Keller Plan) even quite high, but on standardized tests the effects drop significantly. More precisely, the effects range from small to very impressive depending on study features, the tests used, etc. Does this mean that grouping, in the end, does not achieve its objectives? Perhaps the results look like this, but it can be questioned whether the organization of education, when grouping procedures are implemented, is responsible for these effects, or other factors.

Grouping procedures are often not implemented in the way they should be. According to Slavin (1987b), one of the conditions for successful grouping is the capacity of teachers to adapt instruction to individual students' needs. His statements about cooperative learning also seem to confirm the importance of the way grouping is implemented. Discussing their findings, Reezigt and Weide (1989) also point to the implementation of grouping as a possible explanation for their negative conclusions. Teachers are forced to divide their attention among students to a much higher degree than in whole-class instruction. This can cause problems for teachers as well as for students, especially with respect to the allocated time offered to students and the time students are actually engaged in learning. Many grouping procedures require frequent student testing, registration of progress and feedback. Teachers do not necessarily meet these requirements when they group students for instruction. As the meta-analyses on mastery testing by Kulik and Kulik (1986–7, 1987) show, this influences results negatively: when testing is absent in mastery learning, effects on student achievement are substantially reduced.

When teachers start grouping for pragmatic reasons, for instance to handle pacing differences in their classes, they will choose grouping procedures that will solve their problems. However, the attention of teachers to slow or fast learners, and their achievement, may decrease in this process. They take the differences for granted and perhaps do not offer the learning opportunities students need. This might result in negative or small effects of grouping. In his study on the effects of mastery learning, Nuy (1981) also concludes that variations in results are possibly caused by variations between teachers in the way they actually proceed.

Considering the factors that could influence the effects of grouping negatively, it seems important to pay special attention to mastery learning. Mastery learning shows positive effects repeatedly, and combines within-class grouping with a specific approach in instruction.

MASTERY LEARNING

Mastery learning as an instructional model was designed by Bloom (1976) and is theoretically based on Carroll's model of school learning (see Chapter 2). One of Carroll's intentions was to raise new and better questions for research and he certainly succeeded in this respect, because there has been a lot of research on variables that were included in the model. In addition, the Carroll model made substantial contributions to educational practice, for example in the development of the model of mastery learning, the Keller Plan for individualized instruction, research on the length of school days and school years (Wiley and Harnischfeger, 1974) and research on teaching related to learning time (for example, in the Beginning Teacher Evaluation Study, discussed in Chapter 2). According to Anderson and Block (1987, p. 58), mastery learning is in fact a modern translation of a traditional optimistic philosophy about education and learning that 'the teacher can help "dumb", "slow" and "unmotivated" students to learn like "smart", "fast" and "motivated" students' (p. 58).

Bloom (1976) tried to transform Carroll's key concepts into directions for the design of classroom instruction. His assumption is that although students' capacities are normally distributed, the majority of students can be brought up to achieve at a criterion level when they are provided with sufficient learning time and optimal instruction. The mastery criterion is the degree of mastery students should achieve for a learning unit, before they are allowed to start working on the next unit. While only 5 or 10 per cent of highly achieving students used to succeed in achieving these objectives in traditional instruction, mastery learning was supposed gradually to reach full achievement of objectives for 80 per cent of the students (Warries, 1979). The order and quantity of learning units are selected in such a way that they form a logical sequence: delays or cumulative deficiencies are not supposed to occur.

Block and Burns (1976, p. 12) define the essential characteristics of mastery learning as follows:

1   A set of course objectives that students will be expected to master at some high level is pre-specified.
2   The course is broken into a number of smaller learning units so as to teach only a few of the course's objectives at one time.
3   Each unit is taught for mastery – all students are first exposed to a unit's material in a standard fashion, then they are tested for their mastery of the unit's objectives, and those whose test performance is below mastery are then provided with additional instruction.
4   Each student's mastery over the course as a whole is evaluated on the basis of what the student has and has not achieved, rather than on how well he or she has achieved relative to classmates.

McNeil (1969, p. 308) describes the educational practice of mastery learning, which includes quite concrete guidelines of how to proceed:

1   Students have to understand the nature of learning tasks and they should know the procedure they are to follow in learning their tasks.
2   Specific instructional objectives have to be formulated for these tasks.
3   Courses or extensive subjects should be broken down into smaller units, with a test at the end of each unit.
4   After each test, teachers provide feedback to students on their errors and difficulties.
5   Teachers should find ways to alter the time some individuals need to learn.
6   Alternative learning opportunities (for example, materials other than the initial materials) may be profitable.
7   Student effort will increase when small groups of two or three students meet regularly, for about an hour, to review their test results and to help one another to overcome the difficulties identified by means of the test.

Students of Bloom continued to develop the theory and research of mastery learning, as well as its applications for educational practice. The procedure developed by Bloom and his students is mostly directed to classrooms and small groups of students. The individualized form of mastery learning, which had a different origin, is known as the Keller Plan or Personalized System of Instruction (PSI) (Keller, 1968). The Keller Plan also requires a mastery criterion but it is adapted to individual students to a higher extent, concerning curricular materials as well as instructional time. Some whole-class instruction may occur but only to stimulate and motivate students. In the United States and in other countries, such as the Netherlands, the Keller Plan was popular in college courses for some years, especially because of its emphasis on students' responsibilities for their own programmes (Braak, 1974; Plomp, 1974).

Mastery learning is widespread in the United States, becoming so when it became clear that the implementation of mastery learning in individual classrooms was not very effective and that mastery learning should be introduced and implemented at the school level. The ideas of mastery learning successively expanded from classrooms to schools and from schools to school districts. Eventually, a national movement was involved in mastery learning and both educational policy and educational practice were inspired by the thought that education should produce results and, moreover, that the results could be produced by the design of education.

Current ideas about effective schools and effective instruction are therefore certainly not new; they are also reflected in mastery learning. According to Bloom (1984), elements of mastery learning are present in the publications of Washburne (1922) and Morrison (1926), but of course they can also be found in the works of educators such as Comenius, Pestalozzi and Herbart.

A lot of research on mastery learning is available and several reviews have been published (for example, Bloom, 1984; Slavin, 1987a; Guskey and Pigott, 1988; Kulik *et al.*, 1990). Some results of meta-analyses on mastery learning have been provided in the previous section and Table 5.3. The results reported in reviews are not very consistent. Bloom (1984), for example, concludes very optimistically that group-based mastery learning can improve achievement by one standard deviation. However, his conclusion is based on a very limited set of studies by his students at the University of Chicago. Sometimes mastery learning was not implemented accurately and the experimental and control groups were sometimes hard to compare, for example because the control groups were not confronted with traditional instruction but with other individualized programmes. The main problem, however, is that several studies do not control for the sometimes large quantities of extra learning time in the mastery learning condition. Such studies make it impossible to attribute positive effects in the experimental group to mastery learning, because the effects may be caused by the mere provision of extra time. Sometimes it is not clear whether the same curricular contents were offered to the control groups (Arlin, 1984).

The best-evidence synthesis of Slavin (1987a) represents the other end of the continuum. Slavin concludes that group-based mastery learning, although there is an effect on experimenter-made tests, does not succeed in improving student achievement as measured by standardized norm-referenced tests. However, the procedure used by Slavin also shows some problems. Kulik and Kulik (1989) criticize the best-evidence approach because the number of studies included is so limited that the reviews end up being highly speculative. In his best-evidence synthesis, Slavin notes that the individualized form of mastery learning did produce positive effects. However, this implies a contradiction in one of the essential elements of mastery learning as defined by Bloom (1976), the aim to bring individual students to mastery of learning tasks in a group context, by means of classroom organization, allocation of time, provision of curricular materials, tests and feedback. Mastery learning in an individual context resembles tutoring and individual instruction for each student. The teacher–student ratio is one to one in tutoring, which renders it virtually impossible to implement in regular educational settings, even though the effects are substantial: about two standard deviations (Bloom, 1984; Walberg, 1984).

69

In meta-analyses undertaken by Hartley (1977) and Kulik *et al.* (1979), the effects of tutoring were not so strong. In the meta-analysis of Kulik *et al.*, the average effects of tutoring were even smaller than the effects of mastery learning and the Keller Plan (Kulik and Kulik, 1989, pp. 286–7). Kulik *et al.* (1990) report a mean effect size of 0.59. At higher levels of education the effects are strongest (0.68), and overall effect sizes on standardized tests are much lower than those on experimenter-made tests (Table 5.2).

Guskey and Pigott (1988) selected 46 studies on group-based mastery learning from primary, secondary and college education. A large variation in effect sizes was found, with effect sizes largest in primary education, contrary to the results of the meta-analysis of Kulik *et al.* (1990). According to Guskey and Pigott (1988), an explanation is that the effects are likely to be cumulative over the years. In contrast with Slavin, Guskey and Pigott conclude that group-based mastery learning shows great potential.

Even though the results are not very consistent on the size of effects, generally speaking there is sufficient evidence for the effectiveness of mastery learning at the classroom level. However, it seems that the effectiveness of the procedure depends strongly on other factors in the instruction process, which have to be in synchronization with or have to support the essential elements of mastery learning. Feedback and corrective measures of teachers based on tests are essential for the effectiveness of mastery learning. Guskey (1987) points to the 'congruence among instructional components', in that teachers teach what students are supposed to learn and test what they have taught. Studies by Block (1970) and Nordin (1979) support this conclusion. Nordin distinguishes several elements in the quality of instruction:

1 Giving cues or explanations.
2 Participation of students in the learning process.
3 Feedback and corrective measures based on tests.

In an experiment, three groups were formed, one group for each element. Students in the feedback and corrective measures group outperformed both other groups. A meta-analysis on mastery testing by Kulik and Kulik (1986–7), which included studies on individualized instruction and group-based mastery learning as defined by Bloom, supports these findings. When degree of mastery was not assessed by tests, effects were reduced substantially. Testing in itself is not enough and should be followed by feedback and corrective measures to overcome deficiencies in learning. Dutch studies (for example, Westerhof, 1989) also report the positive effects of corrective instruction, which means testing student achievement and subsequently adapting instruction. The effects were small, however.

Dutch research on the effects of mastery learning is summarized by Warries (1979). Several authors (for example, Slavenburg and Creemers, 1979) report the positive effects of mastery learning in primary education. Dutch studies on mastery learning in secondary and post-secondary education that were published later (Weeda, 1982; Nuy, 1981) did not support the results found in studies from the United States. However, Weeda's results partly support the effectiveness of mastery learning, because elements of mastery learning (testing and corrective measures) turn out to be effective.

A combination that is now advocated integrates cooperative and mastery learning (CML). Mastery learning is carried out in small cooperative situations in which team members proceed at the same rate, provide instant help to each other as substitute teachers and so on. Research by Mevarech (1991) showed that pupils performed better in CML than in traditional learning situations.

Perhaps there is no reason for the quite depressing situation that in a room that could hold 750 people during the convention of the American Educational Research Association in 1993, about 25 researchers were celebrating the twenty-fifth anniversary of Bloom's theory of mastery learning.

CONCLUSIONS

In reviewing the results of the analyses of within-class grouping, moderately positive conclusions can be drawn on the basis of the international literature about the effects of grouping procedures. The positive results concern, in descending degrees of effectiveness, grouping on the basis of pacing (forms of mastery learning), grouping on the basis of ability and cooperative learning. The concept of mastery learning, in several forms (and in combination with other grouping procedures and educational strategies), has been shown to be effective at all levels of education.

Analyses from the United States often state that the effectiveness of grouping is dependent on the way teachers implement it (Gamoran, 1986), and Dutch research also points to the importance of teachers and curricula. The effects of grouping within classrooms may be shaped to a higher extent by teachers than by grouping procedures, which might be the most important explanation for the disappointing effects of grouping in Dutch education. Some analyses refer to curricula and the availability of tests and, when linked to the findings in the previous chapter, it can be concluded that effects of grouping procedures are also largely determined by the way teachers use these procedures.

In general, adaptive instruction, which is instruction geared to the learning characteristics and needs of individual students, is more effective than whole-class instruction with respect to cognitive as well as affective measures. This conclusion is empirically affirmed, especially by meta-analytic studies (see, for example, the summary of several meta-analyses by Waxman et al., 1985). They concluded that adaptive instruction improves student learning. The programmes studied were quite different, but programmes in the studies reviewed featured at least one of the following adaptive characteristics:

- instruction is based on the assessed abilities of each student;
- students work at their own pace;
- students receive periodic reports on their mastery;
- students plan and evaluate their own learning;
- alternative materials and activities are provided.

To make it more complicated, adaptive instruction according to these characteristics does not necessarily imply forms of grouping. Adaptive instruction can also be carried out within whole-group teaching. In fact, research on students' time on learning, as in ORACLE (Observational Research And Classroom Learning Evaluation), revealed that very high proportions of time in teacher–whole-class interaction are associated with students spending more time on task during periods of individual activity as well as during other activities (Galton et al., 1980; Croll, 1988).

In the end, grouping procedures aim to increase the effectiveness of instruction by organizing instruction at the classroom level in such a way that instruction can be adapted to the individual characteristics of students. By the grouping of students, time and opportunities for learning can be more adequately allocated. That means that time and opportunities are offered to individuals or groups of students and the learning environment is organized in such a way that their engagement in the learning task, and therefore the outcomes of the instructional process, are maximized. The effects of grouping are strongly determined by the 'quality' of the effective characteristics of the instruction within a grouping procedure. To make the procedure effective it is required that differentiated material is available. For curricular materials, the list of effective characteristics mentioned in Chapter 4 is applicable. Especially important with respect to grouping are the characteristics related to evaluation, feedback and corrective instruction, because in this way teachers can adapt instruction to students, the ultimate objective of grouping procedures. Applying this idea to the earlier-mentioned list of features of adaptive instruction (Waxman *et al.*, 1985), we expect very positive effects of features that can be clearly related to time, opportunity and quality of instruction. Grouping procedures do offer a frame and a structure, as curricula do; however, what actually happens in classrooms is decided by teachers. In the end, they are responsible for achieving effects for several groups of students. This implies that it is now necessary to study the behaviour of teachers in classrooms.

In summary, the framework can now be elaborated as presented in Figure 5.1.

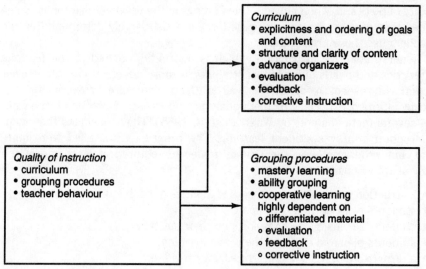

Figure 5.1 *The basic model of educational effectiveness: effective characteristics of grouping procedures.*

Chapter 6

The Effectiveness of Teacher Behaviour

INTRODUCTION

Research on teachers stems from a longstanding tradition. A diversity of measures was used for the independent variables (teachers) as well as for the dependent variables (teacher effects). Dependent variables were often operationalized as levels of student achievement, and sometimes as student attainment (the difference between initial and final achievement). However, other measures were utilized as well, such as students' and parents' satisfaction and school climate. With regard to the independent variables, research initially concentrated on the stable characteristics of personalities of teachers, without a clear relationship with education at classroom level. The teachers themselves were at the centre of attention, not their classroom activities. Variables that were studied included, for example, the intelligence of teachers, their years of teaching experience, and scores on a wide range of personality tests and attitude tests.

Both Gage (1963) and Getzels and Jackson (1963) concluded that research on the relation of personality variables and attitude variables with student achievement does not lead to clear conclusions, not to mention the problems involved in the 'theoretical' interpretation of these results. However, this does not imply that the attention given to the teacher's personality has disappeared; on the contrary, in ordinary daily life people often remember their teachers as persons. They remember their morale, humour and teaching style more than their instructional qualities. In theory and in research the attention given to other components, such as teacher responsiveness and teacher pedagogy, has come up again (Stones, 1992; Oser *et al.*, 1993). And research does reveal a relationship between characteristics such as the ability of teachers, their motivation, their engagement and their expectations, and student outcomes, but it is unclear what these quite unalterable characteristics mean for the teaching and learning process, the main focus of this study.

The findings of Gage and others, and the research results of Coleman among others, on the effects of education on students from different social classes led to the conclusion that schools could make only a small contribution to student achievement, in addition to socioeconomic variables. Actually Coleman did not conclude that schools do not make a difference, but rather that there was no variance in outcomes left unexplained by anything at school level once one put in SES, ethnicity, student, class, etc. As a reaction to Coleman's findings, an attempt was made to focus on variables that did have influence (often expressed as: do teachers make a difference?). Teacher variables used were again characteristics such as years of teaching experience, salary, initial training, academic degree and job satisfaction (Guthrie, 1970).

These studies confirmed Coleman's conclusion that actual teacher behaviour should be the most important teacher characteristic (see, for example, Hanushek, 1970, pp. 79–99). After the criticisms of Gage concerning these studies, more attention was paid to the process–product paradigm, which investigates the relationship between teacher behaviour and effectiveness measures. In the following years, many studies on this relationship were published and reviewed (Rosenshine, 1971a; Gage, 1972; Brophy and Good, 1974; Dunkin and Biddle, 1974; Good et al., 1975). Later, meta-analytic methods were used to reach clear conclusions and for this reason the conclusion of the committee that published A Nation at Risk, concerning the lack of reliable information that explains or proves a causal relation between the instructional behaviour of teachers and growth in student knowledge and skills, is rather surprising (Tomlinson, 1986).

In the following sections, the reliability and validity of research on the relationship between teacher behaviour and student achievement will be discussed. This relationship may not be as linear as is sometimes suggested and a simple relation between teacher behaviour and student achievement and learning cannot be expected. Many variables influence student learning directly or indirectly, as was shown in the models for teaching and learning presented in Chapter 2.

This study concentrates on general aspects of instructional behaviour, in the same way that it concentrated on general aspects of curricula and grouping procedures, and not on subject-specific elements. Specific teacher behaviour in reading or mathematics is not the issue, although all subject-specific teacher activities clearly pre-structure learning, guided or supported by curricula. Research on teacher behaviour tries to find general, stable teacher behaviours, relatively independent of subjects. Teachers are certainly required to have specific knowledge of school subjects and how to teach them, but in addition to that there are more general instructional characteristics that have proved to be effective in various instructional situations, such as different school subjects, for different students and at different school levels. The same holds for textbooks and grouping procedures.

In the next section, we will pay attention to research on teaching, looking for teacher behaviour that is related to student outcomes. In this research a distinction is made between the management behaviour of teachers, which aims to control the class, to prepare the students for learning and to keep them learning, and instructional behaviour, which includes teaching itself. Although this distinction might be useful conceptually, I argue that in instruction both are interwoven: classroom management requires instruction, and instructional behaviour induces control of the class, more or less. Based on research evidence, I will come up with the characteristics of effective teacher behaviour that can contribute to effective instruction at classroom level. Special attention will be given later to direct instruction because, as a teaching strategy, it combines the characteristics of effective teaching more than does research directed to specific elements of the teaching process.

EFFECTIVE TEACHER BEHAVIOUR

In 1954 Ackerman concluded: 'because the actual behaviour of the teacher in the classroom is such an important factor, it is necessary to devise means of observing and recording this behaviour. Methods must be used in which only a minimum of inference is allowed. . . . Such a process suggests a potential wider range of investigation which is hoped to provide more reliable information in the areas of teacher effectiveness and pupil change' (Ackerman, 1954, pp. 286–7). This conclusion is based on an analysis of some studies published at that time. These studies investigated variables such as age, intelligence, teaching experience and scores on personality tests. Teacher behaviour as a dependent variable was scored by students, counsellors or researchers. There were no systematic techniques for the observation of teacher behaviour and this situation called for the development of reliable measures for the recording of teacher behaviour. Another issue then raised in this context was the importance of student outcomes, and so the issue became the development of reliable achievement measures.

Gage can be considered as the stimulator of educational research on the relationship of teacher actions, and other variables at classroom level, to student achievement. According to Rosenshine (1971a, p. 52), Gage declared: 'We have been fooled before in educational research and I for one shall rest uneasy until the evidence on these plausible but undemonstrated connections is investigated.'

Rosenshine and Furst were the first to include in their reviews some of the process–product-oriented studies and other studies that could be related to a similar tradition (Rosenshine, 1971b; Rosenshine and Furst, 1971, 1973). The studies in these reviews all concerned the relationship between teacher behaviour in the classroom and student achievement, the central issue being their correlation. The correlational studies often followed four stages:

1   Instruments were developed which made it possible to record teacher behaviour systematically, and also to measure student achievement.
2   These instruments were used to record teacher and student behaviour.
3   Classrooms were rank-ordered on the basis of student achievement, after corrections for initial achievement differences.
4   Finally, it was investigated which frequency of teacher behaviour correlated with these corrected classroom scores.

The development of observational instruments was an important element in the design and implementation of research on teachers. There are, of course, observational systems that require hardly any interpretation by observers, because the observed behaviour is specific, relatively objective and easy to record (for example, the teacher repeats an answer given by a student, or the teacher asks a question). These systems are the so-called low-inference observational systems. In contrast, high-inference scales often require an interpretation by observers of what is observed to some extent (for example, rating the teachers' enthusiasm, or clarity of presentation). Answering categories varying from 'always' to 'never' are often used, with all kinds of subtle categories in between, which again require interpretational decisions by observers.

The problem with low-inference variables is their lack of highly relevant information on instructional teacher behaviour. High-inference variables, such as enthusiasm and clarity of presentation, are not easily measured in a reliable and valid way. However, it is virtually impossible to transfer high-inference variables into individual low-inference variables. For this reason, rating scales have been used, but observers have been trained and high-inference observational categories have been described more clearly, in order to record relevant information on teacher behaviour.

The development of instruments to collect data on teacher behaviour was based on theories, paradigms, models or just the researcher's ideas or opinions about the relationship between processes in the classroom (especially teacher behaviour) and student outcomes. This led to an overwhelming number of process–product studies and reviews of studies, sometimes more driven by the development of instruments than by careful theoretical analysis.

Simon and Boyer collected instruments in their overview *Mirrors for Behaviour* (1967, 1970). Brophy and Good (1986) give a review of the most important studies and of the development of instruments, some of which are still in use. Flanders's (1970) observation system for the investigation of classroom discourse is well known, and especially for the conclusion of his research that teacher indirectness was positively related to student achievement. Later these findings, contradictory to the results of other studies in the 1970s, were criticized because the teacher's teaching was left out; in fact in the 'indirect classrooms' more teacher's teaching took place, which could have caused the effects.

Other important studies that involved the construction of instruments were the evaluation of Follow Through (Stallings and Kaskowitz, 1974), the teaching of basic reading skills (Stallings *et al.*, 1979), the Texas Teacher Effectiveness Project (Brophy and Evertson, 1976), the Missouri Mathematics Effectiveness Project (Good and Grouws, 1977) and the Beginning Teacher Evaluation Study (Berliner *et al.*, 1978; Fisher *et al.*, 1980).

Initially, the focus of the studies was almost exclusively on the instructional activities of teachers. Later, based on the publication of Kounin (1970), a distinction was made between management behaviour and instructional behaviour. Management behaviour should aim to create a classroom organization that makes it possible for students to learn. Instructional behaviour includes all teacher activities directly aimed at eliciting and consolidating student learning activities. In contrast with instructional behaviour, which is ultimately directed at the individual learning behaviour of students, management behaviour is directed to the students as a group, and the primary focus of the teacher in the pursuit of order is the creation and maintenance of a learning situation.

According to Kounin (1970, p. 74), the following elements of teacher behaviour are important to prevent student activities that are not task-oriented:

1 'Withitness' and overlapping: teachers know what each student is doing; they are able to pay attention to several things at the same time.
2 Transition smoothness: teachers are able to guide student behaviour verbally or non-verbally; they do not have to interrupt teaching to call students to order. Abrupt transitions of student activities do not occur and pacing is maintained.
3 Maintaining alert group focus: teachers succeed in keeping their lessons interesting. Teachers hold all students accountable for their own tasks. Important teacher activities are, for example, asking questions at random turns, the introduction of new materials and mutual student control.
4 Programming to avoid satiation: varying didactic procedures, showing enthusiasm and stimulating students were supposed to raise task-oriented behaviour.

Several researchers (Kounin and Gump, 1974; Kounin and Doyle, 1975; Reiss, 1982) studied these classroom management activities in relation to student achievement. Classroom management and control are important issues in educational practice, which probably explains the number of practice-oriented publications on this topic (for example, Fontana, 1985). In research and improvement projects, special attention is given to management as an essential component of instruction and as providing the basis for teaching and learning at the classroom level (Wragg, 1993). In the Leverhulme Primary Project management is seen as the device to create time for learning and, more specifically, to ensure that students actually spend time on their tasks. Teaching skills, such as explaining and questioning, ensure that effective instruction takes place within this time.

Management behaviour and instructional behaviour can be said to overlap substantially, both on theoretical grounds and on the basis of analyses of classroom events. The way these variables are operationalized and measured underlines this conclusion, as the study of Kounin and Gump (1974) shows.

Doyle's review (1986) shows that many management behaviours concern not only the management, organization and order of classrooms, but also instructional, task-oriented teacher behaviour, as can be seen in the studies of Emmer *et al.* (1980) and Evertson and Emmer (1982). Effective managers continue organizational activities and the academic focus such as through monitoring student activities and clarity of assignments; management and instruction are linked with each other. Actually, instruction not only requires management and control, but seems to create classroom control as well.

Doyle (1984) points out that effective teachers in difficult management situations push their students through the curricula. In a later review (Doyle, 1986), he refers to studies in which the opposite is proved: the subject matter or academic work is shaped by managerial considerations. He concludes, 'Studies of management processes must incorporate information about the academic work that students and teachers are trying to accomplish. Moreover, the evidence suggests that fundamental tension exists between management and instructional processes in classrooms.' However, lower on the same page (p. 425) an example that is utilized about a successful teacher training programme can be seen as an argument for the interrelationship between instruction and management. The student trainees are supposed to carry out a question and answer session in arithmetic with a small group of students, which includes aspects of teacher behaviour, such as monitoring the order of turn-taking and the accuracy of answers, and also monitoring a student who is working alone and independently of the teacher.

On the basis of the arguments mentioned above, I conclude that the management behaviour and instructional behaviour of teachers are closely related, especially when we take into account the different aspects of management behaviour. In a review study by Shipman (1990) a relationship is created between management at classroom and school level and the instructional process at both levels. The studies of Pollard represent interest in a combination of management and instruction. Departing from viewing the class as a social context, he is interested in the way teachers and students behave and interact with each other. For teachers this includes management strategies, but this management is from the beginning directed to enhancing the learning of students. Their combination of skills has to be moniłored constantly, evaluated and revised by teachers in a process of reflective teaching (Pollard, 1982; Pollard and Tann, 1987; Menter and Pollard, 1989). Management is an important characteristic of effectiveness, but it should be combined, as these examples show, with other characteristics of effective instruction.

Rosenshine and Furst (1971, 1973) identified ten teacher behaviour variables that yielded the most consistent results. These variables are:

1 Clarity of teacher presentation.
2 Teacher enthusiasm.
3 Variety of activities during lessons.
4 Achievement-oriented behaviour in classrooms.
5 Opportunity to learn criterion material.
6 Acknowledgement and stimulation of ideas of students by teachers during discussions.
7 Criticism.
8 Use of structuring comments at the beginning of lessons and during lessons.
9 Use of a wide variety of question types.
10 Guiding of student answers by teachers.

With the exception of criticism, these variables correlated positively with student achievement. In the earlier studies, the first five variables showed the highest correlations with achievement measures.

Later, some of these teacher activities, such as clarity of presentation and the enthusiasm of teachers, turned out to correlate not very clearly with student achievement, or at best not significantly (Rosenshine, 1979). Rosenshine blamed this on the reduction of instruction actually provided by teachers in United States education in that period, since students were working alone for up to 70 per cent of their time. Teacher-led discussions, in which the described activities might play an important part, took up only 10–15 per cent of the time. In addition, a variety of activities during lessons, an adequate predictor of student achievement in earlier studies, turned out to correlate negatively in the later studies. Rosenshine explains this finding by pointing to the dangers that a variety of activities can generate in an orderly course of lessons (in the traditional educational and societal situation). The opportunity to learn criterion material, involving the content that is tested later on, and achievement-oriented behaviour remained good predictors. Acknowledging and stimulating the ideas of students during discussions still correlated positively, but no longer significantly, with student achievement. Criticism consistently correlated negatively with student achievement; however, criticism did not occur very frequently and often indicated difficulties in keeping classes and students under control. Other variables, such as the use of structuring statements, a variety of question types and the guiding of student answers, were not studied very frequently between 1971 and 1979, because of their rather low correlations with student achievement in the earlier studies.

As was mentioned in Chapter 3, a vast amount of research arose from the process–product paradigm. Research was quite often instigated by United States researchers like Anderson et al. (1979), Good and Grouws (1979) and Brophy

(1988a), and more recently those in the Louisiana School Effectiveness Study (Teddlie *et al.*, 1989; Teddlie and Stringfield, 1993). The research is summarized in important contributions, for example in the third edition of the *Handbook of Research on Teaching* by Brophy and Good (1986) and Doyle (1986), and in other reviews by Good (1987, 1989), Brophy (1988b), Porter and Brophy (1988) and Walberg (1990). In addition to the research and the reviews of research, the discussion about the generation of theory in research on teachers and teaching went on. The strictly outcome-oriented approach of the process–product research came under fire, and other more cognitive-oriented approaches were developed (Shulman, 1986; Needels, 1988; Gage and Needels, 1989). Nowadays, a balance between approaches is established, or even a combination is found between cognition- and skill-oriented approaches, and meta-cognition (and meta-skills) oriented models or theories for education and research. It is emphasized that cognition and skills are required for the development of meta-cognitive skills, which deserve more attention because they offer teachers and students the strategies for acquiring new knowledge and skills and for solving problems (Jones, 1986; Winne, 1987; Veenman, 1992).

In Europe, perhaps because of the pedagogical background of educational research, more attempts were made to combine the results of research on teaching with a pedagogy of education. In fact, the research revealed the same results as the earlier restricted research on teaching (Bennett *et al.*, 1984; Helmke *et al.*, 1986; Bennett, 1987). The conclusions were translated into guides for educational practice (Perrott, 1982), but more often they were used, implemented and evaluated in a broader context than the classroom environment or the effects of the teaching process, such as from the perspective of their relationship to the educational system and wider society (Delamont, 1987; Bennett, 1988; Galton, 1989a, b; Alexander, 1992).

Just as for grouping, in recent years a large number of meta-analyses have been published on the results of research on teacher behaviour in relation to achievement. Different elements of teacher behaviour, ranging from reinforcement for students to the waiting time between asking questions and requiring the answers, were included in these meta-analyses. Fraser *et al.* (1987) present a review of these meta-analyses on teachers. Often these meta-analyses about instruction concern specific subjects, such as science, mathematics and reading. Table 6.1 shows the elements referring to teacher variables. It shows for each factor the number of meta-analyses, the number of individual studies, the number of relationships tested and the average correlations with achievement. The authors suggest that with large samples any factor that has a correlation with achievement equal to or higher than 0.20 is well worth pursuing, and any correlation higher than 0.30 should be of much interest. Of the factors mentioned, only quality of instruction, quantity of instruction, reinforcement and remediation/feedback show correlations equal to or higher than 0.30. Curricular materials (methods) and grouping procedures, analysed together and independently of each other, show correlations lower than 0.30.

The relationships mentioned in Table 6.1 do not always provide information about which characteristics of a factor are related to achievement. Table 6.2 provides some further information. Discussion of the results of the synthesis of reviews will be restricted to the relevant (>0.20) relationships. However, the corre-

Table 6.1. *Synthesis of meta-analyses*

Factor	No. of meta-analyses	No. of studies	No. of relationships	Average *r*	SD	*z*
Instructor	9	329	1097	0.21	0.13	0.44
Background	1	65	22	0.29	0.00	0.60
Style	8	264	1075	0.20	0.13	0.42
Instruction	31	1854	5710	0.22	0.14	0.47
Quality	1	41	22	0.47	0.00	1.00
Quantity	4	110	80	0.38	0.02	0.84
Methods	26	1763	5668	0.17	0.08	0.36
Science	11	730	1562	0.18	0.06	0.36
Mathematics	6	416	1713	0.16	0.17	0.32
Reading	8	557	2333	0.24	0.14	0.50
Others	1	60	60	0.13	0.00	0.28
Methods of instruction	37	2541	6352	0.14	0.09	0.29
Individualization	5	467	630	0.07	0.07	0.14
Simulation/games	2	151	111	0.17	0.01	0.34
Computer-assisted	11	557	566	0.15	0.07	0.31
Programmed instruction	4	285	220	0.09	0.05	0.18
Tutoring	2	218	125	0.25	0.06	0.50
Learning hierarchies	1	15	24	0.09	0.00	0.19
Mastery learning	3	106	104	0.25	0.04	0.50
Team teaching	1	41	41	0.03	0.00	0.06
Homework	2	44	110	0.21	0.04	0.43
Instructional media	6	657	4421	0.14	0.12	0.30
Learning strategies	12	714	783	0.28	0.17	0.61
Reinforcement	3	76	139	0.49	0.06	1.13
Advance organizers	5	430	387	0.18	0.12	0.37
Behavioural objectives	1	111	111	0.06	0.00	0.12
Remediation/feedback	3	97	146	0.30	0.11	0.65

Partly from Fraser *et al.* (1987, p. 207).

lations do not reflect causal relationships. To prove such relationships, causal analyses (and appropriate research designs) are required. Furthermore, correlations do not imply effect sizes.

In the following I will discuss per unit the correlations mentioned in Tables 6.1 and 6.2.

Instructor. The background of the teacher is restricted in these tables to a background in science. Variables such as age and educational background seem to have positive effects (teacher expectations will be discussed separately later in this section). With regard to instructional style, asking questions that are directed to higher cognitive levels, such as analysis, synthesis and problem-solving, is positively related to student achievement. However, answering such higher order questions presupposes a knowledge based on a lower level of cognitive complexity. Several authors, Borich among others, advise the maintenance of a ratio of 70:30 or 60:40 between questions aimed at the development of lower-order and higher-order skills (Borich, 1988, p. 198). The correlation of general instructor rating and achievement

Table 6.2. *A summary of relationships to school achievement*

Factors	No. of studies	No. of relationships	Overall	References
Instructor				
Background				
In science	65	22	0.29	Druva and Anderson (1983)
Style				
Questioning	14	14	0.34	Redfield and Rousseau (1981)
Instructor rating	41	67	0.43	Cohen (1981)
Indirect–direct	19	34	0.17	Glass *et al.* (1980)
Praise	14	791	0.08	Wilkinson (1981)
Expectations	77	77	0.16	Dusek and Joseph (1983)
Expectations	18	33	0.04	Raudenbush (1983)
Expectations	34	15	0.26	Rosenthal and Rubin (1978)
Expectations	47	44	0.13	Smith (1980)
Instruction				
Quality				
Course ratings	41	22	0.47	Cohen (1981)
Quantity				
Participation	11	28	0.35	Bloom (1976)
Participation	54	22	0.40	Lysakowski and Walberg (1982)
Time on task	35	20	0.38	Frederick (1980)
Engagement time	10	10	0.40	Walberg (1982)
Learning strategies				
Reinforcement				
In general	39	102	0.50	Lysakowski and Walberg (1982)
In general	13	13	0.43	Walberg (1982)
Stimulation	24	24	0.54	Walberg (1982)
Advance organizers				
On achievement	77	99	0.06	Kozlow (1979); Kozlow and White (1980)
On achievement	29	112	0.31	Stone (1983)
On learning	135	110	0.10	Luiten *et al.* (1980)
On retention	135	50	0.12	Luiten *et al.* (1980)
Cues	54	16	0.30	Lysakowski and Walberg (1982)
Behavioural objectives	111	111	0.06	Ascencio (1984)
Remediation/feedback				
Corrective feedback	54	20	0.43	Lysakowski and Walberg (1982)
In science	28	49	0.26	Yeaney and Miller (1983)
Feedback	15	77	0.22	Schimmell (1983)

From Fraser *et al.* (1987).

in the study of Cohen (1981) is rather high. It should be taken into account that this rating overlaps with other factors, such as the quality of courses.

Instruction. The instructional factor is divided into quantity, quality and methods (discussed in Chapter 4). It is interesting to note that the various methods in science, mathematics and reading have an average correlation of 0.19 with achievement, indicating that these methods do have small but positive effects on achievement. Quality of instruction, measured by course ratings of students, shows a substantial effect on achievement. Adequacy of planning, organization and the use of feedback are important elements. Strong relationships with achievement were found for different measures of time on task, engagement time and participation. These results provide evidence for the importance of academic learning time in instructional effectiveness (see Chapter 2).

Methods of instruction. Under this heading, difficult-to-compare activities are summarized, such as grouping and homework. With respect to the grouping procedures discussed in Chapter 5, it is worth mentioning the rather important relationships between mastery learning and associated tutoring with achievement. Homework, which can be seen as expanding the academic learning time when it is structured and monitored properly, shows an interesting relationship with achievement. In this respect, it is quite curious that some practitioners are so reluctant to give homework (Barber, 1986). In the Netherlands, some schools experimented with so-called homework-free schooling, which means that homework is integrated in the curriculum of the school, and students stay in school until they have finished all their homework, which is supervised and supported. The results are encouraging, especially for disadvantaged groups (Simons, 1992).

Learning strategies. Several techniques used by teachers to enhance student learning are presented. In contrast with the suggestion of the term 'learning strategies', teaching strategies are the issue at hand. The strategies mostly refer to 'reinforcement', a general term that can cover feedback, corrective feedback, feedback with further instruction in various ways and remediation. In general, these reinforcement and feedback procedures seem to influence student achievement substantially. As can be concluded from Table 6.1, the correlation between advance organizers and achievement is 0.18. The use of advance organizers is worthwhile, although the effects, as can be seen in Table 6.2, are quite complex. Advance organizers are more likely to show effects when the reading level is appropriate to the grade level, when the pace of introduction of new ideas is slow, when the content is less complex, when comparative rather than expository organizers are used and when students are given more time to process the information provided by the advance organizers.

Several other teacher behaviours, such as redundancy and clarity of teacher presentation, that were studied in process–product research have not been included in meta-analyses as yet, probably because there are not enough studies on these subjects.

Good and Brophy (1978) and Brophy and Good (1986) present an overview of teacher behaviours that are related to achievement to a higher or lesser extent. As well as elements referring to quantity of instruction, active learning time, management and classroom organization, which have been discussed already, the following teacher activities are important for specific parts of lessons.

- When information is given, structuring of the contents of lessons is important by means of advance organizers, review of objectives, outlining contents, signalling transitions between lesson parts, calling attention to the main ideas, summarizing parts of the lessons and reviewing main ideas at the end, and organizing concepts and analogies in order to help students link new materials to already familiar materials.

- Redundancy/sequencing: achievement is higher when information is presented with a degree of redundancy, especially when general rules and key concepts are at stake; structuring of the contents in a sequence according to the task that has to be acquired also appears important.
- Clarity of presentation correlates consistently with student achievement.
- Appropriate pacing can have positive effects: in early grades a rapid pace seems to be appropriate, whereas in higher grades, where teachers present information for longer periods, a slower pace is necessary for new concepts to sink in.
- Questioning: except for the cognitive level of questions, mentioned before in the discussion of meta-analyses, the quality of questions in terms of their relevancy, timing and appropriateness is important (ambiguous questions or two or more questions at the same time raise problems for students; Carlsen, 1991).
- Post-question waiting time: a pause of about three seconds after a question, before calling on one of the students, gives students time to think and has positive effects on achievement.
- Results of studies on reactions to student answers confirm the conclusions about reinforcement and feedback. Correct answers should be acknowledged as such: when answers are partly correct or incorrect, teachers first have to indicate this and then give more information. In a review of research on evaluation practices in classrooms (varying from questions in texts and questions of teachers, to tests after curricular units), Crooks (1988) concludes that evaluation during instruction has important direct effects on student achievement. This is particularly important in special needs programmes (Shapiro and Ager, 1992).
- Seatwork, by which is meant students working alone and independently of their teachers, is probably overused in United States education and cannot substitute for active teacher instruction. Materials for seatwork should be clearly structured and interesting enough to motivate students. Effects also depend on curricular materials and student characteristics, such as age and prior mastery of meta-cognitive strategies. Immediate well-organized exercise after the presentation of new contents increases the effectiveness of instruction. The same holds for homework assignments. Homework is positively related to student achievement when it is assigned adequately and followed by accurate feedback. In this context, the results of a review of the effectiveness of computer-based instruction can also be mentioned. In a large meta-analysis of findings of 254 controlled evaluation studies, Kulik and Kulik (1991) conclude that computer-based instruction usually produces positive effects on student achievement. Positive effects are found in all grade levels, but they are smaller in studies of a longer duration (probably owing to a novelty effect or a Hawthorne effect in short experiments). The effects are also smaller when the same teachers teach the experimental and control classes. An indication of the predominance of the teacher?

As yet, teacher expectations have not been mentioned, because they belong to background characteristics rather than to the behaviours described in this chapter and this book. The importance of teacher expectations has been an integral part of educational research since the study of Rosenthal and Jacobson (1968). Rosenthal and Jacobson gave teachers incorrect information about their students: teachers were told that the IQ scores of certain students suggested that they might achieve significantly better than they actually did. After eight months, the achievement of these students had increased by more than usual. Rosenthal and Jacobson were criticized because of the methods they used and because of the nature of their statistical analysis. However, teacher expectations of achievement can be assumed to influence achievement, because teachers will act according to their expectations. Research on effective schools confirmed these results; not only individual teachers, but also schools can achieve such effects. Schools with high expectations of student achievement show higher levels of achievement than schools that do not expect as much (Levine and Lezotte, 1990; for further information, see Chapter 8). However, some research also indicates a reverse relationship (Goldenberg, 1992), because there might be a discrepancy between what teachers expect and what teachers do. The second is far more important than the first. Sometimes, for instance with respect to the achievement of girls or of ethnic minority groups, high expectations of teachers are recorded together with lower achievement (Jungbluth, 1981). The correlations mentioned in Table 6.2 are also not clear concerning the relationship, since they range from 0.04 (Raudenbush) to 0.26 (Rosenthal and Rubin).

Both traditional literature reviews and meta-analyses point to teacher behaviours that have positive effects on student achievement. Some meta-analyses and syntheses of meta-analyses are more sceptical, perhaps because of the limited range of behaviours being studied. For example, based on analyses only of science studies, Fraser *et al.* conclude that teacher behaviour, even though it is studied very frequently, does not contribute substantially to student achievement. They suggest that this line of research should perhaps be stopped. The average correlation is 'only' 0.22, and larger correlations cannot be expected in future research (Fraser *et al.*, 1987, p. 183), which conclusion is not in line with their own interpretation of their correlations later in the same study (Fraser *et al.*, 1987, p. 208). In their concluding comments concerning several analyses, they put their results in the perspective of the educational productivity model of Walberg (see Figure 2.1). They then conclude that some elements of the quality variable and the number of instruction variables of this model, among them teacher behaviours such as waiting time, question techniques, reinforcement and feedback, contribute to the improvement of student achievement (p. 233). Moreover, some elements that according to Fraser *et al.* do not belong to teacher behaviour, such as homework assignments, use of advance organizers and classroom organization, are in fact part of teacher behaviour or highly dependent on teacher behaviour, and in my opinion they should be included in an overview of effective teaching behaviour. The contributions of Waxman and Walberg (1991) provide the same set of effective teaching characteristics as described above and in one of the predecessors of this study (Walberg, 1979).

In school effectiveness studies, empirical evidence can be found for some of the characteristics of effective teaching. Many studies were not primarily interested in effective teaching since the main focus was on factors at school level, but, as is illustrated by Scheerens and Creemers (1989), several school effectiveness factors should actually be located at classroom level. Studies by Rutter *et al.* (1979) and Mortimore *et al.* (1988) and the overview of Dutch studies by Scheerens (1992) support the importance of effective teaching characteristics, such as evaluation including record keeping (see Mortimore *et al.*, 1988), structured teaching (Mortimore *et al.*, 1988; Scheerens, 1992), classroom management (Rutter *et al.*, 1979; Mortimore *et al.*, 1988), and a positive classroom climate conducive for learning (Brookover *et al.*, 1979; Edmonds, 1979; Mortimore *et al.*, 1988). Levine and Lezotte (1990) summarize even more correlates of teacher effectiveness at classroom level.

The overviews can provide endless lists of elements or correlates. One of the purposes of this study is to find those alterable characteristics of effective instruction that can be used to explain the small but substantial variation in student outcomes. That means that we may find more elements than the simple lists outlined in school effectiveness studies, but at the same time fewer than the vast number shown in the fishing expeditions for the correlates of effectiveness.

DIRECT INSTRUCTION

Because the role of isolated effective teacher behaviours in instruction was not clear, and because isolated behaviours could not be expected to have large effects on student achievement, isolated behaviours were integrated into an instructional approach (Rosenshine, 1987). The term 'direct instruction' had already existed for some time. It was used to describe teaching–learning processes, explicitly directed by teaching, in a stepwise procedure. Other terms came into use later, such as explicit teaching, explicit instruction and active teaching.

Direct instruction is a form of explicit, stepwise instruction, emphasizing student learning and cognitive achievement: 'Direct instruction and the similar terms can be summarized in the phrase: If you want students to learn something, teach it to them directly' (Rosenshine, 1987, p. 258). Guidelines for direct instruction are based on results of correlational and experimental studies on teaching (Rosenshine, 1983). Teachers are most effective, especially in teaching basic skills, when they:

1 Structure learning experiences.
2 Proceed in small steps but at a brisk pace.
3 Give detailed and redundant instructions, explanations and examples.
4 Ask a large number of questions and provide overt student practice.
5 Provide feedback and corrections, especially in the initial stages of learning new material.
6 Have a student success rate of 80 per cent or higher, especially in initial learning.
7 Divide assignments into smaller assignments, and find ways to control frequently.
8 Provide for continued student practice (students may even learn more than is necessary; they may have a success rate of 90–100 per cent and become rapid, firm and self-confident in learning).

These guidelines were further developed by Rosenshine on the basis of experimental studies. In these studies, teachers were trained in real-life educational practice to show behaviours that raised student achievement (see, for example, Rosenshine and Stevens, 1986). Rosenshine made use of the guidelines of Good and Grouws (1979), developed for the Missouri Mathematics Effectiveness Study. Table 6.3 gives an overview. According to Rosenshine and Stevens (1986), direct instruction can be adapted to students. For example, more opportunities for rehearsal and more guided practice might be offered to low achievers, while the opposite holds for high achievers.

Veenman, who introduced direct instruction in the Netherlands (Veenman *et al.*, 1988, 1992), summarized the benefits of direct instruction on the basis of a large number of studies (Veenman, 1992). Direct instruction is best equipped for well-structured school subjects like mathematics, where subjects can be divided into small units. In this area the model is very successful, especially for students from disadvantaged backgrounds. In several projects, like the Missouri programme (Good and Grouws, 1979) and the Gersten and Carnine programme (1986), direct instruction is used. Studies like *What Works* (1986) recommend direct instruction. In educational practice, teachers look upon direct instruction as an instructional approach that resembles their usual daily work.

Direct instruction in fact stems from the behaviouristic process–product tradition in education. As explained before, there is nothing wrong with that. However, schools should not only focus on basic skills and basic cognitive knowledge, they should also promote higher cognitive processes, such as learning strategies, problem solving and meta-cognitive behaviour. This requires more strategic teaching from teachers but it turns out that forms like modelling and scaffolding can be included in the direct instruction model (Veenman, 1992, p. 265). Originally, direct instruction was used only to achieve a set of specific objectives, such as knowledge or skills, but to achieve these objectives learning strategies are important and these strategies can be used in more complex learning situations with the already acquired information and skills. For that purpose, in the different phases of the learning process scaffolds are included in the direct instruction model to structure such strategic learning. These scaffolds contain elements that enable the acquisition of meta-cognitive knowledge and skills, such as the knowledge of how to proceed, modelling, thinking aloud and social support by peers.

CONCLUSIONS

On the basis of research discussed in this chapter, it can be concluded that teacher behaviour in classrooms is positively related to student achievement. Teacher behaviour that is important in this respect encompasses the allocation and use of learning time, and classroom management aimed at generating an orderly atmosphere to promote learning. It also encompasses teacher activities in several educational components, such as structuring the content, the questioning, the evaluation, the feedback and the corrective instruction.

These teacher behaviours have positive effects on student achievement. These effects can be expected to increase, as some experimental studies show, when teachers are trained in showing these behaviours (Bennett and Carré, 1993). On the basis of the effects of the model of direct instruction, as well as derivative or comparable educational models, such combinations of teacher behaviours can be expected to be effective.

Table 6.3. *Instructional functions*

1 *Daily review and checking homework*
 Checking homework (routines for students to check each other's papers)
 Reteaching when necessary
 Reviewing relevant past learning (may include questioning)
 Review prerequisite skills (if applicable)

2 *Presentation*
 Provide short statements of objectives
 Provide overview and structuring
 Proceed in small steps but at a rapid pace
 Intersperse questions within the demonstration to check for understanding
 Highlight main points
 Provide sufficient illustrations and concrete examples
 Provide demonstrations and models
 When necessary, give detailed and redundant instructions and examples

3 *Guided practice*
 Initial student practice takes place with teacher guidance
 High frequency of questions and overt student practice (from teacher and/or materials)
 Questions are directly relevant to the new content or skill
 Teacher checks for understanding (CFU) by evaluating student responses
 During CFU teacher gives additional explanation, process feedback, or repeats explanation – where necessary
 All students have a chance to respond and receive feedback: teacher ensures that all students participate
 Prompts are provided during guided practice (where appropriate)
 Initial student practice is sufficient so that students can work independently
 Guided practice continues until students are firm
 Guided practice is continued (usually) until a success rate of 80 per cent is achieved

4 *Correctives and feedback*
 Quick, firm and correct responses can be followed by another question or a short acknowledgement of correctness (e.g. 'That's right')
 Hesitant correct answers might be followed by process feedback (e.g. 'Yes, Linda, that's right because . . .')
 Student errors indicate a need for more practice
 Monitor students for systematic errors
 Try to obtain a substantive response to each question
 Corrections can include sustaining feedback (e.g. simplifying the question, giving clues), explaining or reviewing steps, giving process feedback, reteaching the last steps
 Try to elicit an improved response when the first one is incorrect
 Guided practice and corrections continue until the teacher feels that the group can meet the objectives of the lesson
 Praise should be used in moderation, and specific praise is more effective than general praise

5 *Independent practice (seatwork)*
 Sufficient practice
 Practice is directly relevant to skills/content taught
 Practise to overlearning
 Practise until responses are firm, quick and automatic
 Ninety-five per cent correct rate during independent practice
 Students alerted that seatwork will be checked
 Student held accountable for seatwork
 Actively supervise students, when possible

6 *Weekly and monthly reviews*
 Systematic review of previously learned material
 Include review in homework
 Frequent tests
 Reteaching of material missed in tests

Note: with older, more mature learners with more knowledge of the subject, the following adjustments can be made: (1) the size of the step in presentation can be larger (more material is presented at one time); (2) there is less time spent on teacher-guided practice and (3) the amount of overt practice can be decreased, replacing it with covert rehearsal, restating and reviewing.
From: Rosenshine and Stevens (1986).

We can now elaborate the model introduced in Chapter 2 as presented in Figure 6.1. As principles for the further development of the model I use the concepts introduced in Chapter 2: time for learning, opportunity to learn and quality of instruction. For the quality of instruction the following characteristics of teacher behaviour are important.

- Management of the classroom to create a situation where learning can take place. This implies an orderly and quiet atmosphere in the classroom, although, as mentioned before, learning itself requires more than a well-organized class. Moreover, effective teaching itself contributes to the management of the class.
- Provision of homework. If properly organized, homework contributes to effectiveness. This implies a clear structure of assignments, and supervision and evaluation of homework.
- Expectations teachers (and schools) have of their abilities to influence student outcomes probably influence what teachers do. We can expect those expectations to become apparent in the actual teacher behaviours.
- Clear goal setting. This includes a restricted set of goals, and an emphasis on basic skills and on cognitive learning and transfer. The content should be chosen in line with these goals.
- Structuring the content. This includes the ordering of the content according to the hierarchically ordered goals. As mentioned in Chapter 4, the use of advance organizers can also structure the content for students. The use of prior knowledge can increase students' own contributions and responsiveness for learning.
- Clarity of presentation, which implies the elements mentioned above but also refers to the transfer process itself (avoiding vagueness and incomplete sentences).
- Questioning (by means of low- and higher-order questions) keeps students at work and can be used to check their understanding.
- Immediate exercise after presentation. Like questioning, exercises provide a check for understanding and can be used to clarify problems.
- Evaluating whether the goals are obtained, by means of testing, providing feedback and corrective instruction.

The characteristics presented are based on research on teaching and to an extent on school effectiveness research. They are not an enumeration of all possible correlates but a choice of characteristics based on empirical evidence on the one hand and on the theoretical notions outlined earlier on the other.

The relationship between teacher behaviour in classrooms and the other elements of the teaching–learning situation, curricula and grouping procedures, should be emphasized. Rosenshine (1983), and later Rosenshine and Stevens (1986), state, in discussing active teaching, that it is important that guidelines for teacher behaviour are collected together in contemporary times. However, they believe the guidelines should also be integrated into curricular teacher manuals and teacher training.

Teacher behaviour is often partly elicited, planned or directed by curricula or grouping procedures, which can be more or less effective in their own way. As Table 6.1 shows, the contribution of methods and grouping to effectiveness is quite small,

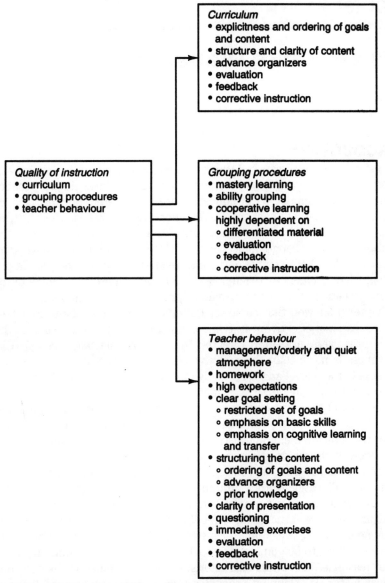

Figure 6.1 *The basic model of educational effectiveness: effective characteristics of teacher behaviour.*

and smaller than teacher behaviour. We can expect that better tuning of the components of instruction will induce a higher correlation with outcome measures. The next step is to check whether it is possible to relate these elements in some way or another, in order to enhance the effectiveness of instruction.

Chapter 7

The Effective Classroom

INTRODUCTION

The previous chapters discussed the separate components of the teaching–learning process: curriculum, grouping and teacher behaviour. These chapters made it clear that these three components of education are interrelated. For instance, curricula are meant to be used by teachers, and teachers will partly base their instruction on curricula. Teachers will also interpret curricula and use them in the way they want to, in that they will change some parts, add some elements and leave some other elements out. Another example of the interrelatedness of the components concerns grouping, which influences teacher behaviour, and where the choice of a specific grouping procedure requires in turn appropriate curriculum material.

Chapter 6 showed that some characteristics of teacher behaviour help to increase educational effectiveness. Some characteristics, however, such as the use of advance organizers, are often directed by the curricula teachers use. Classroom effectiveness is more than the effectiveness of the separate components of education at classroom level and is certainly more than the separate effective characteristics of these components. It is essential to create an optimal composition of the components and the characteristics of these components that can enhance effectiveness. It cannot be expected that the individual characteristics of teacher behaviour or the individual characteristics of the curriculum will result in substantially higher levels of classroom effectiveness, and this certainly holds for characteristics that merely increase learning time, such as the management behaviour of teachers or their time allocation within grouping, because something also has to be done during that time in order to make learning possible. This principle also holds for other characteristics: structuring or feedback may increase learning time or lead to improvement in some areas but, for instruction to become more effective, effective variables will have to be combined in such a way that they are mutually reinforcing. For that reason, effectiveness characteristics were combined in the development of curricular materials, grouping procedures and teacher behaviours. Some of these combinations are presented in earlier chapters.

It turned out decades ago to be of little use to advise teachers to acquire or to present isolated instructional characteristics, so the search for a combination of characteristics, each shown to be effective, started. Teacher behaviour, aimed at higher effectiveness, became known in the United States literature as 'direct instruction', or 'active teaching', or 'direct explicit teaching'. In direct instruction, however, the relations of teacher behaviour with curricula or grouping are not specified.

Another approach that integrates effective variables is mastery learning. Moreover, mastery learning integrates elements of several components. However, in mastery learning the main focus remains only the allocation of time to individual students or groups of students to enhance learning in order to achieve their object-ives. In curriculum development and school improvement projects, like the Education and Social Environment Project (OSM), the characteristics of curricula that have been shown to be effective are put into practice to generate effective text-books and learning material. However, other components, like grouping and teacher behaviour, except as a 'tool' to implement the material, received less attention in projects like this.

With regard to teacher behaviour, it has been made clear that a mix of beha-viours, such as through direct instruction, can result in a higher effectiveness of education than individual elements of behaviour. Direct instruction needs to be related to the other components of education at the classroom level as well, not only because these components can increase effectiveness, but also because curricula and grouping procedures can be seen as elements of effective teacher behaviour. The same holds for the other components of instruction at the classroom level: grouping procedures and curriculum material, such as textbooks. Each component includes effective characteristics, but the effectiveness of the component is in-creased by combination with other components. In reality, in the instructional process the components presuppose each other and I will try to show that this is even more so with respect to the effective characteristics of the components.

In this chapter, an integration of separate elements will be described. Such an integration is necessary, because the effectiveness of curricula and grouping pro-cedures is strongly dependent on the way teachers use curricula and grouping. First, I will present an overview of the empirical evidence for the characteristics included in the model in the previous chapters. Then, I will show how effectiveness can be enhanced by an integration of components. The key concept is the mutually re-inforcing process by which empirically effective characteristics of curricula, group-ing procedures and teacher behaviour succeed in increasing effectiveness.

EMPIRICAL EVIDENCE FOR THE CHARACTERISTICS OF EFFECTIVE INSTRUCTION

In earlier chapters parts of a basic model of educational effectiveness were devel-oped. The basic model itself was based on Carroll's model of school learning. Essen-tial in his model are time for learning and quality of instruction, in addition to the aptitude of students. We added to this model the concept of the opportunity to learn. Time and opportunity are discerned both at the classroom level and at the student level. In this way, we made a distinction between time available and actually used time and opportunity. We distinguished three components within the overall quality of instruction at classroom level: curricular materials, grouping procedures and teacher behaviour. We reviewed the literature to find characteristics of these components that contribute to effectiveness. We included characteristics based on two criteria: their theoretical notions and the empirical evidence.

Theoretical notions are at the core of the basic model, especially the expecta-tion that the characteristics which constitute quality of instruction are related to the time and the opportunities for learning offered to the students. The principal idea was not to include as many characteristics as possible, but to develop an economic and relevant, as well as an insightful, model. As a consequence only major characteristics, which can be considered as 'collections' of several minor characteristics, were included. An example of such a minor characteristic is waiting time, which can explain variance in student outcomes but which is so detailed that it confuses or mixes up the theoretical framework. I regard waiting time, more precisely 'taking at least three seconds between phrasing the question and asking for answers', as a dimension of the more global variable of questioning. There are more guidelines for 'good questioning' than a certain waiting time. For the theoretical model, 'questioning', including all these different aspects, is sufficient.

Characteristics that could be confusing between the components of effective instruction were also left out. An example is pacing, an effective characteristic of teacher behaviour. The way it is usually defined is related to grouping procedures, which take care of the pace of instruction, adapted to groups of students. So I decided to leave pacing out of the list of characteristics of teacher behaviour, but we can assume that the effectiveness of grouping procedures is linked to whether teachers are able to pace the instructional process.

Sometimes characteristics are included in the model even when the empirical evidence for them is quite small. For example, this is the case with 'methods', which turned out not to be a very influential factor in itself (see Chapter 6). We can assume that the contribution of methods to effectiveness will be enlarged when they are developed according to the guidelines described, and when the components are interrelated.

In summary, the model was developed from a theoretical model about the determinants of learning in school. The addition of variables to the model was determined by theoretical notions and empirical evidence.

The three components have received empirical support, but the distinction between curricular materials and teaching behaviour is problematic in this respect. Teacher behaviour is possible (although difficult) without curricular materials, but to investigate the effectiveness of curricular materials we need teachers and teacher behaviour. Research designed to find out the specific contribution of curricular materials is quite complicated to implement in educational practice. So the empirical evidence for the effects of teacher behaviour and grouping procedures is strong, while the empirical evidence for the importance of curricular materials is only moderate.

The characteristics differ from each other with respect to the empirical evidence. For curriculum, a 'specific' kind of research sustains the importance of explicitness and the ordering of goals and content (mastery learning). For structure and clarity of content this is less obvious, but their importance can be assumed based on empirical evidence in the field of teacher behaviour. Moreover, the characteristics in the area of structuring need more research, probably after better conceptualization. For advance organizers, evaluation and feedback the evidence is quite substantial. The importance of corrective instruction has to be assumed on the basis of more 'circumstantial' evidence, such as the importance of adaptive instruction.

Although there is a debate about the research evidence on grouping, some conclusions can be drawn. There is strong empirical evidence for mastery learning, for positive effects of ability grouping the evidence is moderate, and for cooperative learning positive evidence can be expected, but further research is needed. These characteristics receive sufficient empirical support. This also holds for the importance of evaluation, and somewhat less for feedback and corrective instruction. The importance of these characteristics can also be deduced from the negative effects of certain kinds of grouping within educational practice. Empirical evidence is not so clear for differentiated curriculum material.

With respect to teacher behaviour, the empirical support for the characteristics mentioned above is quite strong in general. Management and a quiet and orderly atmosphere were substantially supported. The same holds for use of homework, but the effects are highly dependent on the clarity of assignments, evaluation and feedback. High expectations are empirically supported. The same holds for goal setting. Some evidence for the effectiveness of a restricted set of goals comes from the research on mastery learning; with respect to an emphasis upon basic skills, empirical support stems from school effectiveness studies, but it could not be replicated by other studies. An emphasis on cognitive learning and transfer can be expected to contribute to instructional effectiveness, based upon research on learning. With respect to structuring of contents, the empirical evidence comes from quite different areas of research. The ordering of goals and content again comes from research in the field of mastery learning and the other aspects of structuring are supported by research on teaching. Clarity of presentation is found to be effective in teacher effectiveness studies. Immediate exercise after presentation is moderately supported in empirical studies. In teacher effectiveness research sufficient support can be found for the importance of questioning and evaluation, and moderate support can be found for feedback. Corrective instruction can be expected to be effective. Table 7.1 provides an overview of the empirical evidence for the discerned characteristics.

INTEGRATION OF EFFECTIVE CHARACTERISTICS OF INSTRUCTIONAL COMPONENTS: THE CONSISTENCY PRINCIPLE

Research on education at the classroom level shows that isolated components or effective elements of individual components do not result in strong effects on student achievement. Good curricula need teachers who can make adequate use of them, and who show effective instructional behaviour. The same also holds for grouping procedures. Each component contributes to learning in classrooms, but the other components are necessary for substantial effects. Adequate management behaviour in classrooms will result in learning time, but good curricula, effective grouping procedures and adequate instructional behaviour are necessary to make learning time productive.

An integrated approach to education at the classroom level, with an even higher level of integration than direct instruction or mastery learning, is necessary. In this integrated approach, the educational components of curricula, grouping procedures and teaching behaviour are adapted to each other.

Effective instruction should provide time and opportunities to learn. To achieve that, the three components in general should have the same effective characteristics. The components should all be seen as vehicles, as means to achieve objectives, which are the learning outcomes of students. For that purpose, curricular materials like textbooks should be developed according to certain well-stated and clear goals. In the use of grouping procedures, it should be clear what kind of goals

Table 7.1. *Overview of empirical evidence for the characteristics of effective instruction*

Characteristics	Strong empirical evidence	Moderate empirical evidence	Plausible
Curriculum		x	
Grouping procedures	x		
Teacher behaviour	x		
Curriculum			
Explicitness and ordering of goals and content	x		
Structure and clarity of content		x	
Advance organizers	x		
Evaluation	x		
Feedback	x		
Corrective instruction			x
Grouping procedures			
Mastery learning	x		
Ability grouping		x	
Cooperative learning			x
Differentiated material			x
Evaluation	x		
Feedback		x	
Corrective instruction		x	
Teacher behaviour			
Management/orderly and quiet atmosphere	x		
Homework	x		
High expectations		x	
Clear goal setting		x	
Restricted set of goals		x	
Emphasis on basic skills		x	
Emphasis on cognitive learning and transfer			x
Structuring the content		x	
Ordering of goals and content		x	
Advance organizers	x		
Prior knowledge		x	
Clarity of presentation		x	
Questioning	x		
Immediate exercise		x	
Evaluation	x		
Feedback		x	
Corrective instruction			x

have to be achieved by individual students or by groups of students. Teacher behaviour should be guided by the goals teachers and students have to accomplish, although operationalization of goals is not meant to be a part of the instructional behaviour of teachers. When teachers make use of curricular materials and grouping procedures, it should be clear that the goals they have in mind are also part of the curriculum they are using, together with the grouping procedures and the materials that are used for the grouping of students.

The same holds for structuring. Structuring should be an important characteristic of curricular materials and textbooks. Elements of structuring are the ordering of goals, the availability of advance organizers, links with prior knowledge, the ordering of subjects according to the goals and immediate exercises after presentation of new content. The same characteristics show up in the provision of well-structured instruction. Teachers depend heavily on curricular materials and textbooks, which make it possible to structure instruction. Textbooks are, in a way, scaffolds for teachers. Another effective teacher characteristic, questioning, is also structured by curricular materials and textbooks. These materials provide teachers with all kinds of possibilities to raise questions and to adapt instruction to different groups of students. That is even more so with some other elements of curricular materials, such as evaluation, the provision of tests, generating possibilities for feedback and the inclusion of different kinds of corrective instruction. These elements can provide guidelines for effective teacher behaviour, and are of crucial importance for the effectiveness of grouping procedures.

As was said before, the same characteristics of effective teaching should be apparent in the different components. It is even more important that the actual goals, structuring and evaluation in curricular materials, grouping procedures and teacher behaviour are along the same lines. This does not mean that they have to be the same, but they should support each other; they should be consistent with each other. In this way a synergistic effect can be achieved.

Consistency of the effective characteristics of the main components of instruction can cause a synergistic effect. We can observe such an effect in the implementation of new, experimental curricula in which teachers contribute to the effect of the curriculum, sometimes more than the curriculum itself. The opposite can be seen in the negative results of the introduction of material in situations in which teachers did not have the chance to adapt themselves to the curriculum, or to adapt the curriculum (Olsen and Eaton, 1987; Kuiper, 1993).

The question could be raised as to whether it is possible to create instructional arrangements of the different components, including effectiveness characteristics, that are in line with each other, mutually reinforce each other and have a synergistic effect that exceeds the effectiveness of the separate components. Direct instruction and mastery learning show to some extent that this is possible. Moreover, some successful school improvement projects have been developed more or less in line with the principles explained by this study. The Milwaukee project combines the curriculum, grouping (whole-class instruction at grade level and small-group instruction at performance level) and instruction at the classroom level. The results showed a significant progress of the schools with respect to outcomes on mathematics and reading (McCormack-Larkin, 1985). Other examples are 'Success for All' (Slavin et al., 1989), the project of the Halton Schoolboard (Stoll and Fink, 1992) and the programme in Sederoth (Bashi et al., 1990). In these programmes, empirically effective factors of components in classroom instruction processes are integrated, and supported by effective factors at other educational levels (school level or national level). These levels are discussed in the next chapter.

School improvement projects should be evaluated very carefully, in order to see what contributes to effectiveness and what should be changed. Sometimes school improvement projects are focused on improvement more than on careful evaluation, but the programmes in Sederoth and 'Success for All' are carefully evaluated. The project in Sederoth shows impressive results, although the stimulating Israeli

95

educational context and its high expectations must be taken into account in the interpretation of results. However, high expectations are one of the important factors for increasing effectiveness. Essential for the Sederoth programme at classroom level is the emphasis on achieving intermediate objectives. For that purpose, mastery learning is used, with extra time provided to master objectives.

The programme developed by Slavin also shows favourable results (Slavin *et al.*, 1990). This programme combines effective characteristics of curricular materials, grouping procedures and – again – the provision and effective use of time to master objectives. The emphasis on the prevention of reading problems and the immediate remediation of reading difficulties in a tutoring system is essential and contributes to the results impressively.

Unfortunately, research on effective instructional arrangements is limited in school improvement projects, so that support for synergistic effects cannot be illustrated. In these projects, the evaluation was directed to see if improvements were put into practice by teachers or established in curricular materials. But the ultimate test for effectiveness was not included: achievement test results of students, in connection with the improvements and the changed instructional processes. Some school improvement projects concentrated on factors at the school level, such as team building, the organization of the school and the development of a school evaluation policy. They were not directed primarily at the classroom level, although some of them are supposed to link to increasing effectiveness at the classroom level. These projects hypothesize that teachers become more effective in their instructional behaviour if they follow guidelines they receive from principals. The results of some of these projects are encouraging (Stringfield and Teddlie, 1989), although Freiberg *et al.* (1990) point to the fact that the results tend to decline in schools in severely disadvantaged areas when they are no longer supported.

In the Netherlands, improvement projects and research projects are being prepared or started, based on the principles described in this study. Most of these projects take place in the context of the Dutch Educational Priority Policy for disadvantaged children. An example within this policy is the Amsterdam EGAA project, which strives for a general improvement of education in fourteen disadvantaged schools. This project makes use of the results of research on effective instruction and effective schools and concentrates on reading, language instruction and the implementation of a student monitoring system. The first research results are positive (Haanen *et al.*, 1990). Another programme that focuses on the classroom level is directed to the improvement of reading instruction (Osinga *et al.*, 1993).

The results of these kinds of projects are supported by the results of the evaluation of the Educational Priority Programme. In general, outlier analyses of high- and low-effectiveness schools show that they can be distinguished based on the characteristics of effective instruction, especially in the area of teacher behaviour and curricular materials (van der Werf and Weide, 1991; Weide, 1993).

A similar conclusion on the importance of the combination of characteristics of effectiveness in classroom instruction can be drawn from some of the programmes described earlier, intended to push education towards higher effectiveness. Although these programmes want to change the whole school, the starting point is the classroom level. The Louisiana School Effectiveness Study (Teddlie and Stringfield, 1993) is an empirical argument for starting at the classroom level and for addressing more than one component at the same time. Effective schools in this study are schools that can achieve effective classrooms, showing a combination of the effective characteristics of the different components.

Mostly, this synergy between components is not developed carefully and is more or less arbitrary even in improvement programmes, a result of different development activities which by accident turn out to be congruent or supplementary. Consistency between the components and the effectiveness characteristics should be established systematically, and, once achieved, consistency can be expected to have a synergistic effect, to increase the effects of the separate components and characteristics.

CONCLUSIONS

In the previous section, a plea was made for instructional arrangements of all the components and effective characteristics of components. Most of the time, the improvement of education at classroom level starts with a teacher making a decision about grouping procedures and the choice and use of curricular materials. This is where effective instruction starts. Effective instruction cannot develop from scratch in an empty space. Effective instruction starts with teachers in classrooms. This has two important implications:

1   Teachers as a central factor have to make a lot of decisions at the classroom level: about goals, the allocation of time to groups or individual students, use of material and their own instructional and management behaviour during the instructional process. But the complexity of the instructional process as it appears in the analyses in earlier chapters requires serious planning, in which consistency can be systematically developed.

2   To guide the planning of the instructional process by teachers and the development of effective arrangements, central ideas are of crucial importance. These can be found, in addition to the goals of education, in theories and research about learning and teaching, and in theories and research about the quality and the effectiveness of instruction. Both have to be combined. Time for learning and the opportunity to learn should be used as mediating constructs. They can guide the development of effective instruction.

Ultimately, teachers are the crucial factor in education at the classroom level. They should implement curricular materials and grouping procedures adequately, and show effective instructional behaviours. Considering the actual context, in which education is provided by teachers to a large extent, it is important for teachers to train and to practise these very behaviours.

Teachers have to be convinced that they can enhance learning in this way, and that education will become more effective. When they are convinced, teachers should let themselves be guided by good curricula and effective grouping procedures in preparing and implementing education at classroom level. Moreover, teachers should have a repertoire of capacities that enable them to structure instruction, order content adequately, ask questions, use tests and give feedback to their students.

In addition to this, curricular materials and grouping procedures can be more stable components in the instructional process and can constitute effective instruction together with teachers. Teachers – and that means in pre- and in-service training, in supervision and in team building – should be able to adapt and use

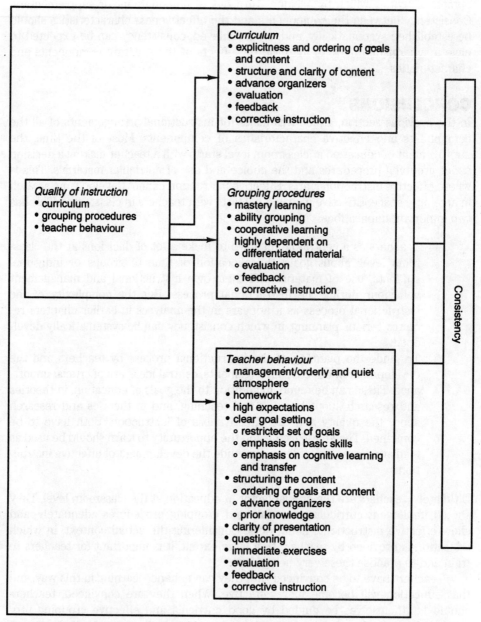

Figure 7.1 *The basic model of educational effectiveness: consistency of effective characteristics and components.*

curricula and grouping procedures to create consistency and, by this, a synergistic effect. Curricula and the specification of grouping procedures should provide teachers with opportunities to do so.

The model developed in the earlier chapters can now be complemented with the additional requirement of consistency between components and effective characteristics (see Figure 7.1).

Chapter 8

Effective Instruction in Effective Schools

INTRODUCTION

So far, this study has been mainly preoccupied with variables within components that are important in classrooms, variables that may raise effectiveness according to research results. However, classrooms are not islands, although they sometimes look like islands when teachers close their doors. Classrooms are parts of schools, and schools in their turn are parts of a broader context formed by other schools and the environment of schools.

School effectiveness is at the centre of much interest nowadays (see, for example, Nuttall *et al.*, 1989; Reynolds, 1989, 1991, 1992; Levine and Lezotte, 1990; Mortimore, 1991; Scheerens, 1992; Teddlie and Stringfield, 1993). Variables at the school level and variables at the classroom level contributing to effectiveness are not always clearly separated in the concept of the effective school (Scheerens and Creemers, 1989). As was argued in earlier chapters, the effectiveness of education is created at the classroom level, because the learning processes of students take place there. The design of education at the classroom level should be adapted to these processes, and the other levels in the system should be adapted to what goes on at the classroom level.

Following the integration of the empirically effective components of instruction at classroom level in Chapter 7, and the introduction of the concept of consistency, this chapter will discuss the conditions in the context of classrooms that may enhance effective instruction: conditions at the school level and conditions in the broader context of schools.

A SEARCH FOR CONDITIONS OF EFFECTIVENESS

The literature on school effectiveness is large and contains hundreds of correlates of effectiveness at the school level (see, for example, Levine and Lezotte, 1990). It is not my purpose to sum these up once again. On the contrary, for the sake of the development of a theory on educational effectiveness, it is important to reduce the number of correlates by theoretical analysis and by empirical research, as well as by replication studies. The correlates are often not sustained in replication studies, which relates to the fact that results of studies depend on chance and on multi-collinearity. The concepts used are sometimes so limited that they are of no use for our understanding of what happens in schools. Even when these concepts and correlates explain some variance, they are so conceptually restricted that they do not offer a real insight into relationships with student achievement. Some correlates at the school level, mentioned in earlier studies (see Scheerens, 1992), are not related empirically or theoretically to student achievement at all. Conceptually, it is unclear what the contribution to effectiveness could be and the empirical evidence is based mostly on technically weak studies.

In the theoretical framework of this book we are restricted to the explanation of outcomes which can be related theoretically and empirically to what happens in classrooms. The same procedure should be followed at other levels. This means that we are not so interested in the personality characteristics of headteachers, but in what they contribute to effectiveness. This implies that we are interested in studies and in theories that can be related to the theoretical framework based on learning and instruction. In this respect, the application of theories that do not focus on instruction and schooling, such as public choice theory at the school level and theories about contextual effects, can be criticized. Approaches to school improvement, like school restructuring, which are quite vague about the relationship between the outcomes of education and the variables at different levels, can also be criticized. From a theoretical perspective, school conditions can be formulated based on the ideas on instructional effectiveness, developed in the previous chapters.

At the classroom level, time, opportunity and quality influence student outcomes, in addition to student background variables. This means that we now need to look for conditions, at levels above the classroom level, that can be related to these three concepts. It is assumed that effective factors at other levels influence the time, the opportunity or the quality of instruction at classroom level. In this way we can make a theoretical analysis of effectiveness across the different levels.

Some of the conditions will contribute more clearly to instructional effectiveness than others. For example, the timetable at school level will clearly influence time at the classroom level. The maximum time for instruction at the classroom level is defined in this way. The same holds for conditions such as an evaluation policy at school level, or the school grouping system (if it exists). The influence of other variables is less clear. The contribution of the school principal or the team depends on the 'activities' they carry out to create conditions for effectiveness at the classroom level. These activities have to be spelled out. The school-level concepts have to be filled in, in terms of time, opportunity and quality, to make clear what can be expected as a contribution to instructional effectiveness, and to make them accessible for empirical research. This is not likely to be as complicated a task for variables directly related to education, such as the components of instruction at the classroom level and the components of the school as an educational system (curriculum, policy on grouping, policy on evaluation).

In addition to these, other influences are possible, especially of factors not strongly related to time, opportunity and quality (see Creemers, 1991; International School Effectiveness Research Programme, 1992; Reynolds, 1993a). For example, Levine and Lezotte (1990) pay attention to home–school relations. Reynolds (1993b) distinguishes all kinds of variables in the school as an organization, even cleaners, but the relation to the main concepts in our framework is not clear (empirically or conceptually), so these variables are not included.

Looking for factors related to these basic concepts is one way to develop a theory, or perhaps equally importantly, to establish educational effectiveness in school improvement projects. Another way builds on the fact that school education and therefore school effectiveness are both longitudinal processes. Students move from one class to another, from one grade level to another and in turn from one school subject to another. Therefore, besides the conditions and factors, we can discern formal criteria for effectiveness. These formal characteristics of effectiveness cannot be seen immediately in schools, but one can conclude that they exist when the same factors and variables are seen across instructional components, subjects, classes and grades. These formal characteristics that induce effective education are:

- Consistency: at the school level, conditions for effective instruction related to curricular materials, grouping procedures and teacher behaviour are in line with each other.
- Cohesion: all members of the school team show a consistency of effectiveness characteristics. In this way effective instruction between classes can be guaranteed.
- Constancy: effective instruction is provided during the total school career of students. Too often students are confronted with differences in instruction between teachers and grade levels. Constancy means that consistency and cohesion are guaranteed over longer periods of time.
- Control: control refers not only to the evaluation of student achievement and teacher behaviour, but also to an orderly and quiet school climate, which is necessary to achieve results. Control also refers to teachers holding each other responsible for effective instruction (Creemers, 1991; Reynolds and Creemers, 1992; Reynolds, 1993b).

So far, we have focused on variables at the school level which influence instructional effectiveness. Conditions for instructional effectiveness can also be formulated at levels above the school. Mostly, these conditions affect the school level, and then the school level creates the conditions for the classroom level. Sometimes, however, these influences are more clear, as, for example, the existence of a national testing system for student achievement affects the classroom level and the school level as well. Again we will try to formulate conditions related to the main principles of effective instruction of time, opportunity and quality.

At the context level, too, formal characteristics can be discerned:

- Consistency at the context level means that conditions for the school level (and the classroom level related to curricular materials, grouping procedures and teacher behaviour are in line with each other.
- Constancy refers to the fact that conditions at the context level should not change abruptly or too often.
- Control refers to procedures that can guarantee that the conditions at the school level are implemented and sustained.

These formal characteristics are still more hypothetical than empirically validated, but in some research the plausibility of these characteristics becomes apparent (Bosker and Scheerens, 1994).

In the following sections I will describe conditions related to time, opportunity and quality at the school level and at the context level.

CONDITIONS FOR EFFECTIVE INSTRUCTION AT THE SCHOOL LEVEL

In this section, I will discuss conditions for effective instruction at the school level. There will be related to the principles in the basic model: time, opportunity and quality. This implies that a description of all possible correlates will not be given, but that a selection will be made according to these principles in the development of a coherent theoretical framework that allows the interpretation of empirical findings.

The school level includes the organization of the school (teachers, students, parents), but also the educational system above the classroom level, which relates to the curriculum of the school, such as the textbooks and the time schedule. This suggests a distinction in the school level as an organizational and an educational system. Both systems are related to each other, but the first can create and sustain the situation in which education takes place to some extent, comparable with what management of the classroom 'does' for instruction. These factors at the school level are conditions for what goes on at the classroom level. Conditions can be clear, such as the curriculum, or less apparent, like the structure of the organization, but they can affect the instructional process by, for example, influencing what happens between principals and teachers (see, for example, Rosenholtz, 1989; Stoll, 1992; Teddlie and Stringfield, 1993).

Conditions for *time* at the school level are connected with the time schedule. For all grade levels, this schedule spells out how much time should be devoted to different subjects, etc. Above that it is important to keep track of the time schedule. In less effective schools, a lot of scheduled time is wasted, because there is no system to control classrooms in this matter.

The time available for learning can be expanded by a homework policy. In this respect good relations with the home environment can contribute to effectiveness. When homework assignments are well controlled and structured, and adequate feedback is given, such assignments can expand effective learning time outside the school. Good contacts between schools and parents and agreements about school policies and activities may lead to effective use of time spent on homework. When parents expect their children to achieve goals set by the school, the effectiveness of education increases.

Measures at the school level can maintain an orderly atmosphere that facilitates teaching and learning at the classroom level. Learning time is increased by an orderly and quiet classroom climate. At the school level such a climate can be fostered; therefore, it is necessary to establish order, a quiet atmosphere and regularity, and support teachers trying to achieve an orderly climate in their classes.

At the school level, conditions can be created that contribute to the *opportunity to learn* at the classroom level, which is especially important, at the school level, between classes and grade levels within the school. At the school level, the opportunity to learn is provided by the development and availability of documents such as a formal curriculum, a school working plan and an activity plan on what has to be done to pursue the goals of the curriculum and the working plan. In this document, the school management team can explain its vision about education and make clear how effectiveness will be pursued in the school. Schools should have a policy that increases effectiveness. Schools should feel responsible for student achievement: it is their 'mission' to contribute to achievement. A school policy based on these principles can yield important effects. It has already been mentioned that school working plans are not very effective, but their effects might be improved by a stronger relationship to instructional effectiveness at classroom level. But not only the document is important: it is also important to use the document and to 'control' what happens in the schools and classrooms with respect to the school curriculum. This is especially important for transitions between classes and grades.

A distinction has been made between educational and organizational aspects of the *quality of instruction*, although both are interrelated. With respect to the *educational* aspects, the rules and agreements in the school concerning the instructional process at the classroom level are of utmost importance, especially those related to curricular materials, grouping procedures and teacher behaviour. It is important to choose curricular materials for specific grade levels that are also used in other grade levels, or at least to ensure that they have the same structure. Earlier chapters discussed the importance of clearly stated goals and subgoals. There should be a policy at the school level which defines educational goals that have to be achieved in classrooms. This does not imply a wide range of goals that may be impossible to achieve by schools and teachers, but realistic goals that can actually be achieved in education and that can give guidance to teacher behaviour. When a specific grouping procedure is chosen, it is important to implement the same grouping procedure in several grade levels because effectiveness is also enhanced by constancy. There should be a policy at the school level to guide the continuity of grouping procedures across grade levels. Schools should have an evaluation policy that directs activities at classroom and student level by means of a student monitoring system. Schools can promote the testing of students and stimulate teachers to give information about test results to students, to take corrective measures, to monitor student progress and to act as necessary based on student progress, providing opportunities for rehearsal, corrective materials and remedial teaching.

The *organizational* aspects of quality of instruction deal with the intervision (mutual supervision of teachers) and the professionalism of teachers and principals. These refer not only to the structure of the organization but also to the way teachers and principals cooperate to promote the effectiveness of instruction at the classroom level and of the school as a whole. In this respect, the school principal as an 'instructional leader', who takes responsibility for the conditions mentioned above, can be an important conditional variable (Smith and Andrews, 1989). Team consensus about the mission of the school and the way to fulfil this mission through shared values will clearly support the activities of individual teachers and result in continuity (see Sashkin and Walberg, 1993). This can create a school culture in principals, teachers, students and parents that promotes and supports effectiveness (Cheng, 1993).

In this respect, the influence of the school board can also be mentioned. School boards, like principals, are not included in the model, but their influence appears in the model because of what they do. School boards can support school effectiveness and the effectiveness of classroom instruction. When they confirm school curriculum documents, they should attend to the elements mentioned above. They should strive for effective education when deciding about personnel, for example when they recruit new teachers or make decisions about career planning. School boards that are more attentive in this respect can increase effectiveness at the classroom level in the end, through the means of school principals, school teams and individual teachers (Hofman, 1993).

In summary, the following important elements increase effectiveness. Conditions at school level can be described for *quality of instruction* with respect to the *educational* aspects:

- rules and agreements about all aspects of classroom instruction, especially curricular materials, grouping procedures and teacher behaviour, and the consistency between them;
- an evaluation policy and a system at school level to check pupil achievement, to prevent learning problems or to correct problems at an early stage. This includes regular testing, remedial teaching, student counselling and homework assistance.

With respect to the *organizational* aspects at the school level, important conditions for *quality of instruction* are:

- a school policy on intervision and supervision of teachers, heads of departments and school principal by higher-ranking persons, and a school policy to correct and further to professionalize teachers who do not live up to the school standards;
- a school culture inducing and supporting effectiveness.

Conditions for *time* at the school level are:

- the development and provision of a time schedule for subjects and topics;
- rules and agreements about time use, including the school policy on homework, pupil absenteeism and cancellation of lessons;
- the maintenance of an orderly and quiet atmosphere in the school.

Conditions for the *opportunity to learn* at the school level are:

- the development and availability of a curriculum, school working plan or activity plan;
- consensus about the 'mission' of the school;
- rules and agreements about how to proceed and how to follow the curriculum, especially with respect to transition from one class to another or from one grade to another (Creemers *et al.*, 1992).

As has been mentioned, it is not my purpose to include all possible variables in the model. This has been done before (Levine and Lezotte, 1990). For the International School Effectiveness Research Programme, Reynolds (1993b) provided a possible list of factors.

The majority of the variables in these lists are comparable with the ones included in our framework, and the variables specified by Reynolds can be used to elaborate further the model, and especially to test it. But no variables connected with resources are included in the model here. It is not expected that resources explain variance in outcomes within countries, and just providing additional finance and resources to schools is not likely to improve them (Cohn and Geske, 1990; Walberg, 1992). Moreover, in the model resources are defined in a way that clarifies their relationship to effectiveness: curricular materials, teachers and other variables that support education.

CONDITIONS FOR EFFECTIVE EDUCATION IN SCHOOLS AND CLASSROOMS

Even further away from the instructional process at classroom level, there are conditions in the context of schools that influence that process. It is expected that these conditions influence the school level mostly, and through the school level affect the classroom level. But some conditions influence the classroom level as well. For example, a testing system affects the school level and the classroom level.

The available correlates at the school and context levels are in part the results of the way studies have been carried out. In survey studies with many schools and variables even small correlations can be significant. In outlier studies with a small set of schools or classes and many variables, always some variables seem to be important. As at the school level, only conditions that can be related to and interpreted in terms of time, opportunity and quality will be considered. It is assumed that all the correlates of effectiveness, if they survive in replication studies, have influence through these basic concepts and the characteristics discerned in our model.

With respect to *quality*, important contextual conditions are:

- national policy that focuses on the effectiveness of education;
- the availability of an indicator system and/or a national policy on evaluation and a national testing system;
- a training and support system promoting effective schools and effective instruction;
- funding of schools based on outcomes (although this policy is heavily criticized, it probably contributes to effectiveness, in combination with the conditions mentioned above, by directing the processes at the school level and the classroom level towards student outcomes and by emphasizing those conditions at the school level and those characteristics at the classroom level by which these outcomes can be achieved.

Conditions with respect to *time* refer to national guidelines for the time schedules of schools and the supervision of the maintenance of schedules. Conditions for the *opportunity to learn* are the national guidelines and rules for the development of the curriculum, working plan and activity plan at the school level, for example by a national curriculum. For resources at the context level, the same holds as with respect to the school level. Resources are important, but should be defined in this framework: availability and quality of material, teachers and other components supporting effective education in schools and classrooms.

I shall now give examples of the conditions described beyond the school level that can affect instruction.

Educational Policy

Educational policy can contribute to effective instruction by stimulating schools to focus on effectiveness. Educational policy should put student achievement and factors contributing to student achievement at the centre of attention. This means that educational policy should pay attention to the testing and evaluation of student achievement, and to the promotion of effective grouping procedures, curricula and teacher behaviour. Educational policy should stimulate the development of effective curricula, training and support of teachers in developing effective instructional behaviour, and the development of an evaluation system that relates achievement and means at the school and classroom levels. A continuing attention to basic knowledge and skills, national goals and core curricula is required at policy level, based on the expectation that education can and should achieve these goals.

Training

Teachers are the crucial factor in education at the classroom level. Moreover, teachers are mainly responsible for the effects of education, because there are so many aspects that cannot be prescribed and structured in curricula and grouping procedures. Teachers should see it as their professional responsibility to create and consolidate a learning environment that enables students to acquire knowledge and insights. This requires a professional teaching force (for literature and research on this topic, see, for example, Darling-Hammond and Goodwin, 1993).

Another implication is that teachers have to acquire skills to implement the factors that can increase effectiveness. These skills do not concern the application of didactic models in the preparation and teaching of lessons, but they do concern the use of an empirically effective curriculum. Students should acquire knowledge about factors contributing to effective instruction, but they should also be trained to show effective behaviours. Teacher training colleges should acknowledge the existence of effective instructional methods and techniques, and they should be willing to train their students accordingly. Veenman *et al.* (1993) report on the positive effects of a programme for teacher preparation and in-service training according to these principles. Hargreaves and Fullan (1992) advocate pre- and in-service training with respect to the characteristics of effective instruction.

Support Services

When teachers have clear ideas about the effectiveness of instruction, and are trained to put these ideas into practice, they will need support services to assist them in their professional activities. Additional training and support of education might contribute to the increase of educational effectiveness, by means of support for individual teachers and by means of team support and the training of teams. For institutions involved in the development of curricular materials, this implies that curricula should have a clear structure, that they can be used by teachers and that effective elements are explicitly incorporated. Such curricula require much more structuring than is usual now. A lot of current materials seem to conflict with the development and promotion of effective education.

CONCLUSIONS

This chapter summarizes the search for factors that can increase the effectiveness of education in the context of classrooms, which were described in the previous chapters. This search resulted in a selection of factors for conditions at the school and context levels that may enhance effective education at the classroom level.

At the school level, in particular, conditions can be created for effective instruction at the classroom level. It is expected that these conditions will be more effective when they are in line with the characteristics of effective instruction. That means that we can formulate the conditions based on the characteristics of effective instruction. For that reason, the general framework of time, opportunity and quality is used.

Conditions can be formulated for effective education in schools and classrooms at the context level as well. The empirical evidence for these conditions is not yet so clear. The selection of conditions is based more on rational analyses than on empirical evidence. The experiences in the improvement projects mentioned earlier (especially in the Sederoth project) confirm the expectation that conditions at the school level and at the context level have a positive effect on classroom instruction, and ultimately on student results.

The model can be extended with the components at school level and with conditions above the school level (see Figure 8.1).

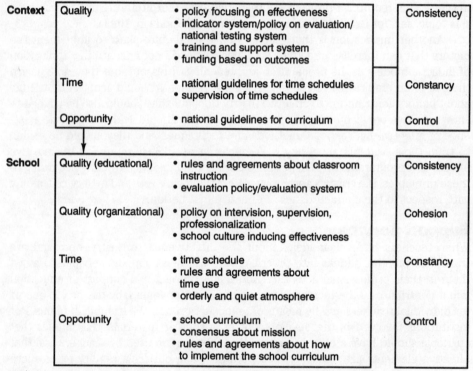

Figure 8.1 *The basic model of educational effectiveness: factors at the school level and the context level.*

Chapter 9

Towards a Theory of Educational Effectiveness

INTRODUCTION

Attention to educational effectiveness has its origins in research and practice with respect to school effectiveness. The early research projects carried out by Brookover *et al.* (1979) and Edmonds (1979) in the United States and by Rutter *et al.* (1979) in the United Kingdom have shown that schools differ from each other with respect to the outcomes of comparable groups of students. Some schools prove to be more effective than other schools and effective schools have some characteristics in common that ineffective schools do not have. In educational policy-making and practice, the idea of effective schools is also now receiving a great deal of attention, which is understandable because it offers the possibility of improving schools to get better results. In educational theory and research these results stimulated the setting up of research projects that looked for factors that could explain effectiveness in education.

Later, serious criticism arose with respect to the methodology, statistical analysis and conceptual frameworks of the school effectiveness research (Purkey and Smith, 1983; Ralph and Fennessey, 1983; Reynolds, 1985). It became clear that effectiveness is achieved at different levels of the system: primarily at the classroom level where instruction and learning take place; other levels in the system, such as the school level, merely provide the conditions for effective instruction at the classroom level.

Educational effectiveness is an important concept within the educational sciences. A comprehensive analysis of the effectiveness of education, taking the different levels of the educational system into account, can in a way be seen as the core of educational science and research. Educational research in this field is aimed at explaining the variance in educational outcomes, based on a theory about causes and effects in education. In this sense, a theory of educational effectiveness can be seen as an integral theory about education which takes into account the outcomes of education, the inputs, the processes and the contexts in which education takes place. In this sense, the concept of educational effectiveness is a welcome addition to educational research in general, and provides a programme for research. Such a programme has to address questions about outcomes and criteria for effectiveness, inputs, processes and contexts.

First, some basic problems with respect to educational effectiveness are discussed. These problems have been touched on at several places in this study, but now the information on educational outcomes and the educational process is brought together. In this final chapter components of the theoretical framework, started in Chapter 2, are combined. In Chapters 4, 5 and 6 the components for effective instruction at the classroom level were introduced, and in Chapter 7 brought together. In Chapter 8 we examined the conditions for effective instruction above the classroom level: the school level and the contextual level. We can now combine the components of the framework into a full integrated model. In large part, the study is based on the results of educational research. In the review of the research on educational effectiveness, the strengths and weaknesses of research in this field became apparent. The chapter ends with some recommendations for research in the future, based on the ideas outlined in this study, together with a conceptual analysis of educational effectiveness.

OUTCOMES OF EDUCATION: CRITERIA, SIZE AND STABILITY

In the past, research on school effectiveness was criticized for its criteria of effectiveness. Research took educational outcomes in the academic field as the only criterion. In addition, the measurement of this criterion was quite poor, involving, for example, the proportion of students going from primary to secondary education, or marks in school exams. At this moment, the best criterion for educational effectiveness is the value education adds to the initial attributes of students. Added value conceptions stress the point that students have a background, an aptitude for learning, a home environment and a peer group, which have already contributed to the knowledge and skills they have acquired at the moment education starts. In examining educational effectiveness, we have to take into account the student's background as well as the student's initial attributes with respect to the specific subjects under study. This requires measurement of general attributes like intelligence and motivation as well as initial attributes with respect to the subjects under study, such as performance in mathematics, reading, etc.

Effectiveness is related to goals in education. Therefore, educational effectiveness is distinguished on the one hand from the study of educational effects, which also takes into account unexpected outcomes of education, such as the results of the hidden curriculum. On the other hand, it is distinguished from the concept of educational efficiency, which is concerned with the relationship between the effects of education and the inputs of education, most of the time in terms of finance.

Effectiveness stresses the point that factors at the different levels of the educational system contribute to educational outcomes: the student level, the classroom level, the school level and the contextual level. In research on educational effectiveness we have to specify the level under study, the factors at the various levels and the ways in which levels are supposed to contribute to the processes at other levels.

As noted earlier, educational effectiveness restricts the criteria for effectiveness to what can be achieved by schools and what schools are for. School effectiveness research was criticized because it took into account only a restricted set of outcomes, such as basic skills and knowledge. Therefore, 'multiple outcomes' are proposed as criteria for effectiveness. The following are some examples of these multiple outcomes:

- Traditional outcomes are *basic skills and knowledge*, such as reading, mathematics and language. Looking at the history of educational effectiveness, it is quite understandable that such a great deal of attention is given to basic skills and knowledge, because disadvantaged students did not succeed in these fields (Brookover *et al.*, 1979; Edmonds, 1979).

- An outcome frequently used in the past for educational effectiveness was *compensation* for initial attributes (equity). The idea of equity is connected with a belief in the school effectiveness movement that schools can to some extent compensate for initial differences. On the basis of educational research so far with respect to effectiveness, one can conclude that the compensatory powers of schools are quite small. Recent studies (van der Werf *et al.*, 1991; Brandsma, 1993) obtain almost the same results as evaluations of so-called compensatory programmes in the past, such as Head-Start, Follow-Through and, in the Netherlands, the Education and Social Environment Project (Scheerens, 1987; Slavenburg and Peters, 1989). Although equity is a longstanding aim in education, it turns out that schools do not contribute much to the reduction of pre-existing differences between students.
- *Social skills and attitudes*, for example towards school and towards different school subjects, were not systematically researched in the past. The idea behind these outcomes is that schools should be more than places for academic development, and that schools should develop not only academic and cognitive skills but also social and aesthetic skills, and, on top of that, should influence attitudes that are important in their own right but can also influence academic outcomes.
- *Higher-order skills*, such as problem solving, are useful criteria for educational effectiveness, especially in higher grades.
- The same holds for *meta-cognitive knowledge and skills*, which refer to learners' knowledge of and control over their cognitive processes by organizing, monitoring and modifying them, and includes strategies of how to learn.
- Finally, a broad range of 'new' educational goals are formulated in different fields, such as educational technology, creativity and moral behaviour.

Some research results can be interpreted as arguments against the immediate adoption of multiple outcomes within school effectiveness research. One of the most striking findings of school effectiveness research in the earlier years was the fact that schools which did not go for a broad range of educational goals but restricted themselves to a small set of academic outcomes had better results than schools with a broad range. This holds especially for low-SES schools (Teddlie and Stringfield, 1993). The recommendation for educational practice of stealing time from other subjects for the basics can be seen as the practical implication of these empirical findings (Levine and Lezotte, 1990). In an evaluation of innovations in primary education in the Netherlands, schools that were the most innovative with respect to educational goals (offering different goals from the past) did not achieve very well. These schools, addressing themselves to new areas of schooling, achieved the worst results not only in the new areas of education but also in the traditional areas, such as reading, mathematics and language. In this case, the findings probably mean that the more you want the less you get (van der Werf, 1988). The suggestion that quality (or excellence) is something different from equity, and that therefore these two

Table 9.1. *Mean language achievement scores of Dutch and immigrant students in different types of schools*

	Quality		Equity		Quality/equity		Overall mean score
	High (*n* = 21)	Low (*n* = 15)	High (*n* = 18)	Low (*n* = 15)	High (*n* = 10)	Low (*n* = 5)	
Dutch students	57	46	50	56	56	50	53
Immigrant students	52	43	50	42	54	40	47

Quality: intercept differences (mean score of all students).
Equity: slope differences (achievement differences between Dutch and immigrant students).
From: van der Werf and Weide (1991, p. 239).

objectives of education should be achieved by different means, does not hold empirically. An argument can be found in research carried out by van der Werf and Weide (1991).

In the evaluation of the Dutch Educational Priority Programme, schools were distinguished on the quality and the equity dimensions, with respect to the results of Dutch as well as of immigrant students. These results are given in Table 9.1, which shows that both Dutch and immigrant students perform relatively well at high-quality schools. The achievement scores of immigrant students are even higher in high-quality schools than in high-equity schools. Immigrant students show the highest achievement scores in schools that are high for quality and equity. Dutch students also perform adequately in these schools. Schools scoring high on the quality dimension but low on the equity dimension were not found in the sample, and nor were schools ranging low on the quality dimension but high on the equity dimension. This means that quality and equity are not necessarily conflicting dimensions. This finding is contrary to results in most research, which shows that quality in Western countries does not go along with equity. For example, the findings in IEA studies show remarkable variations in student outcomes in Western countries and smaller variations in Eastern countries (Walberg, 1989).

In the Educational Priority Programme in the Netherlands, a distinction is made between effective instruction and specific activities for immigrant students to reduce the achievement gap between them and Dutch students. Table 9.2 provides the results of an analysis of effective and ineffective schools with respect to the quality dimension, the equity dimension and a combination of quality and equity.

Unlike what one would expect, there is no difference between effective instruction and specific activities for immigrant students with respect to quality and equity measures. In fact, most of the time activities related to effective instruction count for both high quality and high equity. This means that quality and equity probably are not as independent as suggested in the list of multiple outcomes, and can sometimes be achieved by the same means. This is contrary to the position of Nuttall *et al.* (1989), who suggest that effective schools are differentially effective for different groups of students. Nor do the results shown in Table 9.2 support the so-called Matthew effect (Walberg, 1991), which holds that strategies for underachieving students only result in the higher achievement of students who were already performing rather well. It seems that what is good for the brighter students in

Table 9.2. *Differences between teachers*

	Mean		Scale
	High quality	*Low quality*	
Whole-group education	5.5	4.1	2–10
Orderly climate	39.6	36.1	9–45
Correction of language	12.6	9.9	3–15
Separate language lessons	2.6	2.8	1–5
Activities for immigrant parents	8.1	9.9	4–12
	High equity	*Low equity*	
Whole-group education	5.4	4.1	2–10
Orderly climate	40.3	37.9	9–45
Specific methods	2.9	1.5	1–5
Orientation on content	24.9	21.5	7–35
	High q/e	*Low q/e*	
Orientation on content	26.6	21.6	7–35
Importance of cognitive objectives	40.6	28.0	1–100

From: van der Werf and Weide (1991, p. 240).

effective education could also be appropriate for disadvantaged students. From a research perspective, though, it still remains important to investigate differential effectiveness.

Several studies showed no relationship between the academic and the affective outcomes of education (Mortimore *et al.*, 1988) or a negative relationship (Marsh *et al.*, 1985). In recent publications, Knuver (1993) and Knuver and Brandsma (1993) present the results of research on the relationship between so-called affective outcomes and academic outcomes. In these Dutch studies, academic outcomes do have an effect on attitudes towards arithmetic, attitudes towards school and the well-being of students. This suggests that attitudes, and other affective outcomes, are the result of academic outcomes. The results of the research in this field seem to be quite inconsistent, but one can conclude that there is at least a relationship between affective and cognitive outcomes.

The foregoing deals with criticisms with respect to outcomes, especially the criticism that the criterion for effectiveness in educational research is not well chosen. There are several ways to define outcomes, and from a technical point of view it is no problem to develop instruments to measure them. For a theoretical perspective (what factors contribute to what kinds of outcomes), it is also important to have more measures for school and classroom effectiveness. On the basis of the above research results, however, we should be careful in the selection and definition of outcomes. But this is just one aspect of criticism.

Another point of criticism is that the effects of effective schools are insignificantly small. In fact, this is a more general problem concerning the influence of education as a whole, which has to do with the question of what education contributes to the educational career of students. We know that the largest part of the variation in school results between students is explained by aptitude and social background. Only a small proportion of variance can be explained by variables at the school and instructional levels (see, for instance, Walberg, 1984). The proportion of variance that is left over after controlling for aptitude and SES is at most 20 per cent, although these proportions vary depending on the study (and its statistical procedures). Of this 20 per cent, only a small proportion is accounted for by factors we have studied so far in school effectiveness research (from less than 1 per cent up to at most 2–3 per cent of the total variance, although higher percentages may be presented when only the between-school variance is considered and the 20 per cent between-school variance is seen as the total variance).

When differences between effective and non-effective schools are phrased in terms of their effects on the careers of individual school students, it turns out that these differences (even if they are quite small in the Netherlands) mean that there is a difference for individual students between being referred or not being referred to special education, in grade retention or promotion, and in the choice of a higher level of secondary education. So, even when effects are quite small in a statistical sense, they can be very important for the individual careers of students (Bosker and Scheerens, 1989).

A third point of criticism is that the effects of schools are quite unstable. The discrepancy between the results of different studies is quite large. Most of the time the correlations between school subjects within a grade are rather unstable in primary schools (between 0.55 and 0.80) as well as in secondary schools (between 0.45 and 0.75). Sometimes, this discrepancy is even larger. In primary education, correlations have been found between 0.10 and 0.65, and in secondary education between 0.25 and 0.90 (Bosker, 1991).

To sum up, the first problem for the development of a theory about educational effectiveness has to do with the outcomes of education. Although some arguments are formulated against the use of all kinds of criteria, it is important to use more criteria than before in future research to determine effectiveness, especially in the areas of academic outcomes such as higher-order skills and meta-cognitive knowledge and skills. From a technical point of view multiple outcomes have a preference because they permit the analysis of different constellations of classroom and school factors against each outcome, and it is also possible to deal statistically with the multitude of data that come with them. We have to keep in mind that the educational effects at the classroom and school levels are quite small, but significant. The instability of grades may be improved by a greater cohesion and constancy within schools.

EDUCATIONAL PROCESSES: FACTORS CONTRIBUTING TO EDUCATIONAL EFFECTIVENESS

A theory of educational effectiveness is not concerned in the first place with the outcome effectiveness criteria or the effectiveness criteria alone, but in particular with the question of how these goals can be achieved.

Educational effectiveness deals with the question of why schools with initially comparable students differ in the extent to which they achieve their goals. In a system approach, a distinction is made between the input, context and processes (in addition to outcomes) of education. The input consists of all kinds of variables connected with financial or personnel resources, and the background of students. By context is meant the socioeconomic, political and educational context of schools; for example the guidelines for education and the national evaluation systems.

The most important factors concern the ongoing processes at the classroom and school levels. The question school effectiveness research deals with most of the time is what kind of factors within schools and classrooms make a difference between effective and less effective schools. In fact, this question was the background for the school effectiveness movement that started with the first studies in this field by Brookover *et al.* (1979) and Edmonds (1979). Their research proved that schools differ in the extent to which they can achieve results with comparable groups of students. Early school effectiveness research aimed to find the factors that caused the distinction between effective and less effective schools. In these so-called outlier studies, evidence was found that a small number of factors contribute to effectiveness. Most famous was the five-factor model of Edmonds (1979). Later, this model was criticized from a methodological and conceptual point of view (Scheerens and Creemers, 1989), but in the early days of school effectiveness and school improvement the five-factor model (and later other models with slightly more factors) drew a great deal of attention from educational practice and policymaking. It seemed quite easy to change schools from non-effective to effective by just introducing programmes for the improvement of some factors, such as a programme for the evaluation of student progress in schools or in-service training for the improvement of the educational leadership of principals (Lezotte, 1989).

Later it became clear that it is not that easy to improve schools. Effective and non-effective schools differ on more than just a small amount of factors. This conclusion led to more research to distinguish between effective and non-effective schools. The earlier studies were mostly outlier studies but after criticism of the methodology of the outlier studies, more survey studies were carried out, enlarging the list of characteristics of effective education.

When the idea of effective education spread to countries other than the United States, replication studies were carried out to test whether or not the same characteristics of effective education could be found in other countries. The results of these studies did not confirm the lists of factors produced by research in the United States. Generally speaking, on the one hand the list of characteristics was enlarged and on the other hand replication studies could not find much empirical evidence for the initial 'factors' or characteristics. In addition, a conceptual approach was advocated, whereby a framework or theory should explain the differences between effective and non-effective education, which might be a point of departure for further research.

Recently, the results of these three types of studies (outlier studies, survey studies and theoretical studies) have been reviewed. Creemers and Knuver (1989), Creemers and Lugthart (1989), Reynolds (1989, 1991, 1992), Levine and Lezotte (1990), Scheerens (1990, 1992), Stringfield and Schaffer (1991), Creemers (1992a) and Levine (1992), sum up factors that make a difference between effective and non-effective education within schools and classrooms, each for their own country. The review of research provided by Levine and Lezotte in 1990 is of special interest. They produced a list of effective school correlates, based on 400 studies of school effectiveness in the United States:

- productive school climate and culture;
- focus on student acquisition of central learning skills;

- appropriate monitoring of student progress;
- practice-oriented staff development at the school site;
- outstanding leadership;
- salient parent involvement;
- effective instructional arrangements and implementation;
- high operationalized expectations and requirements for students;
- other possible correlates.

This general list, which contains almost everything that can be found in schools and is enlarged with 'other possible correlates', is broken down into other factors. For example, the correlates for effective instructional arrangements and implementation are:

- successful grouping and related organizational arrangements;
- appropriate pacing and alignment;
- active/enriched learning;
- effective teaching practices;
- emphasis on higher-order learning in assessing instructional outcomes;
- coordination in curriculum and instruction;
- easy availability of abundant, appropriate instructional materials;
- classroom adaptation;
- stealing time for reading, language and maths.

In total, hundreds of correlates of effectiveness are presented. In the correlational studies large numbers of schools and variables are involved, so in this way even small correlations can be significant. In the outlier studies, a few schools or classes but many factors are usually studied. There are always some, or even many, variables that seem to distinguish between these small numbers of schools. That is probably why in replication studies a number of factors do not reappear. The correlates gathered by Levine and Lezotte (1990) are more a result of research methods and techniques than a collection of genuine, clear and relevant concepts in a theory about effectiveness.

In a study in the United Kingdom by Mortimore et al. (1989), only twelve factors could be found:

- purposeful leadership of the staff by the headteacher;
- the involvement of the deputy head;
- the involvement of teachers;
- consistency among teachers;
- structured sessions;
- intellectually challenging teaching;
- a work-centred environment;
- limited focus within sessions;
- maximum communication between teachers and pupils;
- record keeping;
- parental involvement;
- a positive climate.

All these factors are comparable with the factors mentioned by Levine and Lezotte, but Mortimore *et al.* found fewer factors. Quite a few of the American factors did not prove to be related to effectiveness. In twelve Dutch studies even fewer factors could be found to distinguish between effective and non-effective schools, some of which provided evidence for the five factors originally distinguished by Edmonds (Scheerens, 1992). Scheerens and Creemers (1989) conclude that an orderly climate, frequent evaluation, achievement orientation, high expectations and direct instruction seem to contribute to effectiveness in the Netherlands.

Many correlates for effectiveness are available, more or less supported by empirical research, but for the interpretation and understanding of educational effectiveness we need an overarching idea, a conceptual framework that will be developed in the next section.

CONCEPTUAL FRAMEWORK

In this section I will concentrate on the integration of the elements of the conceptual framework for educational effectiveness. The development of a conceptual framework is an important contribution to educational effectiveness research, because it can guide the design of research studies and the interpretation of the results at a later stage.

Based on theoretical notions and studies carried out so far, it is possible to make a list of 'promising' factors of educational effectiveness that have to be taken into account in developing a theory. It became evident that 'time on task' and the 'opportunity to learn' are important intermediating variables that can explain student outcomes. For the selection of 'explanatory' variables, lists of correlates, like the ones mentioned in the previous section, are available.

In recent years, several models for school effectiveness have been developed. The basic idea behind all models for school effectiveness is to distinguish between levels in education. All models include at least the individual student level, the classroom level and the school level, and the higher levels in the models provide the conditions for what happens at the levels below (see Figure 2.5). Factors at the higher levels contribute to the outcomes or are conditional for what happens at the lower levels. This means that not just one level induces results, but a combination of levels.

Further elaborations of this basic multilevel model were provided by Creemers (1991), Scheerens (1991) and Stringfield and Slavin (1992). All these models are based to some extent on Carroll's model for school learning, in which the time needed for mastering the educational objectives is considered as a function of student characteristics, such as aptitude and motivation, and the quality of instruction. Most of the models developed so far are rather detailed at the classroom level.

At the school level, the selection of variables is not so clear. Based on ideas about how the school level can provide conditions for the instructional level, and also on insights from organizational theories, possible factors are discerned at the school level. In the QAIT-MACRO model (Stringfield and Slavin, 1992) these factors are meaningful goals, attention to academic functions, coordination, recruitment and training, and organization. In the model provided by Scheerens (1990), achievement orientation, organization of the school in terms of educational leadership and consensus, quality of the school curricula in terms of content coverage, form and structure, and an orderly atmosphere are distinguished. But how these factors influence what goes on at the classroom level, between classes at the same grade level and between grade levels, remains unclear. The instructional model provided by Creemers (1991) again distinguishes between school curriculum variables and organizational variables. Connected with this idea of a formal relationship between what goes on in classrooms, between classrooms and between the class and the school level are the concepts of consistency, cohesion, constancy and control, which were introduced earlier.

The conceptual model developed in the previous chapters is also based on Carroll's model for school learning. Basic variables, excepting students' aptitude and motivation, at the student level are the time and opportunity they need to master the goals. Education at the classroom level provides time and opportunity for learning. The quality of instruction also contributes to the effectiveness of education, but is mediated by time and opportunity, which are influenced by the quality of instruction. At the school and context levels above the classroom level, variables related to time, opportunity and quality are conditions for instructional effectiveness. In this way, all levels are put in line with each other, which can clarify the way they influence each other and ultimately contribute to students' achievement. The overall framework, which has been developed based on the review here, can be sketched as in Figure 9.1. In the following, some further explanation of the model will be given.

Student Level

The students' backgrounds, motivation and aptitudes strongly determine their achievement. Time on task is the time students are willing to spend on school learning, and on educational tasks, but it is determined not only by the motivation of students, but also by the time provided by the school and by processes at the school and classroom levels. Time on task is the time in which students are really involved in learning, but this time has to be filled by opportunities to learn. These opportunities concern the supply of learning materials, experiences and exercises by which students can acquire knowledge and skills. In fact, learning opportunities are the instructional operationalization of the objectives of education, whereas tests are the evaluative operationalization of the same objectives. In this respect one can speak about the content coverage of the curriculum. Here again a distinction is made between opportunities offered in the instructional process and students' use of the offered experiences.

Classroom Level

As well as time and opportunity, the quality of instruction determines the outcomes of education. Based on theoretical notions and empirical research, it is possible to select effective characteristics of the components of quality of classroom instruction: curriculum, grouping procedures and teacher behaviour. With respect to the curriculum these are the following:

- explicitness and ordering of goals and content;
- structure and clarity of content;
- advance organizers;

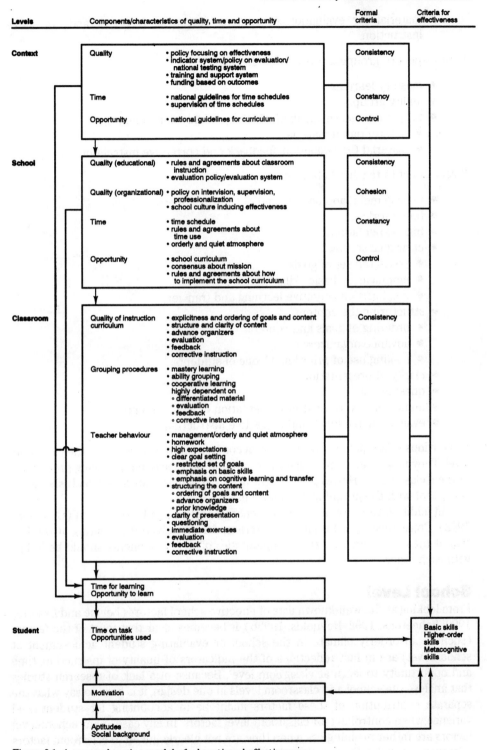

Figure 9.1 *A comprehensive model of educational effectiveness.*

- material for evaluation of student outcomes, feedback and corrective instruction.

With respect to grouping procedures they are:

- mastery learning;
- ability grouping;
- cooperative learning; all of which are highly dependent on
  - differentiated material
  - material for evaluation, feedback and corrective instruction.

With respect to teacher behaviour they are:

- management, and orderly and quiet atmosphere;
- homework;
- high expectations;
- clear goal setting
  - restricted set of goals
  - emphasis on basic skills
  - emphasis on cognitive learning and transfer;
- structuring the content
  - ordering of goals and content
  - advance organizers
  - making use of prior knowledge of students;
- clarity of presentation;
- questioning;
- immediate exercise after presentation of new content;
- evaluation, feedback and corrective instruction.

It is obvious that teachers are the central component in instruction at the classroom level. They make use of curricular materials and they carry out grouping procedures in their classrooms. However, teachers need curricular materials, which should be consistent with the grouping procedure used.

In addition to these, more formal characteristics can be discerned (Creemers, 1992). Consistency is a formal characteristic for effectiveness, pointing at the fact that at the classroom level the characteristics of the components should be in line with each other.

School Level

From looking at the well-known lists of effective school factors (Levine and Lezotte,. 1990; Scheerens, 1992; Reynolds, 1993b), it becomes clear that most of the factors (such as an orderly climate in the school or evaluating student achievement at school level) are in fact reflections of the indicators of quality of instruction, time and opportunity to learn at classroom level. Because of a lack of research studies that analyse the school and classroom levels in one design, it is hard to say what the separate contribution of these factors might be in accounting for student-level variance when controlling for classroom-level factors. In any case, many school-level factors are rather meaningless when they are not clearly linked to classroom factors (Creemers, 1992b). Even if they do have an independent effect on pupil achievement, it is still not clear how this effect comes about and how it should be interpreted.

In the model, all school-level factors are defined as conditions for classroom-level factors. This definition restricts the selection of school level factors to only those factors conditional for and directly related to quality of instruction, time or opportunity to learn. At the school level we can distinguish conditions for the *quality of instruction* with respect to the *educational* aspects:

- rules and agreements about all aspects of classroom instruction, especially curricular materials, grouping procedures and teacher behaviour, and the consistency between them;
- an evaluation policy and a system at school level to check pupil achievement, to prevent learning problems, or to correct problems at an early stage, including regular testing, remedial teaching, student counselling and homework assistance.

With respect to the *organizational* aspects of the school level, important conditions for *quality of instruction* are:

- a school policy on intervision and supervision of teachers, departmental heads and headteachers (educational leadership), and a school policy to correct and further to professionalize teachers who do not live up to the school standards;
- a school culture inducing and supporting effectiveness.

Conditions for *time* at the school level are:

- the development and provision of a time schedule for subjects and topics;
- rules and agreements about time use, including the school policy on homework, pupil absenteeism and cancellation of lessons;
- the maintenance of an orderly and quiet atmosphere in the school.

Conditions for the *opportunity to learn* at the school level are:

- development and availability of a curriculum, school working plan or activity plan;
- consensus about the 'mission' of the school;
- rules and agreements about how to proceed, how to follow the curriculum, especially with respect to transition from one class to another or from one grade to another (Creemers *et al.*, 1992).

At the school level consistency between the components, which are in line with each other, is an important condition for instruction. All members of the school team should take care of that, thereby creating cohesion. Creemers (1991) points out the importance of continuity in all the conditions mentioned above, meaning that schools should not change rules and policies every other year. This implies the constancy principle, which, however, can only be found in a longitudinal setting, by comparing school level factors from year to year. The control principle refers not only to the fact that student achievement should be evaluated, but also to the quiet atmosphere in the school. Control also refers to teachers holding themselves and others responsible for effectiveness.

Context Level

The same components as mentioned before, quality, time and opportunity to learn, can be distinguished at the context level. Quality refers to the following conditions:

- a (national) policy that focuses on effectiveness of education;
- the availability of an indicator system and/or a national policy on evaluation or a national testing system;
- training and support systems promoting effective schools and instruction;
- funding of schools based on outcomes.

Time refers to national guidelines with respect to the time schedules of schools and the supervision of the maintenance of schedules. The opportunity to learn refers to national guidelines and rules with respect to the development of the curriculum, the school working plan and the activity plan at the school level, for example, by a national curriculum.

It is clear that at the different levels, certainly at the context level, resources are also important, but resources should be defined as in this model: availability of materials, teachers and other components supporting education in schools and classrooms. At the context level, consistency, constancy and control are again important formal characteristics, emphasizing the importance of the same material characteristics over time and of mechanisms to ensure effectiveness.

RESEARCH IN EDUCATIONAL EFFECTIVENESS

In this and earlier chapters I reviewed research on instructional effectiveness. On the basis of this review, I made recommendations on how to make instruction more effective. The main principle was to combine the components of instruction and especially to pick up the same effective characteristics in each instructional component, to increase the total influence. This influence could be further enhanced by looking for conditions for effectiveness at the school level and at the context level. I developed a theory based on the key concepts of time, opportunity and quality, to bring together the different levels of effectiveness.

The next phase – and this is a phase that accompanies all theory development – is that of looking for empirical evidence. For that purpose, we need well-designed large survey studies as well as case studies, with an emphasis on the measurement of multiple outcomes and on processes at the classroom level and at the school level. A first step could be a secondary analysis of available large datasets to test the model. Topics in the area of educational effectiveness research are, for example:

- the combination of effective characteristics of the components of instruction in such a way that effective arrangements become available;
- the relationship between the levels with respect to time, opportunity and especially the quality of education;
- the relationship between the organizational and educational system at the school level with respect to effectiveness;
- the variance in effectiveness within schools (related to their effectiveness at classroom level), which implies analysis and research of the formal characteristics of effectiveness.

Recent developments in the area of data analysis techniques will make it possible to combine regression and multilevel techniques at short notice. The topics mentioned earlier refer to fundamental research with respect to the concepts of educational effectiveness and the development of techniques to measure them. Of special importance are international comparative studies, like the IEA and ISERP, which can provide information on factors and variables that are stable between countries, and on the influences of the context on educational effectiveness (Mortimore, 1992). Effectiveness levels themselves are not stable. For the purpose of school improvement, but also for the development of a theory on the question of what induces effective education, we need studies about schools in transition (Freiberg *et al.*, 1990; Chrispeels, 1992; Teddlie and Stringfield, 1993). This implies research on the development of schools as educational organizations, and especially the measures schools take to initiate novice teachers in their organization.

Finally, we need research on and evaluation of school improvement projects based on the results of school effectiveness research (Reynolds, 1993a). This creates a starting point for future theory development and research to increase our body of knowledge about instructional, school and educational effectiveness.

THE FUTURE OF EFFECTIVE INSTRUCTION: THEORY INTO PRACTICE

This chapter describes the development of a theory about educational effectiveness and the empirical research to validate this theory. Instructional effectiveness is incorporated in a theory about the effectiveness of the total educational system. At the end of this chapter it is necessary to pay attention once again to teachers as the key persons in education, to the role that effective instruction can play in the achievement of various educational goals, and to an important condition for successful implementation of effective instruction: an outcomes-oriented climate.

Central in educational effectiveness, as has been made clear, are the teaching and learning processes going on at the classroom level. It turns out that, especially at the classroom level, the characteristics of components that explain variation in student behaviour can be found. They explain differences in learning processes and in the outcomes of learning processes. The components at the classroom level and their effective characteristics are important for improvements in student learning. We found different components at the classroom level, such as teacher behaviour, the curriculum and grouping procedures, and we looked for characteristics of these components that contribute to the effectiveness of the instructional processes. In particular, we were looking for empirical evidence for these effectiveness characteristics. The components and their effective characteristics are interrelated and can be supported by factors at the school level and the contextual level. The characteristics of the components and the interrelationships between them emphasize the importance of teachers in this respect. Teachers create and maintain an environment in their classes in which learning can take place and learning outcomes can be achieved.

At present, a discussion about the goals of education is going on in society. Schools, it is argued, should not restrict themselves to a specific small set of outcomes; they should pursue a variety of educational outcomes (see Chapter 2). For teachers, it is important to know whether different educational outcomes require different kinds of teacher behaviour. It is sometimes suggested that the pursuit of, for example, affective outcomes might need different characteristics of the components from the pursuit of cognitive outcomes. I would like to stress the point that, theoretically, effective instruction does not refer to a small restricted set of outcomes, like knowledge and skills, but to learning outcomes in a broad area, from cognitive knowledge and skills to values, moral education and character education. Brooks and Kann (1993) and Leming (1993) advocate effective instruction in this respect. As yet, there is no convincing empirical evidence to support the hypothesis that teachers should behave differently when they are aiming at different educational goals. Effective instruction can therefore be implemented to enhance student achievement in numerous educational domains. Effective instruction will exert not only direct positive influences on achievement in these domains, but also indirect: if cognitive achievement is promoted, achievement in other areas is also stimulated.

However, I would like to emphasize that in areas such as social and aesthetic outcomes, and values, moral education and character education, there is not a very close relationship between the knowledge provided by schools and the behaviour of students (Lockwood, 1993). In general, cognitive outcomes are determined by school and teacher factors to a much higher extent than are outcomes in other educational domains. This again means an emphasis on the crucial role of teachers in education in general and more specifically in the determination of classroom level processes. Teachers can combine the effective characteristics of the curriculum and grouping procedures with their own instructional behaviour.

Perhaps a lot of teachers are already familiar, through their own experiences, with the characteristics of effective instruction outlined in this study. The characteristics do not involve sophisticated and trendy tricks and they reflect only elements of everyday teaching. They all concern decisions teachers have to make day by day in their classrooms. The major contribution of this book to teacher behaviour is the focus on the linkages between the components, the linkages between the characteristics of the components, and the linkages between factors at the classroom level, the school level and the contextual level. Moreover, all the linkages described in this book are supported by empirical evidence. Even when teachers are acquainted with the knowledge base for effective instruction, they often experience problems when they try to put their knowledge into practice. Teachers are often aware of the importance of effective learning time and opportunity to learn, but many of them show behaviour that does not increase learning time or the opportunity to learn and sometimes even reduces it. Even when they succeed, the long-term effects of their instructional practices can be reduced when the next teacher in line shows different and less effective behaviour. Therefore, the factors mentioned at the school and contextual levels that can promote and foster effective education are also vitally important.

Ultimately it is teachers at the classroom level that have to do it. It became clear in a recent evaluation of primary education in the Netherlands that the biggest problem is not a lack of knowledge about effectiveness but the realization of it in educational practice. Even in an egalitarian society such as the Netherlands, there are great differences in the ways teachers behave, although they probably share the same knowledge base provided by research in educational effectiveness. It can be assumed that this is also the case in other countries. On top of this, it is a problem in education in general that there is neither an outcomes-oriented climate nor an outcomes-oriented policy within schools and classrooms. Research in the Netherlands (Commissie Evaluatie Basisonderwijs, 1994) showed that schools and teachers are more concerned about the well-being of students than about their outcomes in knowledge and skills. Educational effectiveness therefore requires a shift in the orientation of schools and teachers.

The future of effective instruction is situated in the hands of the teaching profession even more than it lies in theory development and empirical research. Teachers have to take the responsibility for learning processes and the outcomes of their students. This book makes it possible for them to use the findings of empirical research concerning instructional effectiveness.

References

Ackerman, W. I. (1954). 'Teacher competence and pupil change'. *Harvard Educational Review*, **24**, 273–89.

Akker, J. J. H. van den (1988). *Ontwerp en implementatie van natuuronderwijs* (The Design and Implementation of Science). Lisse: Swets & Zeitlinger.

Alexander, R. (1992). *Policy and Practice in Primary Education*. London: Routledge.

Allan, S. (1991). 'Ability-grouping research reviews: what do they say about grouping and the gifted'. *Educational Leadership*, **48**(6), 60–5.

Anderson, L. M., Evertson, C. M. and Brophy, J. E. (1979). 'An experimental study of effective teaching in first-grade reading groups'. *Elementary School Journal*, **79**(4), 193–223.

Anderson, L. W. (1991). *Increasing Teacher Effectiveness*. Paris: UNESCO/International Institute for Educational Planning.

Anderson, L. W. and Block, J. H. (1987). 'Mastery learning models'. In M. J. Dunkin (ed.), *International Encyclopedia of Teaching and Teacher Education*, pp. 58–68. Oxford: Pergamon Press.

Arlin, M. N. (1984). 'Time, equality, and mastery learning'. *Review of Educational Research*, **54**(1), 65–86.

Ascencio, C. E. (1984). 'Effects of behavioural objectives on student achievement: a meta-analysis of findings'. *Dissertation Abstracts International*, **45**, 501A (University Microfilm No. 084-12499).

Ausubel, D. P. (1968). *Educational Psychology: A Cognitive View*. New York: Holt, Rinehart & Winston.

Ax, J. (1985). *Planningsgedrag van leraren* (Planning behaviour of teachers). Lisse: Swets & Zeitlinger.

Bangert, R. L., Kulik, J. A. and Kulik, C.-L. C. (1983). 'Individualized systems of instruction in secondary schools'. *Review of Educational Research*, **53**(2), 143–58.

Barber, B. (1986). 'Homework does not belong on the agenda for educational reform'. *Educational Leadership*, **43**(8), 55–7.

Barker Lunn, J. C. (1970). *Streaming in the Primary School*. Slough: NFER.

Barr, R. and Dreeben, R. (1983). *How Schools Work*. Chicago: University of Chicago.

Bashi, J., Sass, Z., Katzit, R. and Margolin, J. (1990) *Effective Schools from Theory to Practice: An Intervention Model and Its Outcomes*. Jerusalem: Nevo Publ. Ltd.

Batenburg, Th. A. van (1988). *Een evaluatie van taalmethoden* (An evaluation of language curricula). Groningen: RION.

Bennett, N. (1987). 'Changing perspectives on teaching–learning processes in the post-Plowden era'. *Oxford Review of Education*, **13**(1), 67–79.

Bennett, N. (1988). 'The effective primary school teacher: the search for a theory of pedagogy'. *Teaching and Teacher Education*, **4**(1), 19–30.

Bennett, N. and Carré, C. (eds) (1993). *Learning to Teach*. London: Routledge.

Bennett, N., Desforges, C., Cockburn, A. and Wilkinson, B. (1984). *The Quality of Pupil Learning Experiences*. London: Lawrence Erlbaum Associates.

Bennett, S. N. (1978). 'Recent research on teaching: a dream, a belief, and a model'. *British Journal of Educational Psychology*, **48**, 127–47.

Berg, G. van den (1987). *Effectief evalueren: een empirische studie naar de doelmatigheid van aanwijzingen voor de evaluatiepraktijk* (Effective evaluation: an empirical study on the effectiveness of guidelines for evaluation practices). Lisse: Swets & Zeitlinger.

Berliner, D., Fisher, C., Filby, N. and Marliave, R. (1978). *Executive Summary of Beginning Teacher Evaluation Study*. San Francisco: Far West Laboratory.

Berman, P. and McLaughlin, M. (1977). *Federal Programs Supporting Educational Change*; Vol. VII, *Implementing and Sustaining Innovations*. Santa Monica, CA: Rand Corporation.

Berman, P. and McLaughlin, M. (1978). *Federal Programs Supporting Educational Change*; Vol. VIII, *Implementing and Sustaining Innovations*. Santa Monica, CA: Rand Corporation.

Block, J. H. (1970). *The Effects of Various Levels of Performance on Selected Cognitive, Affective and Time Variables*. Chicago: University of Chicago Press.

Block, J. H. and Burns, R. B. (1976). 'Mastery learning'. In L. S. Shulman (ed.), *Review of Research in Education*, Vol. 4, pp. 3–49. Itasca, IL: Peacock.

Blok, H. (1992). 'De grootte van het schooleffect in het basisonderwijs: een analyse op basis van vijf jaar Eindtoets Basisonderwijs' (The size of school effects in primary education: an analysis based on five years of results on the final test of primary education). *Tijdschrift voor Onderwijsresearch*, **17**(6), 343–54.

Blok, H. and Hoeksma, J. B. (1993). 'De stabiliteit van het schooleffect in de tijd: een analyse op basis van vijf jaar Eindtoets Basisonderwijs van het Cito' (The stability of school effects over time: an analysis based on five years of results on the final test of primary education). *Tijdschrift voor Onderwijsresearch*, **18**(6), 331–42.

Bloom, B. S. (1963). 'Testing cognitive ability and achievement'. In N. L. Gage (ed.), *Handbook of Research on Teaching*, pp. 379–97. Chicago: Rand McNally.

Bloom, B. S. (1976). *Human Characteristics and School Learning*. New York: McGraw-Hill.

Bloom, B. S. (1984). 'The 2 sigma problem: the search for methods of group instruction as effective as one-to-one tutoring'. *Educational Researcher*, **41**, 4–16.

Boekaerts, M. (1988). 'Emotion, motivation and learning'. *International Journal of Educational Research*, **12**(3), 227–346.

Boekaerts, M. and Simons, P. R. J. (1993). *Leren en instructie: psychologie van de leerling en het leerproces* (Learning and instruction: psychology of the student and the learning process). Assen: Dekker & Van de Vegt.

Bonset, E. H. (1987). *Onderwijs in heterogene groepen: een case-study naar het vak Nederlands in een breed-heterogene brugklas van een reguliere scholengemeenschap, en een literatuurstudie naar heterogeniteit en interne differentiatie* (Teaching in heterogeneous groups: a case study on Dutch-language instruction in a widely heterogeneous first grade of secondary education, and a literature review on heterogeneity and grouping within classes). Purmerend: Muusses.

Borich, G. D. (1988). *Effective Teaching Methods.* Columbus, Ohio: Merrill.

Bosker, R. J. (1991). 'De consistentie van schooleffecten in het basisonderwijs' (The consistency of school effects in primary education). *Tijdschrift voor Onderwijsresearch,* **16**(4), 206–18.

Bosker, R. J. (1992). *De stabiliteit en consistentie van schooleffecten in het basisonderwijs* (The stability and consistency of school effects in primary education). Enschede: Universiteit Twente.

Bosker, R. J. and Scheerens, J. (1989). 'Issues in the interpretation of the results of school effectiveness research'. *International Journal of Educational Research,* **13**(7), 741–51.

Bosker, R. J. and Scheerens, J. (1994). 'Alternative models of school effectiveness put to the test'. *International Journal of Educational Research,* in the press.

Bosker, R. J. and Vries, A. M. de (1982). *Het aanbod van leerwegen op de experimenten middenschool* (Adaptive instruction in experimental comprehensive schools). Haren: RION.

Bosker, R. J. and Vries, A. M. de (1984). *De leerwegen van leerlingen op vier experimentele middenscholen* (Adaptive instruction for students in four experimental comprehensive schools). Haren: RION.

Boyd, W. and Rawson, W. (1965). *The Story of the New Education.* London: Heinemann.

Braak, L. H. (1974). *Geïndividualiseerde onderwijssystemen: constructie en besturing* (Individualized systems of education: construction and management). Eindhoven: Technische Hogeschool.

Brandsma, H. P. (1993). *Basisschoolkenmerken en de kwaliteit van het onderwijs* (Characteristics of primary schools and the quality of education). Groningen: RION.

Brandsma, H. P. and Knuver, J. W. M. (1989a). 'Organisational differences between Dutch primary schools and their effect on pupil achievement'. In D. Reynolds, B. P. M. Creemers and T. Peters (eds). *School Effectiveness and Improvement. Proceedings of the First International Congress, London,* pp. 199–212. Groningen/Cardiff: RION/University of Wales.

Brandsma, H. P. and Knuver, J. W. M. (1989b). 'Effects of school and classroom characteristics on pupil progress in language and arithmetic'. *International Journal of Educational Research,* **13**(7), 777–88.

Brookover, W. B., Beady, C., Flood, P. and Schweitzer, J. (1979). *School Systems and Student Achievement: Schools Make a Difference.* New York: Praeger.

Brooks, B. D. and Kann, M. E. (1993). 'What makes character education programs work?' *Educational Leadership,* **51**(3), 19–21.

Brophy, J. (1988a). 'Educating teachers about managing classrooms and students'. *Teaching and Teacher Education,* **4**(1), 1–18.

Brophy, J. (1988b). 'Research on teacher effects: uses and abuses'. *The Elementary School Journal*, **89**(1), 3–21.

Brophy, J. and Evertson, C. (1976). *Learning from Teaching: A Developmental Perspective*. Boston: Allyn & Bacon.

Brophy, J. and Good, T. L. (1974). *Teacher–Student Relationships: Causes and Consequences*. New York: Holt, Rinehart & Winston.

Brophy, J. and Good, T. L. (1986). 'Teacher behavior and student achievement'. In M. C. Wittrock (ed.), *Handbook of Research on Teaching*, 3rd edn. pp. 328–75. New York: Macmillan.

Bruggencate, C. G. ten, Pelgrum, W. J. and Plomp, T. (1986). 'Eerste resultaten van de Second IEA Science Study in Nederland' (First results of the Second IEA Science Study in the Netherlands). In W. J. Nijhof and E. Warries (eds), *De opbrengst van onderwijs en opleiding* (Outcomes of education and training). Lisse: Swets & Zeitlinger.

Bruner, J. S. (1966). *Toward a Theory of Instruction*. New York: Norton.

Burnstein, L. (1993). 'Indicators of opportunity to learn in the third international mathematics and science study'. Paper presented at the Annual Meeting of the American Educational Research Association, Atlanta.

Carlsen, W. S. (1991). 'Questioning in classrooms: a sociolinguistic perspective'. *Review of Educational Research*, **61**(2), 157–78.

Carnegie Forum on Education and the Economy (1986). *A Nation Prepared: Teachers for the 21st Century*. New York: Carnegie Forum on Education and the Economy.

Carroll, J. B. (1963). 'A model of school learning'. *Teachers College Record*, **64**, 723–33.

Carroll, J. B. (1989). 'The Carroll Model: a 25-year retrospective and prospective view'. *Educational Researcher*, **18**, 26–31.

Chall, J. S. (1967). *Learning to Read: The Great Debate*. New York: McGraw-Hill.

Cheng, Y. C. (1993). 'Profiles of organizational culture and effective schools'. *School Effectiveness and School Improvement*, **4**(2), 85–110.

Chrispeels, J. (1992). *Purposeful Restructuring: Creating a Culture for Learning and Achievement in Elementary Schools*. London: Falmer Press.

Clark, C. M. and Yinger, R. J. (1977). 'Research on teacher thinking'. *Curriculum Inquiry*, **7**(4), 279–394.

Clark, C. M. and Yinger, R. J. (1979). 'Teacher thinking'. In P. L. Peterson and H. J. Walberg (eds), *Research on Teaching*. Berkeley, CA: McCutchan.

Cohen, D. K. and Grant, S. G. (1992). 'America's children in their elementary schools'. *Daedalus*, **122**(1), 177–207.

Cohen, P. A. (1981). 'Student ratings of instruction and student achievement: a meta-analysis of multisection validity studies'. *Review of Educational Research*, **51**(3), 281–309.

Cohn, E. and Geske, T. G. (1990). *The Economics of Education*, 3rd edn. Oxford: Pergamon Press.

Coleman, J. S., Campbell, E., Hobson, C., McPartland, J., Mood, A., Weinfeld, F. and York, R. (1966). *Equality of Educational Opportunity*. Washington, DC: US Government Printing Office.

Commissie Evaluatie Basisonderwijs (1994). *Inhoud en opbrengsten van het basi-*

sonderwijs (Input and output of primary education). The Hague: Staatsuitge-verij.

Creemers, B. P. M. (1983). 'Paradigma of alibi: een reactie op "Heroriëntatie in het onderzoek van het onderwijzen"' (Paradigm or alibi: comments on 'A new orientation in research on teaching'). *Tijdschrift voor Onderwijsresearch*, **8**(6), 270–2.

Creemers, B. P. M. (1985). 'De verdere ontwikkeling van de onderwijskunde' (Development of educational science). *Nederlands Tijdschrift voor Opvoeding, Vorming en Onderwijs*, **1**(1), 30–9.

Creemers, B. P. M. (1991). *Effectieve instructie: een empirische bijdrage aan de verbetering van het onderwijs in de klas* (Effective instruction: an empirical contribution to improvement of education in the classroom). The Hague: SVO.

Creemers, B. P. M. (1992a). 'School effectiveness, effective instruction and school improvement in the Netherlands'. In D. Reynolds and P. Cuttance (eds), *School Effectiveness: Research, Policy and Practice*, pp. 48–70. London: Cassell.

Creemers, B. P. M. (1992b). 'School effectiveness and effective instruction: the need for a further relationship'. In J. Bashi and Z. Sass (eds), *School Effectiveness and Improvement. Proceedings of the Third International Congress, Jerusalem*, pp. 105–32. Jerusalem: The Magnes Press.

Creemers, B. P. M. and Knuver, A. W. M. (1989). 'The Netherlands'. In B. P. M. Creemers, T. Peters and D. Reynolds (eds), *School Effectiveness and School Improvement. Proceedings of the Second International Congress, Rotterdam*, pp. 79–82. Lisse: Swets & Zeitlinger.

Creemers, B. P. M. and Lugthart, E. (1989). 'School effectiveness and improvement in the Netherlands'. In D. Reynolds, B. P. M. Creemers and T. Peters (eds), *School Effectiveness and Improvement. Proceedings of the First International Congress, London*, pp. 89–103. Groningen/Cardiff: RION/University of Wales.

Creemers, B. P. M., Hoeben, W. Th. J. G. and Westerhof, K. J. (1981). 'De functie van leerplannen bij onderwijzen en leren: een andere ingang voor curriculumonderzoek' (Curricula in searching and learning: another perspective for curriculum research). In B. P. M. Creemers (ed.), *Onderwijskunde als opdracht* (Educational science as a mission). Groningen: Wolters-Noordhoff.

Creemers, B. P. M., Reezigt, G. J. and Werf, M. P. C. van der (1992). *Development and Testing of a Model for School Learning*. Groningen: RION.

Creemers, B. P. M., Hoeben, W. Th. J. G. Peschar, J. L. and Snippe, J. (eds) (1993). *Wat is onderwijsonderzoek waard?* (The value of educational research). De Lier: Academisch Boeken Centrum.

Croll, P. (1988). 'Teaching methods and time on task in junior classrooms'. *Educational Research*, **30**(2), 90–7.

Crooks, T. J. (1988). 'The impact of classroom evaluation practices on students'. *Review of Educational Research*, **58**(4), 438–81.

Dar, Y. (1981). *Homogeneity and Heterogeneity in Education: Interaction between Personal Resources and the Learning Environment in Their Effect on Scholastic Achievement*. Jerusalem: Hebrew University Institute for Innovation in Education.

Darling-Hammond, L. and Goodwin, A. L. (1993). 'Progress toward professionalism in teaching'. In G. Cawelti (ed.), *Challenges and Achievements of American Education*, pp. 19–52. Alexandria, VA: Association for Supervision and Curriculum Development.

Davidson, N. and Wilson O'Leary, P. (1990). 'How cooperative learning can enhance mastery teaching'. *Educational Leadership*, **47**(51), 30–3.

De Corte, E., Geerligs, C. T., Lagerweij, N. A. J., Peters, J. J. and Vandenberghe, R. (1974). *Beknopte didaxologie* (Didaxology). Groningen: H. D. Tjeenk Willink.

Delamont, S. (ed.) (1987). *The Primary School Teacher*. London: Falmer Press.

Doyle, W. (1984). 'How order is achieved in classrooms: an interim report'. *Journal of Curriculum Studies*, **16**(3), 259–77.

Doyle, W. (1986). 'Classroom organization and management'. In M. C. Wittrock (ed.), *Handbook of Research on Teaching*, 3rd edn, pp. 392–431. New York: Macmillan.

Druva, C. A. and Anderson, R. D. (1983). 'Science teacher characteristics by teacher behavior and by student outcome: a meta-analysis of research'. *Journal of Research in Science Teaching*, **20**, 467–79.

Dunkin, M. J. and Biddle, B. J. (1974). *The Study of Teaching*. New York: Holt, Rinehart & Winston.

Dusek, J. B. and Joseph, A. (1983). 'The bases of teacher expectations: a meta-analysis'. *Journal of Educational Psychology*, **75**, 327–46.

Edelenbos, P. (1988). *Evaluatie Engels in het basisonderwijs* (Evaluation of English language instruction in primary education). Groningen: RION.

Edelenbos, P. (1990). *Leergangen voor Engels in het basisonderwijs vergeleken* (A comparison of courses for English in Dutch primary education). Groningen: RION.

Edmonds, R. R. (1979). 'Effective schools for the urban poor'. *Educational Leadership*, **37**(1), 15–27.

Eisner, E. W. (1979). *The Educational Imagination: On the Design and Evaluation of School Programs*. New York: Macmillan.

Eisner, E. W. (1987).'Why the textbook influences curriculum'. *Curriculum Review*, **26**(3), 11–13.

Eisner, E. W. and Vallance, E. (1974). *Conflicting Conceptions of Curriculum*. Berkeley, CA: McCutchan.

Elley, W. B. (1992). *How in the World Do Students Read?* IEA Study of Reading Literacy. The Hague: The International Association for the Evaluation of Educational Achievement.

Emmer, E., Evertson, C. and Anderson, L. (1980). 'Effective classroom management at the beginning of the school year'. *Elementary School Journal*, **80**(5), 219–31.

Entwistle, N. J. (ed.) (1990). *Handbook of Educational Ideas and Practices*. London: Routledge.

Evertson, C. M. and Emmer, E. T. (1982). 'Effective management at the beginning of the year in junior high classes'. *Journal of Educational Psychology*, **74**(4), 485–98.

Fend, H. (1984). 'Determinanten von Schulleistungen: wie wichtig sind die Lehrer?' (Determinants of school achievement: how important are teachers?). *Unterrichtswissenschaft*, **12**(1) 68–86.

Fisher, C., Berliner, D., Filby, N., Marliave, R., Cahen, L. and Dishaw, M. (1980). 'Teaching behaviors, academic learning time, and student achievement: an overview'. In C. Denham and A. Lieberman (eds), *Time to Learn*. Washington, DC: National Institute of Education.

Flanders, N. (1970). *Analyzing Teacher Behavior*. Reading, MA: Addison-Wesley.

Flinders, D. J. (1987). 'What teachers learn from teaching: educational criticisms of instructional adaptation'. Doctoral dissertation submitted to the Graduate School of Education, Stanford University.

Fontana, D. (1985). *Classroom Control: Understanding and Guiding Classroom Behaviour*. London: British Psychological Society.

Fraser, B. J., Walberg, H. J., Welch, W. W. and Hattie, J. A. (1987). 'Syntheses of educational productivity research'. *International Journal of Educational Research*, **11**(2), 145–252.

Frederick, W. C. (1980). 'Instructional time'. *Evaluation in Education*, **4**, 117–18.

Freeman, D. J. and Porter, A. C. (1988). 'Does the content of classroom instruction match the content of textbooks?' Paper presented at the Annual Meeting of the American Educational Research Association, New Orleans.

Freeman, D. J. and Porter, A. C. (1989). 'Do textbooks dictate the content of mathematics instruction in elementary schools?' *American Educational Research Journal*, **26**(3), 403–21.

Freiberg, H. J., Prokosch, N., Treister, E. S. and Stein, T. (1990). 'Turning around five at-risk elementary schools'. *School Effectiveness and School Improvement*, **1**(1), 5–25.

Fuchs, L. S., Fuchs, D., Hamlett, C. L. and Stecker, P. M. (1991). 'Effects of curriculum-based measurement and consultation on teacher planning and student achievement in mathematics operations'. *American Educational Research Journal*, **28**(3), 617–41.

Fullan, M. and Pomfret, A. (1977). 'Research on curriculum and instruction implementation'. *Review of Educational Research*, **47**, 335–97.

Gage, N. L. (1963). 'Paradigms for research on teaching'. In N. L. Gage (ed.), *Handbook of Research on Teaching*, pp. 94–141. Chicago: Rand McNally.

Gage, N. L. (1966). 'Research on cognitive aspects on teaching'. In Association for Supervision and Curriculum Development, Seminar on Teaching. *The Way Teaching Is*. Washington, DC: National Education Association.

Gage, N. L. (1972). *Teacher Effectiveness and Teacher Education: The Search for a Scientific Basis*. Palo Alto, CA: Pacific Books.

Gage, N. L. (1977). *The Scientific Basis of the Art of Teaching*. New York: Teachers College Press.

Gage, N. L. (1989). 'The paradigm wars and their aftermath: a "historical" sketch of research on teaching since 1989'. *Teachers College Record*, **91**(2), 135–89.

Gage, N. L. and Giaconia, R. (1983). 'Teaching practices and student achievement: causal connections'. *New York University Education Quarterly*, **12**(3), 2–9.

Gage, N. L. and Needels, M. C. (1989). 'Process–product research on teaching: a review of criticisms'. *The Elementary School Journal*, **89**(3), 253–300.

Gagné, R. M. (1977). *The Conditions of Learning*. New York: Holt, Rinehart & Winston.

Galloway, D. and Edwards, A. (1991). *Primary School Teaching and Educational Psychology*. London: Longman.

Galton, M. (1989a). 'Primary teacher training: practice in search of a pedagogy'. In A. McClelland and V. Varma (eds), *Advances in Teacher Education*. London: Hodder & Stoughton.

Galton, M. (1989b). *Primary Teaching*. London: David Fulton.

Galton, M., Simon, B. and Croll, P. (1980). *Inside the Primary Classroom*. London: Routledge & Kegan Paul.

Gamoran, A. (1986). 'Instructional and institutional effects of ability grouping'. *Sociology of Education*, **59**, 185–98.

Gamoran, A. (1992). 'Is ability grouping equitable?' *Educational Leadership*, **50**(2), 11–17.

Gamoran, A. and Berends, M. (1987). 'The effects of stratification in secondary schools: synthesis of survey and ethnographic research'. *Review of Educational Research*, **57**(4), 415–35.

Gersten, R. and Carnine, D. (1986). 'Direct instruction in reading comprehension'. *Educational Leadership*, **43**(7), 70–8.

Gettinger, M. (1991). 'Learning time and retention differences between nondisabled students and students with learning disabilities'. *Learning Disability Quarterly*, **14**(3), 179–89.

Getzels, J. W. and Jackson, P. W. (1963). 'The teacher's personality and characteristics'. In N. L. Gage (ed.), *Handbook of Research on Teaching*, pp. 506–82. Chicago: Rand McNally.

Glaser, R. (1976). 'Components of a psychology of instruction: toward a science of design'. *Review of Educational Research*, **46**, 1–24.

Glass, G. V. (1976). 'Secondary and meta-analysis of research'. *Educational Researcher*, **11**, 3–8.

Glass, G. V., McGaw, B., White, K. and Smith, M. L. (1980). *Integration of Research Studies: Meta-analysis of Research, Methods of Integrative Analysis*. Final report. Washington, DC: National Institute of Education.

Goldenberg, C. (1992). 'The limits of expectations: a case for case knowledge about teacher expectancy effects'. *American Educational Research Journal*, **29**(3), 517–44.

Good, T. L. (1987). 'Two decades of research on teacher expectations: findings and future directions'. *Journal of Teacher Education*, **38**(4), 32–47.

Good, T. L. (1989). *Classroom and School Research: Investments to Enhance Schooling (ED308191)*. Washington, DC: Office of Educational Research and Improvement.

Good, T. and Brophy, J. (1978). *Looking in Classrooms*. New York: Harper & Row.

Good, T. and Grouws, D. (1977). 'Teaching effects: a process–product study in fourth grade mathematics classrooms'. *Journal of Teacher Education*, **28**, 49–54.

Good, T. L. and Grouws, D. A. (1979). 'The Missouri Mathematics Effectiveness Project: an experimental study in fourth-grade classrooms'. *Journal of Educational Psychology*, **71**(3), 355–62.

Good, T. L., Biddle, B. J. and Brophy, J. (1975). *Teachers Make a Difference*. New York: Holt, Rinehart & Winston.

Goodlad, J. I. (1984). *A Place Called School*. New York: McGraw-Hill.

Graubard, S. R. (1993). 'Preface to the issue "America's Childhood"'. *Daedalus*, **122**(1), V–XII.

Gravemeijer, K., Heuvel-Panhuizen, M. van den, Donselaar, G. van, Ruesink, N., Streefland, L., Vermeulen, W. and Woerd, E. te (1991). *Methoden in het reken-wiskundeonderwijs, een rijke context voor vergelijkend onderzoek* (Mathematics curricula: rich contexts for comparative reserach). Utrecht: Vakgroep OW&OC/ISOR.

Greenwood, C. R. (1991). 'Longitudinal analysis of time, engagement, and achievement in at-risk versus non-risk students'. *Exceptional Children*, **57**(6), 521–35.

Gregory, R. P. (1984). 'Streaming, setting and mixed ability grouping in primary and secondary schools: some research findings'. *Educational Studies*, **10**(3), 209–26.

Groot, A. D. de (1961). *Methodologie* (Methodology). The Hague: Mouton.

Groot, A. D. de (1976). 'Ontwikkelingslijnen in de Nederlandse onderwijsresearch' (Trends in the development of educational research in the Netherlands). *Tijdschrift voor Onderwijsresearch*, **1**(4), 145–60.

Guba, E. G. (1978). *Toward a Methodology of Naturalistic Inquiry in Educational Evaluation*. Los Angeles: Center for the Study of Evaluation.

Guskey, T. R. (1987). 'Rethinking mastery learning reconsidered'. *Review of Educational Research*, **57**, 225–9.

Guskey, T. R. and Pigott, T. J. (1988). 'Research on group-based mastery learning programs: a meta-analysis'. *Journal of Educational Research*, **81**(4), 197–216.

Guthrie, J. W. (1970). 'A survey of school effectiveness studies'. In *Do Teachers Make a Difference?*, pp. 25–55. Washington, DC: Office of Education.

Gutiérrez, R. and Slavin, R. E. (1992). 'Achievement effects of the nongraded elementary school: a best evidence synthesis'. *Review of Educational Research*, **62**(4), 333–76.

Haan, D. M. de (1992). 'Measuring test–curriculum overlap'. PhD thesis, University of Twente, Enschede.

Haanen, M., Lagendaal, P., Roders, R. and Wolf, K. van der (1990). *Kleurrijk en effectief: eindrapportage van de eerste fase van het Amsterdamse EGAA-project* (Colourful and effective: final report of the first phase of the Amsterdam EGAA project). Delft: Eburon.

Haertel, G. D., Walberg, H. J. and Weinstein, T. (1983). 'Psychological models of educational performance: a theoretical synthesis of constructs'. *Review of Educational Research*, **53**(1), 75–91.

Hall, G. and Loucks, S. (1977). 'A developmental model for determining whether the treatment is actually implemented'. *American Educational Research Journal*, **14**, 263–76.

Hallinan, M. T. and Sørensen, A. B. (1983). 'The formation and stability of instructional groups'. *American Sociological Review*, **48**(6), 839–51.

Hamaker, C. (1986). 'The effect of adjunct questions on prose learning'. *Review of Educational Research*, **56**, 212–42.

Hanushek, E. A. (1970). 'The production of education, teacher quality, and efficiency'. In *Do Teachers Make a Difference?* Washington, DC: Department of Health, Education and Welfare, US Government Printing Office.

Hanushek, E. A. (1971). 'Teacher characteristics and gains in student achievement'. *American Economic Review*, **61**, 280–8.

Hargreaves, A. and Fullan, M. G. (eds) (1992). *Understanding Teacher Development*. London: Cassell.

Harnischfeger, A. and Wiley, D. E. (1976). 'The teaching learning process in elementary schools: a synoptic view'. *Curriculum Inquiry*, **6**, 5–43.

Harskamp, E. G. (1988). *Rekenmethoden op de proef gesteld* (Arithmetic curricula put to the test). Groningen: RION.

Harskamp, E. G. and Suhre, C. J. M. (1993). *Beoordeling van onderwijsmethoden in het basisonderwijs* (An evaluation of primary school curricula). Groningen: RION.

Hartley, S. S. (1977). 'Meta-analysis of the effects of individually paced instruction in mathematics'. *Dissertation Abstracts International*, **38**, 4003A (University Microfilms 77–29926).

Helmke, A., Schneider, W. and Weinert, F. E. (1986). 'Quality of instruction and classroom learning outcomes: the German contribution to the IEA classroom environment study'. *Teaching and Teacher Education*, **2**(1), 1–18.

Hoeben, W. Th. J. G. (1981). *Praktijkgericht onderzoek en de groei van kennis* (Applied research and the growth of knowledge). The Hague: SVO.

Hoeben, W. Th. J. G. (1985). 'Evaluatieonderzoek van het onderwijs: stand van zaken' (Evaluation research in education: state of the art). In R. Halkes and R. G. M. Wolbert (eds), *Docent en methode* (Teacher and curriculum), pp. 23–39. Lisse: Swets & Zeitlinger.

Hoeben, W. Th. J. G. (1989). 'Educational innovation or school effectiveness: a dilemma?' In B. P. M. Creemers, T. Peters and D. Reynolds (eds), *School Effectiveness and School Improvement. Proceedings of the Second International Congress, Rotterdam*, pp. 157–66. Lisse: Swets & Zeitlinger.

Hofman, R. H. (1993). *Effectief schoolbestuur* (Effective schoolboards). Groningen: RION.

Horn, A. and Walberg, H. J. (1984). 'Achievement and interest as functions of quantity and quality of instruction'. *Journal of Educational Research*, **77**, 227–32.

Huberman, A. M. and Crandall, D. P. (1982). *Implications for Action. A Study of Dissemination Efforts Supporting School Improvement. People, Policies, and Practices: Examining the Chain of School Improvement*, Volume IX. Andover, MA: The Network.

Husén, T. (1967). *International Study of Achievement in Mathematics: A Comparison of Twelve Countries*. New York: Wiley.

Hymel, G. M. (1990). 'Harnessing the mastery learning literature: past efforts, current status and future directions'. Paper presented at the Annual Meeting of the American Educational Research Association, Boston.

International School Effectiveness Research Programme (1992). *An Outline*. Cardiff: University of Wales.

Jackson, P. W. and Guba, E. G. (1957). 'The need structure of in-service teachers: an occupational analysis'. *School Review*, **65**, 176–92.

Janssens, F. J. G. (1986). *De evaluatiepraktijken van leerkrachten* (Evaluation practices of teachers). Arnhem: CITO.

Jencks, C., Smith, M., Acland, H., Bane, M. J., Cohen, D., Gintis, H., Heyns, B. and

Michelson, S. (1972). *Inequality: A Reassessment of the Effects of Family and Schooling in America*. New York: Basic Books.

Johnson, D. W. and Johnson, R. T. (1989). *Cooperation and Competition: Theory and Research*. Edina, MN: Interaction Book Company.

Jones, B. F. (1986). 'Quality and equality through cognitive instruction'. *Educational Leadership*, **43**(7), 4–11.

Jungbluth, P. (1981). *Docenten over onderwijs aan meisjes* (Teachers' views on the education of girls). Nijmegen: ITS.

Keller, F. S. (1968). 'Good-bye, teacher . . .'. *Journal of Applied Behavioural Analysis*, **1**, 79–89.

Keller, J. M. (1983). 'Motivational design of instruction'. In Ch. Reigeluth (ed.), *Instructional Design Theories and Models*. Hillsdale, NJ: Erlbaum.

Kerckhoff, A. C. (1986). 'Effects of ability grouping in British secondary schools'. *American Sociological Review*, **51**, 842–58.

Klaasman, R. R. P. (1989). *Implementatie van onderwijsprogramma's en leerprestaties* (The implementation of educational programmes and achievement). Rotterdam: Project Onderwijs en Sociaal Milieu.

Klauer, K. J. (1984). 'Intentional and incidental learning with instructional texts: a meta-analysis for 1970–1980'. *American Educational Research Journal*, **21**, 323–39.

Knoers, A. M. P. (1983). 'Vakkenintegratie en kwaliteit van het onderwijs' (Integration of school subjects and quality of education). In A. M. P. Knoers and J. J. R. M. Corten (eds), *Ontwikkelingen in het Nederlandse onderwijs, aspectenvan kwaliteit en beleid* (Trends in Dutch education: quality and policy aspects). Nijmegen: Vakgroep Interdisciplinaire Onderwijskunde.

Knuver, J. W. M. (1993). *De relatie tussen klas- en schoolkenmerken en het affectief functioneren van leerlingen* (The relationship between class and school characteristics and the affective functioning of pupils). Groningen: RION.

Knuver, A. W. M. and Brandsma, H. P. (1993). Cognitive and affective outcomes in school effectiveness research. *School Effectiveness and School Improvement*, **4**(3), 189–204.

Koning, P. de (1973). *Interne differentiatie* (Grouping within classrooms). Purmerend: Muusses.

Koning, P. de (1987). *Programmadifferentiatie in het voortgezet onderwijs* (Grouping in secondary education). Lisse: Swets & Zeitlinger.

Kounin, J. S. (1970). *Discipline and Group Management in Classrooms*. New York: Holt, Rinehart & Winston.

Kounin, J. S. and Doyle, P. H. (1975). 'Degree of continuity of a lesson's signal system and the task involvement of children'. *Journal of Educational Psychology*, **67**, 159–64.

Kounin, J. S. and Gump, P. (1974). 'Signal systems of lesson settings and the task related behavior of preschool children'. *Journal of Educational Psychology*, **66**, 554–62.

Kozlow, M. J. (1979). 'A meta-analysis of selected advance organizer research reports from 1960 to 1977'. *Dissertation Abstracts International*, **39**, 5047–5048A.

Kozlow, M. J. and White, A. L. (1980). 'Advance organiser research'. *Evaluation in Education*, **4**, 47–8.

Kuiper, W. A. J. M. (1993). 'Curriculumvernieuwing en lespraktijk' (Curriculum reform and teaching practice). PhD thesis, University of Twente, Enschede.

Kulik, C.-L. C. (1985). 'Effects of inter-class ability grouping on achievement and self-esteem'. Paper presented at the Annual Meeting of the American Psychologist Association, Los Angeles.

Kulik, C.-L. C. and Kulik, J. A. (1982). 'Effects of ability grouping on secondary school students: a meta-analysis of evaluation findings'. *American Educational Research Journal*, **19**(3), 415–28.

Kulik, C.-L. C. and Kulik, J. A. (1984a). 'Effects of ability grouping on elementary school pupils: a meta-analysis'. Paper presented at the Annual Meeting of the American Psychologist Association, Toronto.

Kulik, C.-L. C. and Kulik, J. A. (1986–7). 'Mastery testing and student learning: a meta-analysis'. *Journal of Educational Technology Systems*, **15**, 325–45.

Kulik, C.-L. C. and Kulik, J. A. (1991). 'Effectiveness of computer-based instruction: an updated analysis'. *Computers in Human Behavior*, **7**, 75–94.

Kulik, C.-L. C., Kulik, J. A. and Bangert-Drowns, R. L. (1990). 'Effectiveness of mastery learning programs: a meta-analysis'. *Review of Educational Research*, **60**(2), 265–99.

Kulik, J. A. and Kulik, C.-L. C. (1984b). 'Effects of accelerated instruction on students'. *Review of Educational Research*, **54**(3), 409–25.

Kulik, J. A. and Kulik, C.-L. C. (1987). 'Effects of ability grouping on student achievement'. *Equity and Excellence*, **23**, 22–30.

Kulik, J. A. and Kulik, C.-L. C. (1989). 'Meta-analysis in education'. *International Journal of Educational Research*, **13**(3), 221–340.

Kulik, J. A., Kulik, C.-L. C. and Cohen, P. A. (1979). 'A meta-analysis of outcome studies of Keller's Personalized System of Instruction'. *American Psychologist*, **34**(4), 307–18.

Kyriacou, C. (1985). 'Conceptualising research on effective teaching'. *British Journal of Educational Psychology*, **55**, 148–55.

Laarhoven, P. van, Bakker, B., Dronkers, J. and Schijf, H. (1986). 'Some aspects of school careers in public and non-public primary schools'. *Tijdschrift voor Onderwijsresearch*, **11**(2), 83–96.

Laarhoven, P. van and Vries, A. M. de (1987). *Effecten van de interklassikale groeperingsvorm in het voortgezet onderwijs: resultaten van een literatuurstudie* (Effects of between-class grouping in secondary education: a literature review). ORD-paper. Groningen: RION.

Lagerweij, N. A. J. (1976). *Handleidingen in het onderwijs* (Teacher manuals in education). Meppel: Boom.

Leming, J. S. (1993). 'In search of effective character education'. *Educational Leadership*, **51**(3), 63–71.

Levine, D. U. (1992). 'An interpretive review of US research and practice dealing with unusually effective schools'. In D. Reynolds and P. Cuttance (eds), *School Effectiveness: Research, Policy and Practice*, pp. 25–47. London: Cassell.

Levine, D. U. and Lezotte, L. W. (1990). *Unusually Effective Schools: A Review and Analysis of Research and Practice*. Madison, WI: National Center for Effective Schools Research and Development.

Levine, D. U. and Ornstein, A. C. (1989). 'Research on classroom and school effectiveness and its implications for improving big city schools'. *Urban Review*, **21**(2), 81–94.

Lezotte, L. W. (1989). 'School improvement based on the effective schools research'. *International Journal of Educational Research*, **13**(7), 815–23.

Lockwood, A. L. (1993). 'A letter to character educators'. *Educational Leadership*, **51**(3), 72–5.

Lugthart, E., Roeders, P. J. B., Bosker, R. J. and Bos, K. T. (1989). *Effectieve school-kenmerken in het voortgezet onderwijs*. Deel 1: *Literatuurstudie* (Effective schools characteristics in secondary education. Part I: Literature review). Groningen: RION.

Luiten, J., Ames, W. and Ackerson, G. (1980). 'A meta-analysis of the effects of advance organizers on learning and retention'. *American Educational Research Journal*, **17**, 211–18.

Lundgren, U. P. (1972). *Frame Factors and the Teaching Process*. Stockholm: Almqvist & Wiksell.

Lundgren, U. P. (1979). 'Background: the conceptual framework'. In U. P. Lundgren and S. Pettersson (eds), *Code, Context and Curriculum Processes*, pp. 5–35. Stockholm: Stockholm Institute of Education.

Lysakowski, R. S. and Walberg, H. J. (1982). 'Instructional effects of cues, participation, and corrective feedback: a quantitative synthesis'. *American Educational Research Journal*, **19**, 578–99.

McCormack-Larkin, M. (1985). 'Ingredients of a successful school effectiveness project'. *Educational Leadership*, **42**(6), 31–7.

McNeil, J. D. (1969). 'Forces influencing curriculum'. *Review of Educational Research*, **39**, 293–318.

Mager, R. (1962). *Preparing Instructional Objectives*. Palo Alto, CA: Fearson.

Mandeville, G. K. (1988). 'School effectiveness indices revisited: cross-year stability'. *Journal of Educational Measurement*, **25**, 349–56.

Marsh, H. W., Smith, I. D. and Barnes, J. (1985). 'Multi-dimensional self-concepts: relations with sex and academic achievement'. *Journal of Educational Psychology*, **77**(5) 581–96.

Marzano, R. J., Hagerty, P. J., Valencia, S. W. and DiStefano, P. P. (1987). *Reading Diagnosis and Instruction: Theory into Practice*. Englewood Cliffs, NJ: Prentice-Hall.

Menter, I. and Pollard, A. (1989). 'The implications of the national curriculum for reflective practice in initial teacher education'. *Westminster Studies in Education*, **12**, 31–42.

Mevarech, Z. R. (1991). 'Learning mathematics in different mastery environments'. *Journal of Educational Research*, **84**(4) 225–31.

Mitzel, H. E. (1960). 'Teacher effectiveness'. In C. W. Harris (ed.), *Encyclopedia of Educational Research*, 3rd edn, pp. 1481–6. New York: Macmillan.

Morrison, H. C. (1926). *The Practice of Teaching in the Secondary School*. Chicago: University of Chicago Press.

Mortimore, P. (1991). 'School effectiveness research: which way at the crossroads?' *School Effectiveness and School Improvement*, **2**(3), 213–29.

Mortimore, P. (1992). 'Issues in school effectiveness'. In D. Reynolds and P. Cuttance (eds), *School Effectiveness: Research, Policy and Practice*, pp. 154–63. London: Cassell.

Mortimore, P., Sammons, P., Stoll, L., Lewis, D. and Ecob, R. (1988). *School Matters: The Junior Years*. Wells: Open Books.

Mortimore, P., Sammons, P., Stoll, L., Lewis, D. and Ecob, R. (1989). 'A study of effective junior schools'. *International Journal of Educational Research*, **13**(7), 753–68.

Müller, H. (1964). *Methoden des Erstleseunterrichts und ihre Ergebnisse* (Curricula for beginning reading instruction and their effects). Meisenheim am Glan: Verlag Anton Hain KG.

Murphy, J. (1988). 'Equity as student opportunity to learn'. *Theory into Practice*, **27**(2), 145–51.

Murphy, J. (1992). 'Instructional leadership: focus on time to learn'. *NASSP Bulletin*, **76**(542), 19–26.

Muther, C. (1987). 'What do we teach and when do we teach it?' *Educational Leadership*, **45**(1), 77–80.

National Commission for Excellence in Education (1983). *A Nation at Risk*. Washington, DC: US Department of Education.

Needels, M. C. (1988). 'A new design for process–product research on the quality of discourse in teaching'. *American Educational Research Journal*, **25**(4) 503–26.

Nordin, A. B. (1979). 'The effects of different qualities of instruction on selected cognitive, affective, and time variables'. Unpublished doctoral dissertation, University of Chicago.

Nuttall, D. L., Goldstein, H., Prosser, R. and Rasbash, J. (1989). 'Differential school effectiveness'. *International Journal of Educational Research*, **13**(7), 769–76.

Nuy, M. J. G. (1981). *Interne differentiatie* (Grouping within classes). Den Bosch: KPC.

Oakes, J. and Lipton, M. (1990). 'Tracking and ability grouping: a structural barrier to access and achievement'. In J. I. Goodlad and P. Keating (eds), *Access to Knowledge: An Agenda for Our Nation's Schools*, pp. 187–204. New York: College Entrance Examination Board.

Oakes, J. and Lipton, M. (1992). 'Detracking schools: early lessons from the field'. *Phi Delta Kappan*, **73**(6), 448–54.

Olson, J. K. and Eaton, S. (1987). 'Curriculum change and the classroom order'. In J. Calderhead (ed.), *Exploring Teachers' Thinking*, pp. 179–94. London: Cassell.

Oser, F. K., Dick, A. and Patry, J. L. (1993). 'Afterword: responsible action as the hallmark of effective teaching'. In F. K. Oser, A. Dick and J. L. Patry (eds), *Effective and Responsible Teaching: The New Synthesis*, pp. 441–6. San Francisco: Jossey-Bass.

Osinga, N., Boersma, R. and Houtveen, Th. (1993). *School Improvement in the Netherlands*. Leeuwarden: GCO.

Palincsar, A. S. and Brown, A. L. (1989). 'Instruction for self-regulated reading'. In L. B. Resnick and L. E. Klopfer (eds), *Toward the Thinking Curriculum: Current Cognitive Research*, pp. 19–39. Alexandria, VA: Association for Supervision and Curriculum Development.

References

Pelgrum, W. J. (1989a). *Educational Assessment: Monitoring, Evaluation and the Curriculum*. De Lier: Academisch Boeken Centrum.

Pelgrum, W. J. (1989b). *IEA Guidebook 1989: Activities, Institutions, People*. Stockholm: IEA.

Pelgrum, W. J., Eggen, Th. J. H. M. and Plomp, Tj. (1983). *Tweede Wiskunde Project: beschrijving van uitkomsten* (The Second Mathematics Study: results). Enschede: Universiteit Twente.

Perrott, E. (1982). *Effective Teaching: A Practical Guide to Improving Your Teaching*. London: Longman.

Plomp, Tj. (1974). *De ontwikkeling van een individueel studiesysteem: konstruktie en evaluatie van een kursus wiskunde voor de propedeuse aan de Technische Hogeschool Twente* (The development of an individualized study system: construction and evaluation of a mathematics course for first-year students). Groningen: H. D. Tjeenk Willink.

Pollard, A. (1982). 'A model of classroom coping strategies'. *British Journal of Sociology of Education*, **3**(1), 19–37.

Pollard, A. (1985). *The Social World of the Primary School*. London: Holt, Rinehart & Winston.

Pollard, A. (1990). 'Towards a sociology of learning in primary schools'. *British Journal of Sociology of Education*, **11**(3), 241–56.

Pollard, A. and Tann, S. (1987). *Reflective Teaching in the Primary School: A Handbook for the Classroom*. London: Cassell.

Porter, A. C. (1989). 'External standards and good teaching: the pros and cons of telling teachers what to do'. *Educational Evaluation and Policy Analysis*, **11**(4), 343–56.

Porter, A. C. and Brophy, J. (1988). 'Synthesis of research on good teaching: insights from the work of the Institute for Research on Teaching'. *Educational Leadership*, **46**, 74–85.

Postlethwaite, T. N. and Ross, K. N. (1992). *Effective Schools in Reading: Implications for Educational Planners. An Exploratory Study*. The Hague: The International Association for the Evaluation of Educational Achievement.

Postlethwaite, T. N. and Wiley, D. E. (1992). *The IEA Study of Science II: Science Achievement in Twenty-three Countries*. Oxford: Pergamon Press.

Prawat, R. S. (1989). 'Promoting access to knowledge, strategy and disposition in students: a research synthesis'. *Review of Educational Research*, **59**, 1–41.

Purkey, S. C. and Smith, M. S. (1983). 'Effective schools: a review'. *The Elementary School Journal*, **83**(4), 427–52.

Ralph, J. H. and Fennessey, J. (1983). 'Science or reform: some questions about the effective schools model'. *Phi Delta Kappan*, **64**(10), 689–94.

Raudenbush, S. W. (1983). 'Utilizing controversy as a source of hypotheses for meta-analysis: the case of teacher expectancy's effects on pupil IQ'. In R. J. Light (ed.), *Evaluation Studies Review Annual*, vol. 8. Beverly Hills, CA: Sage.

Redfield, D. L. and Rousseau, E. W. (1981). 'A meta-analysis of experimental research on teacher questioning behavior'. *Review of Experimental Research*, **51**, 237–45.

Reezigt, G. J. (1993). *Effecten van differentiatie op de basisschool* (Effects of grouping in primary education). Groningen: RION.

Reezigt, G. J. and Weide, M. G. (1989). *Effecten van differentiatie: resultaten survey-onderzoek* (Effects of grouping: a survey study). Groningen: RION.

Reezigt, G. J., Dijk, M. H. van and Bosveld, J. J. F. (1986). *Differentiatie op de basisschool* (Grouping in primary education). The Hague: SVO.

Reiss, V. (1982). *Die Steuerung des Unterrichtsablaufs* (Influencing educational outcomes). Frankfurt am Main: Peter Lan.

Reynolds, D. (ed.) (1985). *Studying School Effectiveness*. London: Falmer Press.

Reynolds, D. (1989). 'School effectiveness and school improvement: a review of the British literature'. In D. Reynolds, B. P. M. Creemers and T. Peters (eds), *School Effectiveness and School Improvement. Proceedings of the First International Congress, London*, pp. 11–29. Groningen/Cardiff: RION/University of Wales.

Reynolds, D. (1991). 'School effectiveness and school improvement in Great Britain'. In B. P. M. Creemers, D. Reynolds, G. Schaffer, S. Stringfield and C. Teddlie (eds) *International School Effects Research Workshop*, pp. 209–27. Kaohsiung: College of Education, National Kaohsiung Normal University.

Reynolds, D. (1992). 'School effectiveness and school improvement: an updated review of the British literature'. In D. Reynolds and P. Cuttance (eds), *School Effectiveness: Research, Policy and Practice*, pp. 1–24. London: Cassell.

Reynolds, D. (1993a). 'Linking school effectiveness knowledge and school improvement practice'. In C. Dimmock (ed.), *School-Based Management and School Effectiveness*, pp. 185–200. London: Routledge.

Reynolds, D. (1993b). 'Conceptualising and measuring the school level'. Paper presented at the Annual Meeting of the American Educational Research Association, Atlanta.

Robitaille, D. F. and Garden, R. A. (1989). *The IEA Study of Mathematics II: Contexts and Outcomes of School Mathematics*. Oxford: Pergamon Press.

Romiszowski, A. J. (1984). *Producing Instructional Systems*. London: Kogan Page.

Rosenholtz, S. J. (1989). *Teachers' Workplace*. New York: Longman.

Rosenshine, B. (1971a). 'Teaching behaviors related to pupil achievement: a review of research'. In I. Westbury and A. A. Bellack (eds), *Research into Classroom Processes: Recent Developments and Next Steps*, pp. 51–98. New York: Teachers College Press.

Rosenshine, B. (1971b). *Teaching Behaviours and Student Achievement*. Windsor: NFER.

Rosenshine, B. (1979). 'Content, time and direct instruction'. In P. L. Peterson and H. J. Walberg (eds), *Research on Teaching*. Berkeley, CA: McCutchan.

Rosenshine, B. (1983). 'Teaching functions in instructional programs'. *Elementary School Journal*, **83**(4), 335–51.

Rosenshine, B. (1987). 'Direct instruction'. In M. J. Dunkin (ed.), *International Encyclopedia of Teaching and Teacher Education*, pp. 257–62. Oxford: Pergamon Press.

Rosenshine, B. and Furst, N. (1971). 'Research on teacher performance criteria'. In B. O. Smith (ed.), *Research in Teacher Education*, pp. 37–72. Englewood Cliffs, NJ: Prentice-Hall.

Rosenshine, B. and Furst, N. (1973). 'The use of direct observation to study teaching'. In R. M. W. Travers (ed.), *Second Handbook of Research on Teaching*, pp. 122–83. Chicago: Rand McNally.

Rosenshine, B. and Stevens, R. (1986). 'Teaching Functions'. In M. C. Wittrock (ed.), *Handbook of Research on Teaching*, 3rd edn, pp. 376–91. New York: Macmillan.

Rosenthal, R. and Jacobson, L. (1968). *Pygmalion in the Classroom: Teacher Expectations and Pupils' Intellectual Development*. New York: Holt, Rinehart & Winston.

Rosenthal, R. and Rubin, D. B. (1978). 'Interpersonal expectancy effects: the first 345 studies'. *Behavior and Brain Sciences*, **3**, 377–86.

Rutter, M., Maughan, B., Mortimore, P. and Ouston, J. (1979). *Fifteen Thousand Hours*. London: Open Books.

Sashkin, M. and Walberg, H. J. (eds) (1993). *Educational Leadership and School Culture*. Berkeley, CA: McCutchan.

Saylor, J. G. and Alexander, W. M. (1974). *Planning Curriculum for Schools*. New York: Holt, Rinehart & Winston.

Scheerens, J. (1987). *Enhancing Educational Opportunities for Disadvantaged Learners*. Amsterdam: North-Holland.

Scheerens, J. (1990). 'School effectiveness research and the development of process indicators of school functioning'. *School Effectiveness and School Improvement*, **1**(1), 61–80.

Scheerens, J. (1991). 'Foundational and fundamental studies in school effectiveness: a research agenda'. Unpublished paper commissioned by the Institute for Educational Research (SVO) in the Netherlands.

Scheerens, J. (1992). *Effective Schooling: Research, Theory and Practice*. London: Cassell.

Scheerens, J. and Creemers, B. P. M. (1989). 'Conceptualizing school effectiveness'. *International Journal of Educational Research*, **13**(7), 691–706.

Scheerens, J., Nanninga, H. C. R. and Pelgrum, W. J. (1989). Generalizility of instructional and school effectiveness indicators across nations; preliminary results of a secondary analysis of the IEA second mathematics study. In B. P. M. Creemers, T. Peters and D. Reynolds (eds), *School Effectiveness and School Improvement. Proceedings of the Second International Congress, Rotterdam*, pp. 199–209. Lisse: Swets & Zeitlinger.

Schimmell, B. J. (1983). 'A meta-analysis of feedback to learners in computerized and programmed instruction'. Paper presented at Annual Meeting of American Educational Research Association, Montreal.

Shapiro, E. S. and Ager, C. (1992). 'Assessment of special education students in regular education programs: linking assessment to instruction'. *Elementary School Journal*, **92**(3), 283–96.

Sharan, S. (1980). 'Cooperative learning in small groups: recent methods and effects on achievement, attitudes, and social relations'. *Review of Educational Research*, **50**, 241–71.

Shavelson, R. J. (1983). 'Review of research on teachers' pedagogical judgements, plans and decisions'. *Elementary School Journal*, **83**(4), 392–413.

Shipman, M. (1990). *In Search of Learning: A New Approach to School Management*. Oxford: Basil Blackwell.

Shulman, L. S. (1986). 'Paradigms and research programs in the study of teaching: a contemporary perspective'. In M. C. Wittrock (ed.), *Handbook of Research on Teaching*, 3rd edn, pp. 3–36. New York: Macmillan.

Simon, A. and Boyer, E. (eds) (1967). *Mirrors for Behavior: An Anthology of Observation Instruments*. Philadelphia: Research for Better Schools.

Simon, A. and Boyer, E. (eds) (1970). *Mirrors for Behavior: An Anthology of Observation Instruments Continued, 1970 Supplement*, Volumes A and B. Philadelphia: Research for Better Schools.

Simons, P. R. J. (1992). 'Onderwijs en ontwikkeling' (Education and development). In R. F. W. Diekstra (ed.), *Jeugd in ontwikkeling: wetenschappelijke inzichten en overheidsbeleid* (The development of children: scientific notions and national policy). The Hague: SDU/WRR.

Slavenburg, J. H. (1986). *Onderwijsstimulering en gezinsactivering* (Compensatory education and family involvement). The Hague: SVO.

Slavenburg, J. H. (1989). 'Implementatiewaarde, doeleffectiviteit en transfereffectiviteit van stimulerings- en activeringsprogramma's' (Implementation value, goal effectiveness and transfer effectiveness of compensatory programmes). In J. H. Slavenburg and T. A. Peters (eds), *Het project Onderwijs en Sociaal Milieu: Een Eindbalans* (The Education and Social Environment Project: a final evaluation), pp. 91–116. Rotterdam: Rotterdamse School Advies Dienst.

Slavenburg, J. H. and Creemers, B. P. M. (1979). 'Leren lezen door beheersingsleren' (Learning to read by mastery learning). In E. Warries (ed.), *Beheersingsleren een leerstrategie* (Mastery learning a learning strategy), pp. 65–80. Groningen: Wolters–Noordhoff.

Slavenburg, J. H. and Peters, T. A. (eds) (1989). *Het project Onderwijs en Sociaal Milieu: Een Eindbalans* (The Education and Social Environment Project: a final evaluation). Rotterdam: Rotterdamse School Advies Dienst.

Slavenburg, J. H., Leune, J. M. G., Creemers, B. P. M. and Peters, T. A. (1989). 'Conclusies en aanbevelingen' (Conclusions and recommendations). In J. H. Slavenburg and T. A. Peters (eds), *Het Project Onderwijs en Sociaal Milieu: Een Eindbalans*, pp. 285–316. Rotterdam: Rotterdamse School Advies Dienst.

Slavin, R. E. (1983). *Cooperative Learning*. New York: Longman.

Slavin, R. E. (1987a). 'Mastery learning reconsidered'. *Review of Educational Research*, **57**(2), 175–213.

Slavin, R. E. (1987b). 'Ability grouping and student achievement in elementary schools: a best-evidence synthesis'. *Review of Educational Research*, **57**(3), 293–336.

Slavin, R. E. (1990a). 'Ability grouping in secondary schools'. *Review of Educational Research*, **60**(3), 471–99.

Slavin, R. E. (1990b). *Cooperative Learning: Theory, Research and Practice*. Englewood Cliffs, NJ: Prentice-Hall.

Slavin, R. E. (1991). 'Ability grouping in the middle grades: effects and alternatives'. Paper presented at the Annual Meeting of the American Educational Research Association, Chicago.

Slavin, R. E., Karweit, N. L. and Madden, N. A. (1989). *Effective Programs for Students at Risk*. Boston: Allyn & Bacon.

Slavin, R. E., Madden, N. A., Karweit, N. L., Livermon, B. J. and Dolan, L. (1990).

'Success for All: first-year outcomes of a comprehensive plan for reforming urban education'. *American Educational Research Journal*, **27**(2), 255–78.

Smith, B. O. (1987). 'Definitions of teaching'. In M. J. Dunkin (ed.), *International Encyclopedia of Teaching and Teacher Education*, pp. 11–15. Oxford: Pergamon Press.

Smith, M. L. (1980). 'Teacher expectations'. *Evaluation in Education*, **4**, 53–5.

Smith, W. F. and Andrews, R. L. (1989). *Instructional Leadership: How Principals Make a Difference*. Alexandria, VA: Association for Supervision and Curriculum Development.

Snippe, J. (1991). *In-service training voor leerkrachten: een studie naar het effect van in-service training op de implementatie van een curriculum en op de leerprestaties* (In-service training for teachers: a study on the effectiveness of in-service training on the implementation of a curriculum and pupils' achievement). Groningen: RION.

Sørensen, A. B. and Hallinan, M. T. (1986). 'Effects of ability grouping on growth in academic achievement'. *American Educational Research Journal*, **23**(4), 519–42.

Squire, J. R. (1988). 'Studies of textbooks: are we asking the right questions?' In P. W. Jackson (ed.), *Contributing to Educational Change*, pp. 127–69. Berkeley, CA: McCutchan.

Stallings, J. and Kaskowitz, D. (1974). *Follow Through Classroom Observation Evaluation 1972–1973* (SRI Project URU-7370). Stanford, CA: Stanford Research Institute.

Stallings, J., Needels, M. and Stayrook, N. (1979). *The Teaching of Basic Reading Skills in Secondary Schools, Phase II and III*. Menlo Park, CA: SRI International.

Starren, J., Bakker, S. J. and Wissel, A. van der (1988). *Inleiding in de onderwijspsychologie: instructie, beoordeling en behandeling* (An introduction to educational psychology: instruction, evaluation and treatment). Muiderberg: Coutinho.

Stodolsky, S. S. (1989). 'Is teaching really by the book?' In P. W. Jackson and S. Haroutunian-Gordon (eds), *From Socrates to Software: The Teacher as Text and the Text as Teacher*. Chicago: University of Chicago Press.

Stoel, W. G. R. (1980). *De relatie tussen de grootte van scholen voor voortgezet onderwijs en het welbevinden van de leerlingen*. Deel I en II (The relationship between school size and attitudes towards schooling of pupils in secondary education. Parts I and II). Groningen: RION.

Stokking, K. M., Dekker, E. M. and Leenders, F. J. (1987). *Zorgverbreding of selectieverscherping? Nascholing Speerpunt Lezen: voorlopige conclusies uit het evaluatieonderzoek* (Mainstreaming or selection? Preliminary conclusions of evaluation research). Utrecht: ISOR.

Stoll, L. (1992). 'Teacher growth in the effective school'. In M. Fullan and A. Hargreaves (eds), *Teacher Development and Educational Change*, pp. 104–22. London: Falmer Press.

Stoll, L. and Fink, D. (1992). 'Reorganization for effectiveness: the Halton approach'. In J. Bashi and Z. Sass (eds), *School Effectiveness and Improvement. Proceed-

ings of the Third International Congress, Jerusalem, pp. 370–80. Jerusalem: Magnes Press.

Stone, C. L. (1983). 'A meta-analysis of advance-organizer studies'. *Journal of Experimental Education*, **51**, 194–9.

Stones, E. (1992). *Quality Teaching: A Sample of Cases*. London: Routledge.

Stringfield, S. C. and Schaffer, G. (1991). 'Results of school effectiveness studies in the United States of America'. In B. P. M. Creemers, D. Reynolds, G. Schaffer, S. Stringfield and C. Teddlie (eds), *International School Effects Research Workshop*, pp. 139–56. Kaohsiung: College of Education, National Kaohsiung Normal University.

Stringfield, S. C. and Slavin, R. E. (1992). 'A hierarchical longitudinal model for elementary school effects'. In B. P. M. Creemers and G. J. Reezigt (eds), *Evaluation of Educational Effectiveness*, pp. 35–69. Groningen: ICO.

Stringfield, S. and Teddlie, C. (1989). 'The first three phases of the Louisiana school effectiveness study'. In B. P. M. Creemers, T. Peters and D. Reynolds (eds), *School Effectiveness and School Improvement. Proceedings of the Second International Congress, Rotterdam*, pp. 281–94. Lisse: Swets & Zeitlinger.

Taba, H. (1962). *Curriculum Development, Theory and Practice*. New York: Harcourt, Brace and World.

Teddlie, C. and Stringfield, S. (1993). *Schools Make a Difference: Lessons Learned from a 10-year Study of School Effects*. New York: Teachers College Press.

Teddlie, C., Kirby, P. C. and Stringfield, S. (1989). 'Effective versus ineffective schools: observable differences in the classroom'. *American Journal of Education*, **97**(3), 221–36.

Tilborg, I. A. J. van (1987). *De betekenis van het arbeidersgezin voor het leerniveau en de schoolloopbaan van het kind* (The importance of the working class family to the level of achievement and the school career of the child). The Hague: SVO.

Tomlinson, T. M. (1986).'A nation at risk: background for a working paper'. In T. M. Tomlinson and H. J. Walberg (eds), *Academic Work and Educational Excellence*, pp. 3–28. Berkeley, CA: McCutchan.

Tyler, R. W. (1949). *Basic Principles of Curriculum and Instruction*. Chicago: University of Chicago Press.

Vedder, P. H. (1985). *Cooperative Learning: a Study on Processes and Effects of Cooperation between Primary School Children*. The Hague: SVO.

Veenman, S. (1987). 'Leraren voor de school van morgen' (Teachers for the future school). *IDEE*, **9**(2), 58–62.

Veenman, S. (1992). 'Effectieve instructie volgens het directe instructiemodel' (Direct instruction). *Pedagogische Studiën*, **69**(4), 242–69.

Veenman, S., Lem, P. and Nijssen, F. (1988). *Omgaan met combinatieklassen: een programma voor schoolverbetering* (Mixed-age classes: a programme for school improvement). The Hague: SVO.

Veenman, S., Lem, P., Roelofs, E. and Nijssen, F. (1992). *Effectieve instructie en doelmatig klassemanagement* (Effective instruction and adequate classroom management). Amsterdam: Swets & Zeitlinger.

Veenman, S., Leenders, Y., Meyer, P. and Sanders, M. (1993). 'Leren lesgeven met het directe instructiemodel' (Learning to teach according to the model of direct instruction). *Pedagogische Studiën*, **70**(1), 2–16.

Vermeulen, A. and Koning, P. de (1985). *De ene brugklas is de andere niet: groeperingsvorm in de eerste drie leerjaren van scholengemeenschappen voor MAVO/HAVO/VWO. Interimrapport II* (Not all first grades are the same: grouping in the first three years of comprehensive schools. Report II). Amsterdam: SCO.

Vries, A. M. de (1986). 'Differentiatie op middenscholen' (Grouping in comprehensive schools). In A. Reints and P. Span (eds), *Differentiatie in het onderwijs* (Grouping in education), pp. 117–30. Lisse: Swets & Zeitlinger.

Walberg, H. J. (ed.) (1979). *Educational Environments and Effects: Evaluation, Policy and Productivity*. Berkeley, CA: McCutchan.

Walberg, H. J. (1982). 'What makes schooling effective? A synthesis and critique of three national studies'. *Contemporary Education Review*, **1**, 23–34.

Walberg, H. J. (1984). 'Improving the productivity of America's schools'. *Educational Leadership*, **41**(8), 19–27.

Walberg, H. J. (1986a). 'Syntheses of research on teaching'. In M. C. Wittrock (ed.), *Handbook of Research on Teaching*, 3rd edn, pp. 214–29. New York: Macmillan.

Walberg, H. J. (1986b). 'What works in a nation still at risk'. *Educational Leadership*, **44**(1), 7–10.

Walberg, H. J. (1989). 'Science, mathematics, and national welfare: retrospective and prospective achievements'. In A. Purves (ed.), *Education in International Perspective*. Alexandria, VA: Association for Supervision and Curriculum Development.

Walberg, H. J. (1990). 'Productive teaching and instruction: assessing the knowledge base'. *Phi Delta Kappan*, **71**, 470–8.

Walberg, H. J. (1991). 'Improving school science in advanced and developing countries'. *Review of Educational Research*, **61**(1), 25–69.

Walberg, H. J. (1992). 'Educational indicators for educational progress'. In B. P. M. Creemers and W. Th. J. G. Hoeben (eds), *Indicatoren van onderwijseffectiviteit* (Indicators of educational effectiveness). Groningen: ICO.

Walker, D. A. (1976). *The IEA Six Subject Survey*. Stockholm: International Studies in Evaluation, IX.

Wang, M. C., Haertel, G. D. and Walberg, H. J. (1990). 'What influences learning? A content analysis of review literature'. *Journal of Educational Research*, **84**(1), 30–43.

Warries, E. (ed.) (1979). *Beheersingsleren een leerstrategie* (Mastery learning a learning strategy). Groningen: Wolters-Noordhoff.

Washburne, C. W. (1922). *Adjusting the School to the Child*. Yonkers, NY: World Book.

Waxman, H. C. and Walberg, H. J. (eds) (1991). *Effective Teaching: Current Research*. Berkeley, CA: McCutchan.

Waxman, H. C., Wang, M. C., Anderson, K. A. and Walberg, H. J. (1985). 'Synthesis of research on the effects of adaptive education'. *Educational Leadership*, **43**(1), 27–9.

Weeda, W. C. (1982). 'Beheersingsleren: het model getoetst in de praktijk' (Mastery learning: testing of the model in educational practice). PhD thesis, University of Tilburg.

Weide, M. G. (1993). 'Effective provisions for ethnic minorities in primary schools'. *Tijdschrift voor Onderwijsresearch*, **18**(2), 74–84.

Weinert, F. E. (1990). 'Theory building in the domain of motivation and learning in school'. In P. Vedder (ed.), *Fundamental Studies in Educational Research*, pp. 5–6. Lisse: Swets & Zeitlinger.

Werf, M. P. C. van der (1988). *Het schoolwerkplan in het basisonderwijs* (The school working plan in primary education). Lisse: Swets & Zeitlinger.

Werf, M. P. C. van der and Weide, M. G. (1991). 'Effectief onderwijs voor allochtone leerlingen' (Effective instruction for immigrant students). *Tijdschrift voor Onderwijsresearch*, **16**(4), 231–43.

Werf, M. P. C. van der, Weide, M. G. and Tesser, P. (1991). *Het Onderwijsvoorrangs-beleid in de school en in de klas: de eerste meting in het basisonderwijs* (Educational priority policy in the school and in the class: a first measurement in primary education). Groningen/Nijmegen: RION/ITS.

Westerhof, K. J. (1989). 'Effectiviteit van leerkrachtgedrag: een empirische studie naar leerkrachtgedrag en de samenhang met leerwinst' (Productivity of teacher behaviour: an empirical study of teacher behaviour and its correlation with learning gain). PhD thesis, University of Groningen.

What Works (1986). *Research about Teaching and Learning*. Washington, DC: Department of Education.

Wheeler, B. K. (1967). *Curriculum Process*. London: Hodder & Stoughton.

Wiley, D. E. and Harnischfeger, A. (1974). 'Explosion of a myth: quantity of schooling and exposure to instruction, major educational vehicles'. *Educational Researcher*, **3**, 7–12.

Wilkinson, S. S. (1981). 'The relationship of teacher praise and student achievement: a meta-analysis of selected research'. *Dissertation Abstracts International*, **41**, 3998A.

Winne, P. H. (1987). 'Why process–product research cannot explain process–product findings and a proposed remedy: the cognitive mediational paradigm'. *Teaching and Teacher Education*, **3**(4), 333–56.

Wittrock, M. C. (ed.) (1986). *Handbook of Research on Teaching*, 3rd edn. New York: Macmillan.

Wolbert, R., Schaap, W. and Span, P. (1986). *Individualisering en differentiatie in de basisschool* (Individualization and grouping in primary education). The Hague: SVO.

Woods, P. and Pollard, A. (eds) (1988). *Sociology and Teaching: A New Challenge for the Sociology of Education*. London: Croom Helm.

Wragg, E. C. (1993). *Primary Teaching Skills*. London: Routledge.

Yeaney, R. H. and Miller, P. A. (1983). 'Effects of diagnostic/remedial instruction in science learning: a meta-analysis'. *Journal of Research in Science Teaching*, **20**, 19–26.

Index

Ability 3, 13, 15, 57
  see also Student
    background
Ability grouping 58
Academic
  focus 77
  work 77
Academic learning time
  (ALT) 27, 28
Achievement 55, 79, 103
  academic 66
  student 12, 28, 39, 66, 75,
    78, 86, 100
Achievement tests 12
Advance organizers 50
Allocated time 29
  see also Academic learning
    time
Aptitude (student) 13, 25, 28
Autonomy of teachers 37

Behavioural goals 48

Capacities (student) 26
Characteristics
  of curricula 50
  of effective instruction 103
  see also Cohesion;
    Consistency;
    Constancy; Control
  of grouping 62
Classroom 4
  learning 5
  level 4, 7, 13, 18, 97, 101,
    118
  management 77
  observation 30
  organization 17, 84
Cohesion 103, 118
Comparative research 41
Compensation (school
  function) 12
Components
  of education 4, 10
  of instruction 93, 97, 100
  of teachers 46
Comprehensive
  education 31
  school 41
Conceptual framework 117
Consistency (principle) 93,
  95, 102, 118

Constancy 103, 118
Context
  educational 9
  level 122
  national 37
  of innovations 8
  of the school 18
Contextual differences 3
Control 103, 118
Co-operative learning 41, 70
  see also Grouping
Correlates of effectiveness
  116
Course 68
Cultural differences 22
Curricula 11, 55, 74
  goals 48
  language 39
  mathematics 39
  variations in 39
Curricular materials 37, 91,
  94, 98
Curriculum 11, 17, 37, 52,
  118
  analysis 30
  characteristics 50
  development 24
  documents 47
  implementation 36, 40
  intensity of use 40
  structure of 49

Decentralization 37
Deficiencies 68
  in education 38
Design of education 28, 40
Development strategies 48
Didactical approach 17
Differences between
  students 2
Differentiation 42
Direct instruction 85
Disadvantaged students 39
Dutch educational system 41

Educational
  arrangements 28
  contents 47
  context 9
  factors 13
  goals 3
  leadership 22

innovations 38
interventions 15
management 21
objectives 3, 55, 117
outcomes 5, 7
policy 21
practice 12, 24, 39, 79
productivity 13
psychology 25
system 30
technology 53
Effective
  classroom 90
  curricula 46, 51
  education 7
  instruction 9, 91, 92, 100,
    106
  learning time 22, 29
  schools 100
  teachers 44, 77
  teaching 41
Effectiveness
  instructional 6, 15
  of education 8, 9, 103
  school 5
Effects of education 107
Empirical research 44
Environment
  student 13
Ethnicity 15
  see also Student
    background
Evaluation 16, 85
Evaluative capacity 22
Examination regulations 21
External variables 3

Feedback 83
Fidelity (implementation) 51

Gender 14, 15
  see also Student
    background
General education 41
Goals 3, 16
  for lessons 16, 18
  general 14
  in curricula 48
  national 22
  non-academic 12
Grouping 11, 41
  ability 41, 59

Grouping *cont.*
  between-class 41
  characteristics 62
  pacing 59
  procedures 6, 64, 91, 99, 119
  within-class 31, 41, 61, 71

Homework assignments 84
Homogenization 59

Implementation
  of curricula 36
  of innovations 38
  sufficient 52
Improvement of education 16
Individualization 31
Initial differences between
  students 2, 4, 15
  see also Student
    background
Innovations (educational) 38
Instruction 8, 10, 81
  adaptive 70, 71
  corrective 70
  direct 85
  individualized 67
  methods of 82
  traditional 69
Instructional
  behaviour 17, 39, 74, 76
  characteristics/factors 24, 90
  effectiveness 6
  functions 87
  objectives 68
  processes 37
  time 68
Interaction
  teacher-whole class 71
Interventions (educational) 15

Language curricula 39
Leadership (educational) 22
Learning 13, 74
  conditions 26
  environment 15, 25
  experiences 85
  opportunities 51
  outcomes 6, 35
  processes 11
  strategies 25, 82
  task 25
  time 19
  unit 67
Lessons 16, 78
Local educational boards 37
Lower-ability class 31

Management (teachers') 17
  behaviour 76
Mastery learning 41, 62, 67, 90, 93

Mathematics curricula 39
Meta-analysis 41, 79
Metacognition 25
Model
  Carrol's 25, 28
  for 'classroom
    teaching' 18, 20
  of didactical analysis 15
  of educational
    effectiveness 27, 56, 72, 89, 91, 98, 108, 119
  prescriptive 15
Motivation 12
Mutual adaption 53

National
  context 37
  goals 22
  policy 106
Non-cognitive areas 66
Non-graded school 59
Non-intended outcomes 12

Objectives 3
Opportunities used 27
Opportunity to learn 22, 25, 30, 55, 91, 103, 105, 117, 121
Organizational aspects 105
Outcomes
  of education 1, 8, 101
  of learning 6, 35
  student 5
Output variables 44

Parent(s) 104
  involvement 22
Perseverance (to learn) 25
Planning documents 17
Preparation (of lessons) 17, 50
Prescriptive models 15
Primary education 22
Prior achievement 14
  see also Student
    background
Process-product
  (-oriented) studies 30, 75, 76, 79, 86
  paradigm 44
Processes of education 1
Productivity (educational) 13

Quality
  of education 21
  of instruction 19, 88, 105, 121
Qualitative research 5, 45
Quantitative research 5, 45
Quantity of subjects 34, 48
Question techniques 84
Questioning 95

Reflective teaching 78
Reinforcement 83
Research
  comparative 41
  empirical 44
  qualitative 5
  quantitative 5
  traditions 36
Results of education 1, 3

School
  activity plan 37
  context 37
  education 101
  effectiveness 5, 100
  improvement projects 22, 95–6
  learning 24
  level 18, 101, 103, 120
  working plan 17, 37, 103
Secondary education 12
Self-paced instruction 41
Setting 57
  see also Grouping
Skills 25
Social
  class 73
  context 77
Socioeconomic status 13, 15, 57
  see also Student
    background
Special education 57
Streaming 41
  see also Grouping
Structure of a curriculum 49
Structured teaching 22
Structuring 94
  principles 50
Student
  achievement 12, 28, 75, 78, 100
  aptitude 13, 25, 28
  attainment 73
  background/
    characteristics 13, 14, 24, 34, 38, 57
  capacities 26
  environment 13
  learning 11, 18, 23, 49
  level 118
  outcomes 5
Subjects (school-) 31
Support services 107

Task difficulty 29
  see also Academic learning
    time
Task-oriented
  behaviour 76
  time 49
Task relevance 29
  see also Academic learning
    time

Index

Teacher(s') 6, 51, 97, 107
  activities 10, 16, 17, 78
  behaviour 9, 73, 74, 82–3,
    88–9, 90, 119
  capacities 42
  characteristics/
    personality 42
  expectations 84
  experience 73
  expertise 54
  interventions 29
  knowledge and
    experience 40
  management 17
  teaching 11, 76
  training of 39, 107

  variables 30, 44
Teaching 10, 74
  effective 40, 84
  experience 44
  – learning process 18
  paradigms 15
  principles of 40
  reflective 78
  structured 85
  style 73
Tests (in curricula) 50
Textbook 6, 50, 94
Time (spent on learning) 25,
  105, 121
Time allocation 28
  see also Learning time

Time on task 29, 117
  see also Academic learning
    time
Tracking 41
Training 107
Transfer of knowledge 10, 34

Vocational education 41

Waiting time 92
What works 47
Whole-class grouping 62
  see also Grouping
Whole-word method of
  teaching 47

150